Essential
TRUTHS
OF THE
CHRISTIAN
FAITH

Essential
TRUTHS OF THE

RC

TYNDALE HOUSE PUBLISHERS, INC.

CHRISTIAN FAITH

SPROUL

CAROL STREAM, ILLINOIS

Visit Tyndale's exciting Web site at www.tyndale.com

TYNDALE and Tyndale's inkwell logo are registered trademarks of Tyndale House Publishers, Inc.

Essential Truths of the Christian Faith

Library of Congress Cataloging-in-Publication Data
Sproul, R. C. (Robert Charles), date.
    Essential truths of the Christian faith / R.C. Sproul.
        p.   cm.
    Includes bibliographical references and index.
    ISBN-13: 978-0-8423-2001-6 (sc)
    ISBN-10: 0-8423-2001-6 (sc)
        1. Theology, Doctrinal—Popular works.   2. Reformed Church—Doctrines.   3. Evangelicalism.   I. Title.
BT77.S718   1992
230'.57—dc20   92-23300

Printed in the United States of America

13 12 11 10 09 08
17 16 15 14 13 12

CONTENTS

Preface *vii*
Introduction *ix*

I. Revelation
1. Divine Revelation *3*
2. Paradox, Mystery, and Contradiction *7*
3. Immediate and Mediate General Revelation *11*
4. Special Revelation and the Bible *15*
5. The Law of God *17*
6. The Prophets of God *19*
7. The Canon of Scripture *21*
8. Interpreting the Bible *25*
9. Private Interpretation *27*

II. The Nature and Attributes of God
10. The Incomprehensibility of God *31*
11. The Triunity of God *35*
12. The Self-Existence of God *37*
13. The Omnipotence of God *39*
14. The Omnipresence of God *43*
15. The Omniscience of God *45*
16. The Holiness of God *47*
17. The Goodness of God *49*
18. The Justice of God *53*

III. The Works and Decrees of God
19. Creation *57*

20. Providence *61*
21. Miracles *65*
22. The Will of God *67*
23. Covenant *71*
24. Covenant of Works *73*

IV. Jesus Christ
25. The Deity of Christ *77*
26. The Subordination of Christ *79*
27. The Humanity of Christ *81*
28. The Sinlessness of Christ *83*
29. The Virgin Birth *85*
30. Jesus Christ as the Only Begotten *87*
31. The Baptism of Christ *91*
32. The Glory of Christ *93*
33. The Ascension of Christ *95*
34. Jesus Christ as Mediator *99*
35. The Threefold Office of Christ *101*
36. The Titles of Jesus *103*

V. The Holy Spirit
37. The Deity of the Holy Spirit *109*
38. The Personality of the Holy Spirit *111*
39. The Internal Testimony of the Holy Spirit *113*
40. The Illumination of the Holy Spirit *115*
41. The Baptism of the Holy Spirit *117*

42. The Holy Spirit as Comforter *121*
43. The Holy Spirit as Sanctifier *123*

VI. Human Beings and the Fall
44. Knowledge of Self and Knowledge of God *127*
45. Human Beings Created in the Image of God *131*
46. Human Beings as Body and Soul *133*
47. Human Beings as Flesh and Spirit *137*
48. Satan *139*
49. Demons *141*
50. Sin *143*
51. Original Sin *145*
52. Human Depravity *147*
53. Human Conscience *151*
54. The Unforgivable Sin *153*
55. Syncretism *155*

VII. Salvation
56. Salvation *159*
57. Predestination *161*
58. Predestination and Reprobation *165*
59. Effectual Calling *169*
60. Rebirth *171*
61. Atonement *173*
62. Definite Atonement *175*
63. Free Will *179*
64. Faith *183*
65. Saving Faith *187*
66. Justification by Faith *189*
67. Faith and Works *191*
68. Repentance *193*
69. Merit and Grace *195*
70. Perseverance of the Saints *197*
71. The Assurance of Salvation *201*
72. The Intermediate State *205*

73. The Last Resurrection *209*
74. Glorification *211*

VIII. The Church and Sacraments
75. The Apostles *215*
76. The Church *217*
77. The Marks of a True Church *219*
78. Excommunication *221*
79. The Sacraments *223*
80. Baptism *225*
81. Infant Baptism *227*
82. The Lord's Supper *231*
83. Transubstantiation *235*
84. The Sabbath *239*
85. Oaths and Vows *241*

IX. Spirituality and Living in This Age
86. The Fruit of the Spirit *245*
87. Love *247*
88. Hope *249*
89. Prayer *251*
90. Antinomianism *253*
91. Legalism *255*
92. The Threefold Use of the Law *257*
93. Perfectionism *259*
94. Civil Government *261*
95. Marriage *265*
96. Divorce *267*

X. End Times
97. The Antichrist *273*
98. The Return of Christ *275*
99. The Kingdom of God *277*
100. Heaven *279*
101. The Beatific Vision *281*
102. Hell *285*

Notes *289*
Suggested Reading *291*
Scripture Index *297*

Every Christian is a theologian. We are always engaged
in the activity of learning about the things of God. We
are not all theologians in the professional or academic
sense, but theologians we are, for better or for worse.
The "for worse" is no small matter. Second Peter warns
that heresies are destructive to the people of God and are
blasphemies committed against God. They are destructive because theology touches every dimension of our
lives.

The Bible declares that as a man thinks in his heart,
so is he. This declaration sounds strange. It is almost as
if the biblical writer blunders. He seems to confuse the
mind and the heart. We normally associate thought with
the brain and feelings with the heart. So what does it
mean to say a man *thinks* in his *heart?* The phrase *to
think in the heart* refers to thoughtful reflection. Many
ideas are briefly entertained by the mind without ever
penetrating the heart. Those ideas that do grasp us in our
innermost parts, however, are the ideas that shape our
lives. We are what we think. When our thoughts are corrupted, our lives follow suit.

We all know that people can recite the creeds flaw-
lessly and make *A*'s in theology courses while living
godless lives. We can affirm a sound theology and live
an unsound life. Sound theology is not enough to live a
godly life. But it is still a requisite for godly living. How
can we *do* the truth without first *understanding* what the
truth is?

No Christian can avoid theology. Every Christian has
a theology. The issue, then, is not, do we want to have a
theology? That's a given. The real issue is, do we have a
sound theology? Do we embrace true or false doctrine?

This is not a textbook of formal theology. It is a
layperson's introduction to the essential doctrines of
Christianity. To understand the Bible's message we must
first understand the concepts by which the message is set

forth. Hence, the purpose of this book is to introduce the reader to the key concepts that together make up the biblical message.

Each concept is set forth in brief, bite-size portions. Suggested biblical references are added to flesh out the skeletal treatment of each concept. The book is both basic and elementary. It is designed to be simple, though not simplistic. I have tried to crystallize into a few pages the essence of theological concepts that are each worthy of a full volume to plumb their depths.

Those who read and study this book will not become experts in theology. But they will become familiar with the key concepts that are the framework for a full-orbed theology. It is my hope that those who read this book will be provoked into a deeper study of theology, which is a lifelong enterprise.

My thanks to Wendell Hawley of Tyndale House for suggesting this work, to Donna Mack for preparing the manuscript, to David Freeland for helping with the graphics, and to my son, R. C., for his editorial skill.

INTRODUCTION

In the decade of the 1980s, a massive and comprehensive study of religion in American life was undertaken by the Gallup organization. Though the sharpest trends and indicators of the study were published and evaluated in various magazines, the mountain of data collected was generally not made public. George Gallup then submitted the data to *Christianity Today,* who, in turn, selected a few theologians to examine and evaluate the significance of the information. I was among the group who had the privilege of analyzing the complete data.

The results of the study were as terrifying as they were revealing. Among the more noteworthy elements were the following: (1) more than sixty million Americans claim to have had a personal conversion experience, and (2) an extraordinarily high percentage of Americans said they believed the Bible to be the Word of God.

Counterbalancing these affirmations, however, was the clear revelation that Americans, even *evangelical* Americans, are woefully ignorant of the content of Scripture and even more ignorant of the history of Christianity and classical Christian theology. Perhaps most alarming was the realization that the mass of people who claim to have biblical faith have had little or no impact on the structures and values of American culture. For example, some recent studies concerning sexual ethics and the question of abortion suggest that the difference in behavior between evangelical Christians and secularists is negligible. In other words, the clear message of these studies is this: Christian "faith" is making little or no difference in people's lives and in American culture. How accurate these studies are is a matter of debate.

How can this be? One possibility quickly comes to mind. Perhaps many of those who claim to have had a conversion experience are mistaken or lying about their conversion. However, if only half of those who claim to be born again are in fact regenerate, we must conclude that America has experienced a revival more widespread than the Great Awakening.

If such a revival has happened, then we must ask why there is so little evidence of its impact on culture. We seem to have had a huge revival with little or no reformation. Indeed, the discrepancy between revival and reformation would be the greatest ever to occur in the history of Christianity. Such a revival is mere fiction. It is spurious. It is not true biblical faith that has been "revived."

A more optimistic view of this anomaly would be this: The chief reason we observe so little evidence of the revival's impact on life and culture is because it is too early to discern it. The millions of people who have been born again are still in their spiritual infancy. When they arrive at spiritual maturity their impact on the nation will surely be felt.

In the secular culture, teenagers tend to have a powerful impact on the shape of values, but not as great an impact as those adults who are in positions of power and influence. Infants, however, have virtually no impact on the shaping of cultural values. Their voice is not heard save in their cries for more milk. Infants have not developed their thinking and skills to a level whereby their counsel is sought in the family or the community. They must mature, they must come of age before they are put in positions of family or community leadership.

We hope that those who remain in spiritual infancy will indeed grow to maturity and have a strong impact on the family, the community, the nation, and the world. So far that has not happened. It may never happen. But for a true spiritual revival and reformation to take place, several barriers must be overcome. It is crucial for the Christian to understand these.

What follows is a brief sketch of ten causes that work against the Christian goal of spiritual maturity. I will list them separately and give definition to each.

Cause #1: The Childlike Faith Error

In some Christian circles the biblical call to a childlike faith has been elevated to a spiritual ideal that radically distorts the biblical meaning of faith. The New Testament does describe a certain childlike faith as a virtue.

Jesus said, "Whoever does not receive the kingdom of God as a little child will by no means enter it" (Mark 10:15).

But what is this childlike faith? The word *like* suggests some sort of analogy. The analogy is obvious. As little children trust their parents and take them at their word, so we, in similar fashion, are to trust God. An infant's life depends on trusting in the care of parents. When a curious toddler reaches for the flame on a stove, the parent says, "No!" There is no time to explain the intricacies of thermal energy, and such sophisticated explanations would be wasted on the child anyway.

However, as children begin to grow, their capacity for trusting in their parents' leadership begins to wane. Before long they begin to ask why, and not long after that, they are openly defiant.

Such defiance has no place in the kingdom of God. God's children are to remain forever in a state of childlike awe and trust of their heavenly Father. There is an appropriate exercise of implicit faith here. God deserves to be trusted implicitly. Indeed, it is foolish as well as foolhardy not to trust Him implicitly. He is altogether trustworthy. The mature Christian never outgrows this sort of childlike faith.

There is a vast difference, however, between a child*like* faith and a child*ish* faith, though the two are often confused. A childish faith balks at learning the things of God in depth. It refuses the meat of the gospel while clinging to a diet of milk. For this, the childish Christian receives an admonition:

For though by this time you ought to be teachers, you need someone to teach you again the first principles of the oracles of God; and you have come to need milk and not solid food. For everyone who partakes only of milk is unskilled in the word of righteousness, for he is a babe. But solid food belongs to those who are of full age, that is, those who by reason of use have their senses exercised to discern both good and evil. (Hebrews 5:12-14)

The call of the New Testament is to maturity. The apostle Paul says, "When I was a child, I spoke as a child, I understood as a child, I thought as a child; but

when I became a man, I put away childish things"
(1 Corinthians 13:11). Paul makes a further distinction
between the way in which we are to remain as babes and
the way in which we are called to adulthood. He says,
"Brethren, do not be children in understanding; however, in malice be babes, but in understanding be
mature" (1 Corinthians 14:20).

**Cause #2:
Fear of
Theological
Skepticism**

There is a deep distrust in the Christian subculture for
theology. In many cases this aversion to theology flows
from a distrust of theologians.

J. V. Langmead Casserley, the noted Anglican apolo-
gist, devoted an entire chapter in his book *Apologetics
& Evangelism* to the theme, "The Treason of the Intellec-
tuals."[1] Casserley observed that the Christian public's
growing distrust for theologians has been provoked by
the radical skepticism toward the Bible and historic
Christianity exhibited by modern higher-critical scholars. It was theologians in the church who declared the
death of God. It is seminary professors and Christian college professors who are most vocal in their attack on the
trustworthiness of Scripture. At the turn of this century
the Dutch theologian Abraham Kuyper remarked, "Biblical criticism has become biblical vandalism."

Undoubtedly many theological seminaries in America
have become citadels of unbelief. Christian parents are
often shocked and dismayed when their children return
home from "Christian" colleges filled with doubt and skepticism they learned from their professors. The reaction to
this theological treason is often, "If this is what studying
theology leads to, then I'm going to avoid it altogether."

No doubt there is bad theology. No doubt the serious
study of theology exposes the student to skeptical criticism. No doubt much of what passes for Christian theology is merely the theologian's attempt to justify his own
unbelief.

We must remember, however, that though skeptical
theology is currently rampant in our institutions, its presence is not new. The chief opponents of Jesus during His
earthly ministry were clergy. The theologians of Jesus'
day hated His theology. But to reject all theology and
theological education in order to avoid bad theology is
to commit spiritual suicide. It is the exercise of another

kind of treason. To reject theology is to reject the knowledge of God. This is not an option for the Christian.

Cause #3: The Error of Easy Believism

Easy believism is a modern form of the ancient heresy of antinomianism. It asserts that once a person makes a decision for Christ or prays to receive Jesus as Savior, it is not necessary to embrace Him as Lord. There are no requirements of law that bind the Christian.

There are few Christian teachers, if any, who declare that one who embraces Christ as Savior shouldn't also embrace Him as Lord. Rather, they encourage the "carnal Christian" to become more spiritual and obedient. But they shrink from declaring that embracing Christ as Lord is necessary for salvation. Indeed, they insist that it is not necessary for attaining salvation. They allow for the reality of a carnal Christian.

This type of antinomianism is so pervasive in American evangelicalism that it may even be the majority report. The current "Lordship Salvation" controversy focuses on this issue.

Recently a pastor spoke to me about a young man in his congregation who was using drugs and living in an illicit relationship with his girlfriend. The pastor tried to counsel the young man about his life-style. The young man said casually, "It's OK, Pastor, I'm a carnal Christian."

To be a Christian in the biblical sense of the word is to be a disciple of Christ. A disciple is a "learner." He enrolls in the school of Christ. The disciple, as the name suggests, is called to a disciplined study of the things of God.

Cause #4: Neo-Monasticism

The monastic movement in church history involved the glorification of withdrawal from this world. Those who made the flight to the cloister were seeking refuge from the despoiling influences of evil society. The monastery was a haven for those seeking spiritual purity.

Many of those who entered monastic life did so to pursue a life of prayer and spiritual devotion. For others, it was an opportunity for secluded study. An element in classical monasticism that is missing from neo-monasticism is devotion to theological scholarship.

When I speak of neo-monasticism, I am referring to the tendency among some evangelicals to "drop out" of the world. I am describing an attitude as well as a lifestyle. It is a kind of world denial that includes far more than a rejection of worldliness. It involves a rejection of the world as the primary arena of Christian activity. It restricts the Christian's activity to a spiritual ghetto. It includes a willful rejection of the study of anything that is not clearly "evangelical."

I remember the second year of my Christian life. As a sophomore in college, I was stirred in my soul in a class on Western philosophy. The professor was lecturing on an essay written by St. Augustine. The lecture awakened my mind to a whole new plane of understanding the character of God. As a young Christian I yearned to go deeper in my faith. I saw the work of Augustine and others like him as a tremendous help to that end.

I decided to change my academic major from Bible to philosophy. When I made that change I was all but drummed out of the evangelical corps on our campus. My friends were horrified at my apparent apostasy. The Bible verse I heard quoted too many times to count was "Beware lest anyone cheat you through philosophy and empty deceit" (Colossians 2:8).

I was both confused and hurt by the reactions of my friends. I had turned to philosophy to strengthen my understanding of God, not to weaken it. Though I was no longer a Bible major, by no means had I rejected the Bible or my study of it. I couldn't figure out how one could "beware" of something without first being "aware" of it. My study of secular philosophy only increased my appreciation for the depths and riches of the things revealed in Scripture. It also provided me with an understanding of those issues crucial to the Christian task of apologetics. It never occurred to me that we were supposed to abandon the world to the pagans.

Neo-monasticism breeds ignorance—ignorance not only of culture and the ideas that shape culture, but ignorance of theology as well. It displays more lack of faith than strength of faith.

The effects of neo-monasticism are catastrophic. By retreating from engagement with the world we have suffered defeat by default. We wring our hands at the secularization of American culture and wonder how it could have happened.

**Cause #5:
Fear of
Controversies**

Theology breeds controversies, no question about it. Whenever theology is studied, arguments inevitably follow. We all desire relationships that are marked by peace and unity. We also understand that the Bible forbids us from being contentious, divisive, argumentative, and judgmental. We are to manifest the fruit of the Spirit, which includes gentleness, meekness, patience, and kindness.

Our reasoning then goes: If we are to avoid a quarrelsome spirit and show forth the fruit of the Spirit we must avoid the study of theology. An American axiom is "Never discuss religion or politics." The reason this statement has been elevated to the level of a prime axiom is because discussions about religion or politics often generate more heat than light. We are tired of witch hunts, nit-picking, persecutions, and even wars that are triggered by theological controversy.

Yet controversy accompanies theological commitment. John Stott, in a book entitled *Christ the Controversialist,*[2] stated what should be obvious to anyone who reads the Bible—Jesus' life was a storm of controversy. The apostles, like the prophets before them, could hardly go a day without controversy. Paul said that he debated daily in the marketplace. To avoid controversy is to avoid Christ. We can have peace, but it is a servile and carnal peace where truth is slain in the streets.

We are called to avoid god*less* controversies. We are called to god*ly* controversies. One positive aspect of Christian controversy is that Christians tend to argue with each other about theology because they understand that truth, especially theological truth, is of eternal consequence. Passions rise because the stakes are so high.

Often godless controversies arise, not because the combatants know too much theology, but because they know too little. They fail to discern the difference between weighty matters of dispute and minor points that should never serve to divide us. We have another maxim: "A little knowledge is a dangerous thing." It is the immature student of theology who is the nitpicker. It is the half-trained theologian who is brittle and quarrelsome. The more one masters the study of theology, the more one is able to discern what issues are negotiable and tolerable and what issues demand that we contend with all our might.

Cause #6:
Antirational
Spirit of the Age

I believe that we are living in the most anti-intellectual era of Christian history ever known. I do not mean anti-academic, antitechnological or antiscientific. By anti-intellectual, I mean *against the mind.*

We live in a period that is allergic to rationality. The influence of existential philosophy has been massive. We have become a sensuous nation. Even our language reveals it. My seminary students repeatedly write like this on their exam pages: "I feel it is wrong that . . ." or "I feel it is true that . . ." I invariably cross out their word *feel* and substitute the word *think.* There is a difference between feeling and thinking.

There is a primacy of the mind in the Christian faith. There is also a primacy of the heart in the Christian faith. Surely that paradoxical declaration sounds like a contradiction. How can there be two primacies? Something must be ultimately prime. Of course we cannot have two different primacies at the same time and in the same relationship. When I speak of two different primacies, I mean with respect to two different matters.

With respect to the primacy of *importance,* the heart is first. If I have correct doctrine in my head but no love for Christ in my heart, I have missed the kingdom of God. It is infinitely more important that my heart be right before God than that my theology be impeccably correct.

However, for my heart to be right, there is a primacy of the intellect in terms of *order.* Nothing can be in my heart that is not first in my head. How can I love a God or a Jesus about whom I understand nothing? Indeed, the more I come to understand the character of God, the greater is my capacity to love Him.

God reveals Himself to us in a book. That book is written in words. It communicates concepts that must be understood by the mind. Certainly mysteries remain. But the purpose of God's revelation is that we understand it with our minds that it might penetrate our hearts. To despise the study of theology is to despise learning the Word of God.

Cause #7:
The Seduction of
Worldliness

We remember that the first detour from the pathway to heaven encountered by Christian in John Bunyan's *Pilgrim's Progress* came when Christian was seduced by the counsel of Mr. Worldly Wiseman.[3] Mr. Worldly Wiseman was not named Mr. False Theologian, but it was a false theology he taught.

We understand how worldliness seduces us in terms of sensuality, materialism, hedonism, and the like. But one of the most powerfully seductive forces of the secular world is the temptation to embrace the view of truth currently popular in American culture.

Allan Bloom, in his book *The Closing of the American Mind*,[4] has documented modern education's almost universal embrace of relativism as its governing epistemology. The American mind has become closed to objective truth that can be known rationally. Relativism is ultimately irrational. To say that truth is relative is mindless. It is a statement that cannot possibly be true. The statement "All truth is relative" would itself be relative and have no truth value.

The mind-set, or rather, anti-intellectual mind-set, of secular education has infiltrated and all but conquered evangelicalism. Evangelicals are sublimely happy to affirm both poles of contradictory ideas and accept radically inconsistent and mutually exclusive theologies.

To be sure, evangelicals do not call this relativism or subjectivism. The philosophy is baptized and spiritualized, being thinly veiled in religious jargon. The "leading of the Spirit" is the license for a multitude of epistemological sins. People are "led by the Spirit" to do things explicitly prohibited by Scripture. But the subjective leading may overrule Scripture because truth is relative. The affirmation of irrational contradictions (a redundancy) is justified by appeals to a "higher order of logic" found in the mind of God.

If we seek a coherent, logical, consistent, and rational understanding of the Bible, we are immediately accused of worshiping at the shrine of Aristotle. Because the philosophy of rationalism has often been hostile to Christianity, we flee from anything that remotely seems like rationalism. Because Christianity has truth that reason cannot discover by its own naked speculative efforts, we assume that reason itself is negotiable.

Christianity is not rationalism. But it is rational. It may have truth beyond what reason can fathom. But it is more than rational, not less. It is a virtue, not a vice to seek a coherent understanding of the Word of God. God's Word is not irrational. It was designed to be understood by the mind.

Cause #8: Pietistic Substitution of Devotion for Study

Is it possible that devotional reading of the Bible can be a hindrance to Christian growth? If it becomes a substitute for serious study of the Bible, I answer categorically yes.

I must concede, however, that I really am not sure I understand the difference between "devotional Bible reading" and serious Bible study. Studying the Bible seriously is an act of devotion. C. S. Lewis once observed:

> The present book is something of an experiment. The translation is intended for the world at large, not only for theological students. If it succeeds, other translations of other great Christian books will presumably follow. In one sense, of course, it is not the first in the field. Translations of the *Theologia Germanica,* the *Imitation,* the *Scale of Perfection*, and the *Revelations* of Lady Julian of Norwich, are already on the market, and are very valuable, though some of them are not very scholarly. But it will be noticed that these are all books of devotion rather than of doctrine. Now the layman or amateur needs to be instructed as well as to be exhorted. In this age his need for knowledge is particularly pressing. Nor would I admit any sharp division between the two kinds of book. For my part, I tend to find the doctrinal books often more helpful in devotion than the devotional books, and I rather suspect that the same experience may await many others. I believe that many who find that "nothing happens" when they sit down, or kneel down, to a book of devotion, would find that the heart sings unbidden while they are working their way through a tough bit of theology with a pipe in their teeth and a pencil in their hand.[5]

There are many helps available for daily devotional reading. Those who read the Bible daily for fifteen to thirty minutes are in the minority. But surely fifteen minutes a day reading the Bible is better than no reading.

The problem emerges when we think we can plumb the depths of Scripture by a simple regimen of fifteen to thirty minutes a day. Few disciplines can be mastered by such brief attention. To grow into a mature understanding of God's Word requires a more concerted effort than that gained by short periods of devotional reading. Devotional reading is a great complement to serious study but is not an adequate substitute for it. A study of the Scripture references at the end of each chapter in this book, and the commentary on them within the chapters, can be an excellent beginning to such serious study.

Cause #9: Slothfulness

Karl Barth once remarked that the three most basic and primal sins of fallen humanity are pride, dishonesty, and slothfulness. I'm not sure if Barth was correct in his ranking of them, but they are certainly severe sins about which the Bible has much to say.

If, by our fallen nature we have a strong proclivity toward slothfulness, we must be careful to be on guard against it. It is by no means safe to assume that rebirth immediately and fully delivers us from being lazy. We are no more instantly cured from indolence than we are from pride or dishonesty.

The Christian life requires hard work. Our sanctification is a process wherein we are coworkers with God. We have the promise of God's assistance in our labor, but his divine help does not annul our responsibility to work. "Work out your own salvation with fear and trembling; for it is God who works in you both to will and to do for His good pleasure" (Philippians 2:12-13).

This work is not something that earns merit or gains us our justification. It is the labor that follows justification, the outworking of faith. Lazy Christians will remain immature because they fail to apply themselves to a diligent study of God's Word.

I often startle my seminary students by saying that theological errors are sins. They recoil from this charge assuming that there is no moral culpability for making mistakes. I argue that the primary reason we misinterpret the Bible is not because the Holy Spirit has failed to do His work, but because we have failed to do ours. We fall short of loving God with all our minds and neglect the responsibility to apply ourselves to a rigorous study of the things of God.

Cause #10: Disobedience

Perhaps it is misleading to include disobedience as a separate causal influence for our failure to grow to maturity, since it is at least implicit in all the others. We will list it, then, as a kind of generic summary of all the rest.

While we have considered a number of reasons why Christians sometimes neglect the study of theology, there are also important positive reasons for such study. It is imperative that we press beyond whatever obstacles lie in our path to a diligent pursuit of deeper theological understanding.

Theology Feeds the Soul
For the soul of a person to be inflamed with passion for the living God, that person's mind must first be informed about the character and will of God. There can be nothing in the heart that is not first in the mind. Though it is possible to have theology in the head without its piercing the soul, it cannot pierce the soul without first being grasped by the mind.

An intellectual understanding of doctrine is a necessary condition for spiritual growth. It is not, however, a sufficient condition for such growth. A necessary condition is a condition that must be present for a desired result to happen. Without it, the result will not be forthcoming. For example, oxygen is a necessary condition for fire. However, the mere presence of oxygen is not enough to guarantee that a fire will occur. That is fortunate for us, since the world would be in flames if oxygen automatically produced fire. Oxygen is therefore necessary for fire, but in itself is not sufficient or enough to make a fire. As oxygen is necessary but not sufficient for a fire to ignite, so doctrine is necessary but not sufficient to light a fire in our hearts. Without the gracious operation of the Holy Spirit in our hearts, the mere presence of doctrine, even sound doctrine, will leave us cold.

God Commands Us to Be Diligent in Study
The second positive reason to pursue a knowledge of theology is that God, who is the subject matter of theology, commands us to progress in doctrinal understanding. Let us follow the apostle Paul's exhortation to "put away childish things" (1 Corinthians 13:11) so that we might press forward to the goal of Christian understanding. In

evil we are to be babes, but in understanding we seek mature adulthood (1 Corinthians 14:20). We don't do this to become arrogant in our knowledge, but that we might grow in grace. Mature understanding is the foundation for mature living.

Growing in the knowledge of God is a great joy and privilege. It is a matter of delight for us. Yet it is more than a privilege; it is also a duty. God commands us to grow up into the fullness of Christ. Consider the Shema of Old Testament Israel:

Hear, O Israel: The LORD our God, the LORD is one! You shall love the LORD your God with all your heart, with all your soul, and with all your strength. And these words which I command you today shall be in your heart. You shall teach them diligently to your children, and shall talk of them when you sit in your house, when you walk by the way, when you lie down, and when you rise up. You shall bind them as a sign on your hand, and they shall be as frontlets between your eyes. You shall write them on the doorposts of your house and on your gates. (Deuteronomy 6:4-9)

At the heart of this sacred command is the solemn duty of learning the law of God, of mastering His revelation. It is by no means a casual or cavalier enterprise. To master God's Word is to be deeply immersed in the study of theology.

We remind the reader that it is possible to have a sound theology without having a sound life. But we cannot have a sound life without having a sound theology. In this sense, theology must never be viewed as an abstract science. It is a matter of life and death, even eternal life and eternal death. This book is intended as a guided tour through those life-and-death issues on the theological landscape.

Part

I

REVELATION

1 DIVINE REVELATION

Everything we know about Christianity has been revealed to us by God. To *reveal* means "to unveil." It involves removing a cover from something that is concealed.

When my son was growing up, we developed an annual tradition for the celebration of his birthday. Instead of the normal pattern of distributing presents, we did it by way of our homemade version of the television game show "Let's Make a Deal." I hid his presents in secret places such as in a drawer, under the sofa, or behind a chair. Then I gave him options: "You can have what's in the desk drawer or what's in my pocket." The climax of the game focused on the "big deal of the day." I arranged three chairs that were covered with blankets. Each blanket concealed a gift. One chair had a small gift, a second chair had his big present, and a third chair had a crutch he had used after breaking his leg at age seven.

For three years in a row my son selected the chair containing the crutch! (I always ended up letting him exchange the crutch for his real gift.) The fourth year he was determined not to choose the chair with the crutch under the blanket. This time I concealed his big present alongside the crutch and allowed the top of the crutch to peek out beneath the blanket. Spying the crutch tip he studiously avoided choosing that chair. I got him again!

The fun part of the game was in trying to guess where the treasure was hidden. But it was sheer guesswork, pure speculation. Discovery of the real treasure could not be made until the blanket was removed and the gift lay unveiled.

So it is with our knowledge of God. Idle speculation about God is a fool's errand. If we wish to know Him in truth, we must rely on what He tells us about Himself.

The Bible indicates that God reveals Himself in various ways. He displays His glory in and through nature.

He revealed Himself in ancient times via dreams and visions. The mark of His providence is shown in the pages of history. He reveals Himself in the inspired Scripture. The zenith of His revelation is seen in Jesus Christ becoming a human being—what theologians call "the incarnation."

The author of Hebrews writes:

> God, who at various times and in various ways spoke in time past to the fathers by the prophets, has in these last days spoken to us by His Son, whom He has appointed heir of all things, through whom also He made the worlds. (Hebrews 1:1-2)

Although the Bible speaks of the "various ways" that God reveals Himself, we distinguish between two chief types of revelation—general and special.

General revelation is called "general" for two reasons: (1) it is general in content, and (2) it is revealed to a general audience.

General Content

General revelation provides us with the knowledge that God exists. "The heavens declare the glory of God," says the psalmist. God's glory is displayed in the works of His hands. This display is so clear and manifest that no creature can possibly miss it. It unveils God's eternal power and deity (Romans 1:18-23). Revelation in nature does not give a full revelation of God. It does not give us the information about God the Redeemer that we find in the Bible. But the God who is revealed in nature is the same God who is revealed in Scripture.

General Audience

Not everyone in the world has read the Bible or heard the gospel proclaimed. But the light of nature shines upon everyone in every place, in every time. God's general revelation takes place every day. He is never without a witness to Himself. The visible world is like a mirror that reflects the glory of its maker.

The world is a stage for God. He is the chief actor who appears front and center. No curtain can fall and obscure His presence. We know from one glimpse of creation that nature is not its own mother. There is no such "mother" as Mother Nature. Nature itself is powerless to produce life of any kind. In itself, nature is barren. The power to produce life resides in the Author of nature—God. To substitute nature as the source of life is to confuse the creature with the Creator. All forms of nature worship are acts of idolatry that are detestable to God.

Because of the force of general revelation, every human being knows that God exists. Atheism involves the utter denial of something that is known to be true. This is why the Bible says, "The fool has said in his heart, 'There is no God'" (Psalm 14:1). When the Scripture so chastens the atheist by calling him a "fool," it is making a moral judgment upon him. To be a fool in biblical terms is not to be dim-witted or lacking in intelligence; it is to be immoral. As the fear of God is the beginning of wisdom, so the denial of God is the height of foolishness.

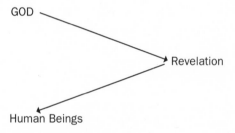

GOD

Revelation

Human Beings

The agnostic, likewise, denies the force of general revelation. The agnostic is less strident than the atheist; he does not flatly deny the existence of God. Rather, the agnostic declares that there is insufficient evidence to decide one way or the other about God's existence. He prefers to suspend his judgment, to leave the issue of God's existence as an open question. However, in light of the clarity of general revelation, the stance of agnosticism is no less detestable to God than that of the militant atheist.

But for anyone whose mind and heart are open, the glory of God is wonderful to see—from the billions of universes in the heavens to the subatomic particles that make up the tiniest of molecules. What an incredible God we serve!

Summary

1. Christianity is a revealed religion.
2. God's revelation is a self-disclosure. He removes the veil that keeps us from knowing Him.
3. We do not come to know God through speculation.
4. God revealed Himself in various ways throughout history.
5. General revelation is given to all human beings.
6. Atheism and agnosticism are based on a denial of what people know to be true.
7. Foolishness is founded on the denial of God.
8. Wisdom is founded on the fear of God.

Biblical passages for reflection:

Psalm 19:1-14
Ephesians 3:1-13
2 Timothy 3:14-17
Hebrews 1:1-4

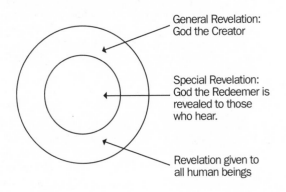

General Revelation: God the Creator

Special Revelation: God the Redeemer is revealed to those who hear.

Revelation given to all human beings

2 PARADOX, MYSTERY, AND CONTRADICTION

The influence of various movements within our culture such as New Age, Eastern religion, and irrational philosophy have led to a crisis of understanding. A new form of mysticism has arisen that exalts the absurd as a hallmark of religious truth. We think of the Zen-Buddhist maxim that "God is one hand clapping" as an illustration of this pattern.

To say that God is one hand clapping sounds profound. It puzzles the conscious mind because it strikes against normal patterns of thought. It sounds "deep" and intriguing until we analyze it carefully and discover that at root it is simply a nonsense statement.

Irrationality is a type of mental chaos. It rests upon a confusion that is at odds with the Author of all truth who is not an author of confusion.

Biblical Christianity is vulnerable to such strands of exalted irrationality because of its candid admission that there is much paradox and mystery in the Bible. Because there are thin but crucial lines that divide paradox, mystery, and contradiction, it is important that we learn to distinguish among them.

We are quickly confounded when we seek to plumb the depths of God. No mortal can exhaustively comprehend God. The Bible reveals things about God that we know are true in spite of our inability to understand them fully. We have no human reference point, for example, to understand a being who is three in person and one in essence (Trinity), or a being who is one person with two distinct natures, human and divine (the person of Christ). These truths, as certain as they may be, are too "high" for us to penetrate.

We face similar problems in the natural world. We understand that gravity exists, but we do not understand it, nor do we seek to define it in irrational or contradictory terms. Most everyone agrees that motion is an integral part of reality, yet the essence of motion itself has perplexed philosophers and scientists for millennia. There is much that is mysterious about reality and much that we do not understand. But that does not warrant a leap into absurdity. Irrationality is fatal both to religion and science. Indeed, it is deadly to any truth.

The late Christian philosopher Gordon H. Clark once defined a paradox as a "charley horse between the ears." His witty remark was designed to point out that what is sometimes called a *paradox* is often nothing more than sloppy thinking. Clark, however, clearly recognized the legitimate role and function of paradox. The word *paradox* comes from the Greek root that means "to seem or to appear." Paradoxes are difficult for us because at first glance they "seem" to be contradictions, but under closer scrutiny resolutions can often be found. For example, Jesus said, "He who loses his life for My sake will find it" (Matthew 10:39). On the surface this sounds akin to a statement like "God is one hand clapping." It sounds like a self-contradiction. What Jesus meant, however, is that if someone loses his life *in one sense,* he will find it *in another sense.* Because the losing and saving are in two different senses, there is no contradiction. I am a father and a son at the same time, but obviously not in the same relationship.

Because the term *paradox* has been misunderstood so often as a synonym for contradiction, it now appears in some English dictionaries as a secondary meaning of the term *contradiction.* A contradiction is a statement that violates the classical law of noncontradiction. The law of noncontradiction declares that *A* cannot be *A* and *non-A* at the same time and in the same respect. That is, something cannot be what it is and not be what it is at the same time and in the same respect. This is the most fundamental of all the laws of logic.

No one can understand a contradiction because a contradiction is *inherently unintelligible.* Not even God can understand contradictions. But He can certainly recognize them for what they are—falsehoods. The word *contradiction* comes from the Latin "to speak against." It is sometimes called an *antinomy,* which means "against law." For God to speak in contradictions would be for Him to be intellectually lawless, to speak with a forked tongue. It is a great insult and unconscionable blasphemy to even suggest that the Author of truth would ever speak in contradictions. Contradiction is the tool of the one who lies—the father of lies who despises the truth.

There is a relationship between mystery and contradiction that easily reduces us to confusing the two. We do not understand mysteries. We cannot understand contradictions. The point of contact between the two concepts is their unintelligible character. Mysteries may not be clear to us now simply because we lack the information or the perspective to understand them. The Bible promises further light in heaven on mysteries we are unable to understand now. Further light may resolve present mysteries. However, there is not enough light in heaven and earth to ever resolve a clear-cut contradiction.

Biblical passages for reflection:
Matthew 13:11
Matthew 16:25
Romans 16:25-27
1 Corinthians 2:7
1 Corinthians 14:33

Summary

1. Paradox is an *apparent* contradiction that under closer scrutiny yields resolution.
2. Mystery is something unknown to us now, but which may be resolved.
3. Contradiction is a violation of the law of noncontradiction. It is impossible to resolve, either by mortals or God, either in this world or the next.

3

IMMEDIATE AND MEDIATE GENERAL REVELATION

When I was a boy and my mother required that I do something without delay, she punctuated her orders to me by using the adverb *immediately.* She would say, "Son, go to your room immediately."

She used the word *immediately* to refer to an event in time that occurs without any intervening block of time. In theology the term *immediate* means something else. It means that something happens without passing through any intervening agent, thing, or means. It is an action that takes place without an intermediary.

In biblical theology we distinguish between two types of general revelation—that which is communicated through an intermediary and that which is direct. When we speak of mediate general revelation, we refer to revelation that is transmitted *through* something. When the heavens reveal God, they become the medium or means through which God displays His glory. In this sense, the whole universe is a medium of divine revelation. The creation bears witness to its Creator.

The Bible says that the whole earth is full of the glory of God. Sadly, we often miss the very glory that surrounds us. We tend to live on the surface of things. We are asleep to the wonder and awe that God provides in His glorious creation. We have tuned out. We are out of touch. Religious ideas are worthless if they do not express something real.

The sublime presence of God is all around us. Yet we are often blind and deaf to it. We don't understand its language. It takes more than stopping to smell the flowers. The flower contains more than a sweet aroma or fragrance. It exudes the glory of its Creator. We are all in touch with divine revelation when we are aware of God's glory in nature. Nature is not divine. But God's glory fills nature and is revealed in and through it.

In addition to revealing His glory indirectly through

creation, God also reveals Himself directly to the human mind. This revelation is called immediate general revelation.

The apostle Paul speaks of the law of God that is written upon our hearts (Romans 2:12-16). John Calvin spoke of a sense of the divine that God implants in the mind of every person. He said:

> That there exists in the human mind, and indeed by natural instinct, some sense of Deity, we hold to be beyond dispute, since God himself . . . has endued all men with some idea of his Godhead, the memory of which he constantly renews and occasionally enlarges.[1]

Cultures everywhere attest to the presence of some kind of religious activity, confirming humankind's incurably religious nature. Human beings are religious at their core. The character of such religion may be crassly idolatrous, but even idolatry, indeed, especially idolatry, gives evidence of this innate knowledge that can be distorted but never obliterated.

Deep within our souls we know that God exists and that He has given His law to us. We seek to suppress this knowledge in order to escape God's commands. But no matter how hard we try, we cannot silence this inner voice. It can be muffled but not destroyed.

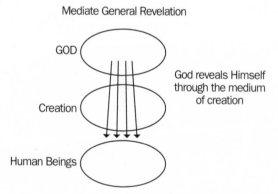

Mediate General Revelation

GOD

Creation

Human Beings

God reveals Himself through the medium of creation

Summary

1. God's glory is evident all around us. It is *mediated* through God's creation.
2. Human beings are religious by nature.
3. God implants in all human beings an innate knowledge of Himself. This is called *immediate* general revelation.

Biblical passages for reflection:
Psalm 19:1-14
Acts 14:8-18
Acts 17:16-34
Romans 1:18-23
Romans 2:14-15

Immediate General Revelation

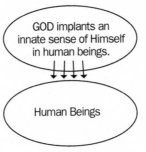

GOD implants an innate sense of Himself in human beings.

Human Beings

4 SPECIAL REVELATION AND THE BIBLE

When Jesus was tempted by Satan in the wilderness, He rebuked the devil with the words, "Man shall not live by bread alone, but by every word that proceeds from the mouth of God" (Matthew 4:4). Historically, the church has echoed the teaching of Jesus by affirming that the Bible is the *vox Dei,* the "voice of God" or the *verbum Dei,* the "Word of God." To call the Bible the Word of God is not to suggest that it was written by God's own divine hand or that it fell from heaven in a parachute. The Bible itself clearly calls attention to its many human authors. In a careful study of Scripture we notice that each human author has his own peculiar literary style, vocabulary, special emphasis, perspective, and the like. Since the production of the Bible involved human effort, how can it be regarded as the Word of God?

The Bible is called the Word of God because of its claim, believed by the church, that the human writers did not merely write their own opinions, but that their words were inspired by God. The apostle Paul writes: "All Scripture is given by inspiration of God" (2 Timothy 3:16). The word *inspiration* is a translation from the Greek word meaning "God-breathed." God breathed out the Bible. Just as we must expel breath from our mouths when we speak, so ultimately Scripture is God speaking.

Although Scripture came to us from the pens of human authors, the *ultimate* source of Scripture is God. That is why the prophets could preface their words by saying, "Thus says the Lord." This is also why Jesus could say, "Your word is truth" (John 17:17), and "Scripture cannot be broken" (John 10:35).

The word *inspiration* also calls attention to the process by which the Holy Spirit *superintended* the production of Scripture. The Holy Spirit guided the human authors so that their words would be nothing less than the word of God. How God superintended the original writings of the Bible is not known. But inspiration does not mean that God dictated his messages to those who wrote the Bible. Rather, the Holy Spirit communicated through the human writers the very words of God.

Christians affirm the infallibility and inerrancy of the Bible because God is ultimately the author of the Bible. And because God is incapable of inspiring falsehood, His word is altogether true and trustworthy. Any normally prepared human literary product is liable to error. But the Bible is not a normal human project. If the Bible is inspired and superintended by God, then it cannot err.

This does not mean that the Bible translations we have today are without error, but that the original manuscripts were absolutely correct. Nor does it mean that every statement in the Bible is true. The writer of the book of Ecclesiastes, for instance, declares that "there is no work or device or knowledge or wisdom in the grave where you are going" (Ecclesiastes 9:10). The writer was speaking from the standpoint of human despair, and we know his statement to be untrue from other parts of Scripture. Even in revealing the false reasonings of a despairing man, the Bible speaks truth.

Biblical passages for reflection:
Psalm 119
John 17:17
1 Thessalonians 2:13
2 Timothy 3:15-17
2 Peter 1:20-21

Summary

1. Inspiration is the process whereby God breathed out His word.
2. God is the ultimate *source* of the Bible.
3. God is the ultimate *superintendent* of the Bible.
4. Only the original manuscripts of the Bible were without error.

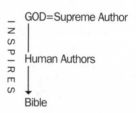

INSPIRES

GOD=Supreme Author

Human Authors

Bible

5 THE LAW OF GOD

God rules His universe by law. Nature itself operates under His providential government. The so-called laws of nature merely describe God's normal way of ordering His universe. These "laws" are expressions of His sovereign will.

God is not accountable to any laws outside of Himself. There are no independent, cosmic rules that God is obligated to obey. Rather, God is a law unto Himself. This simply means that God acts according to His own moral character. His own character is not only morally perfect, it is the ultimate standard of perfection. His actions are perfect because His nature is perfect, and He always acts according to His nature. God is therefore never arbitrary, whimsical, or capricious. He always does what is right.

As God's creatures, we are also required to do what is right. God demands that we live according to His moral law, which He has revealed to us in the Bible. God's law is the ultimate standard of righteousness and the supreme norm for judging right and wrong. As our sovereign, God has the authority to impose obligations on us, to command our obedience, and to bind our conscience. He also has the power and right to punish disobedience when we violate His law. (Sin may be defined as disobedience to God's law.)

Some laws in the Bible are directly based on the character of God. These laws reflect the permanent, transcultural elements of relationships, both divine and human. Other laws were intended for temporary conditions of society. This means that some laws are absolute and eternal, while others may be annulled by God for historical reasons, such as the dietary and ceremonial laws of Israel. Only God Himself may set aside such laws. Human beings never have the authority to set aside God's law.

We are not autonomous. That is, we may not live

according to our own law. The moral condition of humankind is that of heteronomy: we live under the law of another. The specific form of heteronomy under which we live is theonomy, or the law of God.

Biblical passages for reflection:
Exodus 20:1-17
Psalm 115:3
Matthew 5:17-20
Romans 7:7-25
Galatians 3:23-29

Autonomy = *Auto nomos*
Self–law

Heteronomy = *Hetero nomos*
Other–law

Theonomy = *Theos nomos*
God–law

Summary

1. God rules the universe by law. Gravity is one example of God's laws of nature. God's moral law is exhibited in the Ten Commandments.
2. God has the authority to impose obligations upon His creatures.
3. God acts according to the law of His own character.
4. God reveals His moral law to our conscience and in Scripture.
5. Only God has the authority to do away with His laws.

6 THE PROPHETS OF GOD

The prophets of the Old Testament were persons uniquely called of God and supernaturally given God's messages to pass on to us. God spoke His word through the lips and writings of the prophets.

Prophecy involved both future prediction (*fore*telling) and present proclamation and exhortation of God's word (*forth*telling). The prophets were so endowed by the Holy Spirit that their words were God's words. That is why prophetic messages were often prefaced by the phrase, "Thus says the Lord."

The prophets were reformers of Israel's religion. They called the people back to pure worship and obedience to God. Although the prophets were critical of the way Jewish worship often degenerated into mere ritual, they did not condemn or attack the original forms of worship that God had given His people. The prophets were not revolutionaries or religious anarchists. Their task was to purify, not destroy; to reform, not replace the worship of Israel.

The prophets were also deeply concerned about social justice and righteousness. They were the conscience of Israel, calling the people to repentance. They also functioned as God's covenantal lawsuit prosecutors. They "served subpoenas" on the nation for violating the terms of the covenant with God.

Prophets spoke with divine authority because God specifically called them to be His spokesmen. They did not inherit their office, nor were they elected to it. The immediate call from God coupled with the Holy Spirit's power constituted the prophets' credentials.

False prophets were a constant problem in Israel. Instead of speaking the oracles of God, they related their own dreams and opinions—telling people only what they wanted to hear. The true prophets were frequently severely persecuted and rejected by their contemporaries for refusing to compromise the proclamation of the whole counsel of God.

Sometimes the books of the prophets are divided into the "major prophets" and the "minor prophets." This distinction is a reference not to greater or lesser importance of the prophets, but to the volume of their canonical writings. Isaiah, Jeremiah, Ezekiel, and Daniel are called major prophets because they wrote so much, while Amos, Hosea, Micah, Jonah, etc., are referred to as the minor prophets because their books are much smaller.

The New Testament apostles possessed many of the characteristics of the Old Testament prophets. The apostles and the prophets together are called the foundation of the church.

Biblical passages for reflection:
Deuteronomy
18:15-22
Isaiah 6
Joel 2:28-32
Matthew 7:15-20
Ephesians 4:11-16

Summary

1. The Old Testament prophets were agents of divine revelation.
2. Prophecy involved foretelling and forthtelling.
3. The prophets were reformers of Israelite worship and life.
4. Only those directly called by God had the authority to be His prophets.
5. False prophets expressed their own opinions and told people only what they wanted to hear.
6. Major and minor prophets are so designated according to the volume of their written works, not the importance of those works.

7 THE CANON OF SCRIPTURE

We usually think of the Bible as one large book. In reality, it is a small library of sixty-six individual books. Together these books comprise what we call the *canon* of sacred Scripture. The term *canon* is derived from a Greek word that means "measuring rod," "standard," or "norm." Historically, the Bible has been the authoritative rule for faith and practice in the church.

With respect to the books included in the New Testament, there is complete agreement between Roman Catholics and Protestants. However, there is strong disagreement between the two groups concerning what should be included in the Old Testament. Roman Catholics consider the books of the Apocrypha as canonical, whereas historic Protestantism does not. (The books of the Apocrypha were written after the Old Testament was completed and before the New Testament was begun.) The debate concerning the Apocrypha focuses on the broader issue of what was considered canonical by the Jewish community. There is strong evidence that the Apocrypha was not included in the Palestinian canon of the Jews. On the other hand, it seems that Jews living in Egypt may have included the Apocrypha (in its Greek translation) in their Alexandrian canon. Recent evidence has surfaced, however, which casts some doubt upon that.

Some critics of the Bible argue that the church didn't have a Bible as such until almost the beginning of the fifth century. But this is a distortion of the whole process of canonical development. The church met in council on several occasions in the early centuries to settle disputes about which books properly belong in the Canon. The first formal canon of the New Testament was created by the heretic Marcion who produced his own expurgated version of the Bible. To combat this heretic, the church found it necessary to declare the exact content of the New Testament.

Although the vast majority of books that are now included in the New Testament clearly functioned with canonical authority from the time they were written, there were a few books whose inclusion in the New Testament canon was disputed. These included Hebrews, James, 2 Peter, 2 and 3 John, Jude, and Revelation.

There were also several books vying for canonical status that were not included. The overwhelming majority of these were spurious works written by second-century Gnostic heretics. These books were never given serious consideration. (This point is missed by critics who allege that over two thousand contenders yielded a list of twenty-seven. Then they ask, "What are the odds that the correct twenty-seven were selected?") In fact, only two or three books that were not included ever had real consideration. These were *1 Clement, The Shepherd of Hermas,* and *The Didache.* These books were not included in the canon of Scripture because they were not written by apostles, and the writers themselves acknowledged that their authority was subordinate to the apostles.

Some Christians are bothered by the fact that there was an historical selection process at all. They are nagged by the question, how do we know that the New Testament canon includes the proper books? Traditional Roman Catholic theology answers this question by appealing to the infallibility of the church. The church is then viewed as "creating" the Canon, thereby having authority equal to Scripture itself. Classical Protestantism denies both that the church is infallible and that the church "created" the Canon. The difference between Roman Catholicism and Protestantism may be summarized as follows:

Roman Catholic view: The Canon is an infallible collection of infallible books.

Classical Protestant view: The Canon is a fallible collection of infallible books.

Liberal Critical view: The Canon is a fallible collection of fallible books.

Though Protestants believe that God gave special

providential care to insure that the proper books be included, He did not thereby render the church itself infallible. Protestants also remind Roman Catholics that the church did not "create" the Canon. The church recognized, acknowledged, received, and submitted to the canon of Scripture. The term the church used in Council was *recipimus,* "We receive."

By what criteria were books evaluated? The so-called marks of canonicity included the following:

1. They must have apostolic authorship or endorsement.

2. They must be received as authoritative by the early church.

3. They must be in harmony with the books about which there is no doubt.

Though at one stage in his life Martin Luther questioned the canonicity of James, he later changed his mind. There is no serious reason to be the least bit doubtful that the books presently included in the New Testament canon are the proper ones.

Biblical passages for reflection:
Luke 24:44-45
1 Corinthians 15:3-8
2 Timothy 3:16-17
2 Peter 1:19-21
2 Peter 3:14-16

Summary

1. The term *canon* is derived from Greek, and it means "norm" or "standard." Canon is used to describe the authoritative list of books that the church acknowledged as sacred Scripture and thus the "rule" for faith and practice.
2. In addition to the sixty-six books of the Bible accepted by Protestants, Roman Catholics also accept the Apocrypha as authoritative Scripture.
3. To combat heresy, the church found it necessary to declare which books had been recognized as authoritative.
4. There were a few books in the Canon that were a matter of dispute (Hebrews, James, 2 Peter, 2 and 3 John, Jude, and Revelation) and some books that were considered for inclusion that were not admitted to the Canon, including *1 Clement, The Shepherd of Hermas,* and *The Didache.*
5. The church did not *create* the Canon but merely *recognized* the books that bore the marks of canonicity and were therefore authoritative within the church.

6. The marks of canonicity included: (1) apostolic authorship or endorsement, (2) being recognized as authoritative within the early church, and (3) being in harmony with the books that were undoubtedly part of the Canon.

8 INTERPRETING THE BIBLE

Any written document must be interpreted if it is to be understood. The United States of America has nine highly skilled individuals whose daily task is to interpret the Constitution. They comprise the Supreme Court of the land. To interpret the Bible is a far more solemn task than to interpret the U.S. Constitution. It requires great care and diligence.

The Bible itself is its own Supreme Court. The chief rule of biblical interpretation is "sacred Scripture is its own interpreter." This principle means that the Bible is to be interpreted by the Bible. What is obscure in one part of Scripture may be made clear in another. To interpret Scripture by Scripture means that we must not set one passage of Scripture against another passage. Each text must be understood not only in light of its immediate context but also in light of the context of the whole of Scripture.

In addition, properly understood, the only legitimate and valid method of interpreting the Bible is the method of literal interpretation. Yet there is much confusion about the idea of literal interpretation. Literal interpretation, strictly speaking, means that we are to interpret the Bible *as it is written.* A noun is treated as a noun and a verb as a verb. It means that all the forms that are used in the writing of the Bible are to be interpreted according to the normal rules governing those forms. Poetry is to be treated as poetry. Historical accounts are to be treated as history. Parables as parables, hyperbole as hyperbole, and so on.

In this regard, the Bible is to be interpreted according to the rules that govern the interpretation of any book. In some ways the Bible is unlike any other book ever written. However, in terms of its interpretation, it is to be treated as any other book.

The Bible is not to be interpreted according to our own desires and prejudices. We must seek to understand what it actually says and guard against forcing our own views upon it. It is the sport of heretics to seek support from Scripture for false doctrines that have no basis in the text. Satan himself quoted Scripture in an illegitimate way in an effort to seduce Christ to sin (Matthew 4:1-11).

Biblical passages for reflection:
Acts 15:15-16
Ephesians 4:11-16
2 Peter 1:16-21
2 Peter 3:14-18

The basic message of the Bible is simple enough and clear enough for a child to understand. Yet the meat of Scripture requires careful attention and study to understand it properly. Some matters treated by the Bible are so complex and profound that they keep the finest scholars perennially engaged in an effort to sort them out.

There are a few principles of interpretation that are basic for all sound study of the Bible. They include the following: (1) Narratives should be interpreted in light of "teaching" passages. For example, the story of Abraham offering Isaac on Mount Moriah might suggest that God didn't know that Abraham had true faith. But the didactic portions of Scripture make it clear that God is omniscient. (2) The implicit must always be interpreted in light of the explicit; never the other way around. That is, if a particular text seems to imply something, we should not accept the implication as correct if it goes against something explicitly stated elsewhere in Scripture. (3) The laws of logic govern biblical interpretation. If, for example, we know that all cats have tails, we cannot then deduce that some cats do not have tails. If it is true that some cats do not have tails, then it cannot also be true that all cats have tails. This is not a matter merely of technical laws of inference; it is a matter of common sense. Yet the vast majority of erroneous interpretations of the Bible are caused by illegitimate deductions from the Scripture.

Summary:

1. The Bible is its own interpreter.
2. We must interpret the Bible literally—*as it is written.*
3. The Bible is to be interpreted like any other book.
4. Obscure parts of the Bible are to be interpreted by the clearer parts.
5. The *implicit* is to be interpreted in light of the *explicit.*
6. The rules of logic govern what can reasonably be drawn or deduced from Scripture.

9 PRIVATE INTERPRETATION

Two of the great legacies of the Reformation were the principle of private interpretation and the translation of the Bible into the common language of the people. Luther himself brought the issue into sharp focus. When Luther appeared before the Diet of Worms (a council charging him with heresy for his teaching), he declared,

Unless I am convicted by Scripture and plain reason— I do not accept the authority of popes and councils, for they have contradicted each other—my conscience is captive to the Word of God. I cannot and I will not recant anything, for to go against conscience is neither right nor safe. God help me. Amen.[1]

Luther's declaration, and his subsequent translation of the Bible into his native tongue, did two things. First, it took from the Roman Catholic church its sole right of interpretation. No longer would the people be at the mercy of church doctrine, having to accept tradition or church teaching as an authority equal to God's Word. Second, it put interpretation in the hands of the people. This change has been more problematic. It has led to the very excesses about which the Roman Catholic church was concerned—subjective interpretations of the text that depart from historic Christian faith.

Subjectivism has been the great danger of private interpretation. Yet the principle of private interpretation does not mean that God's people have the right to interpret the Bible in whatever manner they wish. Along with the "right" to interpret Scripture comes the responsibility to interpret it *properly*. Believers are free to discover the truths of Scripture, but they are not free to fabricate their own truth. Believers are called to understand sound principles of interpretation and to avoid the danger of subjectivism.

Biblical passages for reflection:
Nehemiah 8:8
2 Timothy 2:15
2 Timothy 3:14-17
Hebrews 1:1-4
2 Peter 1:20-21

In seeking an objective understanding of Scripture we do not thereby reduce Scripture to something cold, abstract, and lifeless. What we are doing is seeking to understand what the Word says in its context before we go about the equally necessary task of applying it to our lives. A particular statement may have numerous possible personal applications, but it can only have one correct meaning. The right to interpret Scripture carries with it the obligation to interpret it accurately. The Bible is not a "waxed nose" to be shaped and formed to suit the views of the interpreter.

Summary

1. The Reformation gave to the church a translation of the Bible in the common language, and to each believer, the right and responsibility of private interpretation of the Bible.
2. Church tradition, though instructive as a guide, does not have equal authority with Scripture.
3. Private interpretation is not a license for subjectivism.
4. The principle of private interpretation carries with it the obligation to seek the correct interpretation of the Bible.
5. Though each biblical text may have multiple applications, it has only one correct meaning.

Part
II

THE NATURE
AND ATTRIBUTES
OF GOD

10 THE INCOMPREHENSIBILITY OF GOD

The Swiss theologian Karl Barth was asked by a student during a seminar in the United States, "Dr. Barth, what is the most profound thing you have ever learned in your study of theology?" Barth thought for a moment and then replied, "Jesus loves me, this I know, for the Bible tells me so." The students giggled at his simplistic answer, but their laughter was of a nervous sort as they slowly realized Barth was serious.

Barth gave a simple answer to a question of profundity. In doing so he was calling attention to at least two vitally important notions. (1) That in the simplest Christian truth there resides a profundity that can occupy the minds of the most brilliant people for a lifetime. (2) That even in learned theological sophistication, we never really rise above a child's level of understanding the mysterious depths and riches of the character of God.

John Calvin used another analogy. He said that God speaks to us in a kind of lisping. As parents engage in "baby talk" when addressing their infant children, so God, in order to communicate with us lowly mortals, must condescend to speak to us in lisps.

No human being has the ability to understand God exhaustively. There is a built-in barrier that prohibits a total, comprehensive understanding of God. We are finite creatures; God is an infinite being. Therein lies our problem. How shall the finite comprehend the infinite? Medieval theologians had a phrase that has become a dominant axiom for all subsequent study of theology, "The finite cannot grasp (or contain) the infinite." Nothing is more obvious than that an infinite object cannot be squeezed into a finite space.

This axiom conveys one of the most important doctrines of orthodox Christianity. It is the doctrine of the *incomprehensibility of God.* The term can be misleading. It may suggest to us that since the finite cannot "grasp" the infinite, that we can know nothing about God. If God is beyond human comprehension, does that not suggest that all of our religious talk is only so much theological babbling and that we are left with, at best, an altar to an unknown God?

This is by no means the intent. The incomprehensibility of God does not mean that we know nothing about God. Rather, it means that our knowledge is partial and limited, falling short of a total or comprehensive knowledge. The knowledge that God gives of Himself through revelation is both real and useful. We can know God to the degree that He chooses to reveal Himself. The finite can "grasp" the infinite, but the finite can never hold the infinite within its grasp. There is always more to God than we apprehend.

The Bible says it this way: "The secret things belong

Biblical passages for reflection:
Job 38:1–41:34
Psalm 139:1-18
Isaiah 55:8-9
Romans 11:33-36
1 Corinthians
    2:6-16

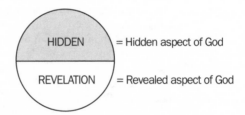

HIDDEN = Hidden aspect of God

REVELATION = Revealed aspect of God

to the LORD our God, but those things which are revealed belong to us and to our children forever" (Deuteronomy 29:29). Martin Luther referred to two aspects of God—the hidden and the revealed. A portion of the divine knowledge remains hidden to our gaze. We work in the light of what God has revealed.

Summary

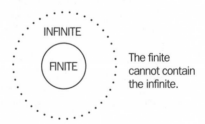

INFINITE

FINITE

The finite
cannot contain
the infinite.

1. There is profound meaning in even the simplest of Christian truths.
2. No matter how deep our knowledge of theology, there will always be much about the nature and character of God that will remain a mystery to us.
3. No human being can have a comprehensive knowledge of God.
4. The doctrine of the incomprehensibility of God does not mean that we can know nothing about God. It means that our knowledge is limited, bounded by our humanity.

11

THE TRIUNITY OF GOD

The doctrine of the Trinity is difficult and perplexing to us. Sometimes it is thought that Christianity teaches the absurd notion that 1+1+1=1. That is clearly a false equation. The term *Trinity* describes a relationship not of three gods, but of one God who is three persons. Trinity does not mean tritheism, that is, that there are three beings who together are God. The word *Trinity* is used in an effort to define the fullness of the Godhead both in terms of His unity and diversity.

The historic formulation of the Trinity is that God is one in essence and three in person. Though the formula is mysterious and even paradoxical, it is in no way contradictory. The unity of the Godhead is affirmed in terms of essence or being, while the diversity of the Godhead is expressed in terms of person.

Though the term *Trinity* is not found in the Bible, the concept is clearly there. On the one hand the Bible strongly affirms the unity of God (Deuteronomy 6:4). On the other hand the Bible clearly affirms the full deity of the three persons of the Godhead: the Father, Son, and Holy Spirit. The church has rejected the heresies of modalism and tritheism. Modalism denies the distinction of persons within the Godhead, claiming that Father, Son, and Holy Spirit are just ways in which God expresses Himself. Tritheism, on the other hand, falsely declares that there are three beings who together make up God.

The term *person* does not mean a distinction in essence but a different *subsistence* in the Godhead. A subsistence in the Godhead is a *real* difference but not an *essential* difference in the sense of a difference in being. Each person subsists or exists "under" the pure essence of deity. Subsistence is a difference within the scope of being, not a separate being or essence. All persons in the Godhead have all the attributes of deity.

There is also a distinction in the work done by each member of the Trinity. The work of salvation is in one sense common to all three persons of the Trinity. Yet in the manner of activity, there are differing operations assumed by the Father, the Son, and the Holy Spirit. The Father initiates creation and redemption; the Son redeems the creation; and the Holy Spirit regenerates and sanctifies, applying redemption to believers.

The Trinity does not refer to parts of God or even to roles. Human analogies such as one man who is a father, son, and a husband fail to capture the mystery of the nature of God.

The doctrine of the Trinity does not fully explain the mysterious character of God. Rather, it sets the boundaries outside of which we must not step. It defines the limits of our finite reflection. It demands that we be faithful to the biblical revelation that in one sense God is one and in a different sense He is three.

Biblical passages for reflection:
Deuteronomy 6:4
Matthew 3:16-17
Matthew 28:19
2 Corinthians 13:14
1 Peter 1:2

Summary

1. The doctrine of the Trinity affirms the triunity of God.
2. The doctrine of the Trinity is not a contradiction: God is one in essence and three in person.
3. The Bible affirms both the oneness of God and the deity of Father, Son, and Holy Spirit.
4. The Trinity is distinguished by the work assumed by the Father, Son, and Holy Spirit.
5. The doctrine of the Trinity sets the limits of human speculation about the nature of God.

12 THE SELF-EXISTENCE OF GOD

When the Bible declares that God is the Creator of the universe it indicates that God Himself is not created. There is a crucial distinction between the Creator and the creation. The creation bears the stamp of the Creator and witnesses to His glory. But the creation is never to be worshipped. It is not Supreme.

It is impossible for something to create itself. The concept of self-creation is a contradiction in terms, a non-sense statement. I ask the reader to pause and reflect a bit. Nothing can be self-created. Not even God can make Himself. For God to create Himself He would have to be before He is. Even God can't do that.

Every *effect* must have a *cause.* That is true by definition. But God is not an effect. He has no beginning and therefore no antecedent cause. He is eternal. He always was or is. He has, within Himself, the power of being. He requires no assistance from outside sources to continue to exist. This is what is meant by the idea of *self-existent.* Granted, it is a lofty and awesome concept. We know of nothing else quite like it. Everything we perceive in our frame of reference is dependent and creaturely. We can't fully comprehend anything as self-existent.

But just because it is impossible (by definition) that a creature be self-existent does not mean it is impossible for the Creator to be self-existent. God, like us, cannot be self-created. But God, unlike us, can be self-existent. Indeed, this is the very essence of the difference between the Creator and creation. This is what makes Him the Supreme Being and the *source* of all other beings.

The concept of self-existence violates no law of reason, logic, or science. It is a rationally valid notion. By contrast, the concept of self-creation violates the most basic law of reason, logic, and science—the law of non-contradiction. Self-existence is rational; self-creation is irrational.

The notion of something being self-existent is not only rationally *possible,* it is rationally *necessary.* Again, reason demands that if anything is, then something must have, within itself, the power of being. Otherwise there would be nothing. Unless something existed in itself, nothing could possibly exist at all.

Perhaps the oldest and deepest question of all is, why is there something rather than nothing? A necessary answer to at least part of the question is because God exists. God exists in Himself eternally. He is the source and fountainhead of all being. He alone has, within Himself, the power of being. Paul declares our dependence upon the power of God's being for our own existence when he says: "In Him we live and move and have our being" (Acts 17:28).

Biblical passages for reflection:

Psalm 90:2
John 1:1-5
Acts 17:22-31
Colossians 1:15-20
Revelation 1:8

Summary

1. Every effect must have a cause.
2. God is not an effect; He has no cause.
3. Self-creation is an irrational concept.
4. Self-existence is a rational concept.
5. Self-existence is not only rationally possible, but rationally necessary.

13 THE OMNIPOTENCE OF GOD

Every theologian is sooner or later asked a question by a student that is posed as an impossible nut to crack. The old query is this: Can God make a rock so big that He cannot move it? At first glance this question seems to impale the theologian on the horns of an unsolvable dilemma. If we answer yes, then we are saying that there is something God cannot do; He cannot move the rock. If we answer no, then we are saying that God cannot build such a rock. Either way we answer we are forced to place limits on God's power.

This problem resembles the other teaser: What happens when an irresistible force meets an immovable object? We can conceive of an irresistible force. We can likewise conceive of an immovable object. What we cannot conceive of is the coexistence of the two. If an irresistible force ever met an immovable object and the object moved, it could no longer properly be called immovable. If the object did not move, then our "irresistible" force could no longer properly be called irresistible. We see, then, that reality cannot contain both—an irresistible force *and* an immovable object.

Meanwhile, back to the immovable rock. The dilemma posed here (as in the case of the irresistible force) is a *false dilemma.* It is false because it is erected on a false premise. It assumes that "omnipotence" means that God can do anything. Yet, as a theological term, omnipotence does not mean that God can do anything. The Bible indicates several things that God cannot do. He cannot lie (Hebrews 6:18). He cannot die. He cannot be eternal and created. He cannot act against His nature. He cannot be God and not be God at the same time and in the same respect.

What omnipotence does mean is that God holds all power over His creation. No part of creation stands outside the scope of His sovereign control. Therefore, there

Biblical passages for reflection:
Genesis 17:1
Psalm 115:3
Romans 11:36
Ephesians 1:11
Hebrews 1:3

is a correct answer to the dilemma of the rock. The nut can be cracked. The answer is no. God cannot build a rock so big that He could not move it. Why? If God ever built such a rock He would be creating something over which He had no power. He would be destroying His own omnipotence. God cannot stop being God; He cannot not be omnipotent.

When the Virgin Mary was puzzled by Gabriel's announcement to her of the conception of Jesus in her womb, the angel said to her: "For with God nothing will be impossible" (Luke 1:37). Here the angel was reminding Mary of God's omnipotence. I guess even angels are capable of using hyperbole. Narrowly considered, the angel expressed bad theology. But the broader biblical understanding points to the meaning that God's power reaches far beyond that of the creature. What may be impossible for us is possible with Him. To say that nothing is impossible with God means that He can do whatever He wills to do. His power is not limited by finite limitations. Nothing or "no thing" can restrict His power. Yet His power is still restricted by what and who He is. Sin is impossible for Him because one cannot sin without willing to sin. God cannot commit sin because He never wills it. Job got to the heart of this matter when he said: "I know that You can do everything, and that no purpose of Yours can be withheld from You" (Job 42:2).

For the Christian, God's omnipotence is a great source of comfort. We know that the same power God displayed in creating the universe is at His disposal to assure our salvation. He showed that power in the Exodus from Egypt. He displayed His power over death in the resurrection of Christ. We know that no part of creation can frustrate His plans for the future. There are no maverick molecules loose in the universe that could possibly disrupt His plans. Though powers and forces of this world threaten to undo, we have no fear. We can rest in the knowledge that nothing can withstand the power of God. He is the One who is almighty.

Summary

1. Omnipotence does not mean that God can do anything. He cannot act against His nature.
2. Omnipotence refers to God's sovereign power, authority, and control over the created order.

3. Omnipotence, though a threat to the wicked, is a source of comfort to the believer.
4. The same power God exhibited in creation is displayed in our redemption.
5. Nothing in the universe can thwart or frustrate God's plans.

14 THE OMNIPRESENCE OF GOD

Astral projection is a fantasy. People may make claims that they can leave their bodies and make junkets to California or India and return without the benefit of trains, planes, or ships, but they are either deluded or deceitful when they make such claims. Yet even if the soul or spirit of a person could be so "projected" to wander the globe, such trips could include only one stop at a time. Our human spirits are still finite spirits and are not now, nor ever will be, capable of being in more than one place at the same time. Only an infinite Spirit is capable of omnipresence.

When we speak of God's omnipresence we usually mean that His presence is in all places. There is no place where God is not. Yet, as spirit, God does not occupy any place, in the sense that physical objects occupy space. He has no physical qualities that can occupy space. The key to understanding this paradox is to think in terms of another dimension. The barrier between God and us is not a barrier of space or time. To meet God, there is not a "where" to go or a "when" to occur. To be in the immediate presence of God is to step into another dimension.

There is a second aspect to God's omnipresence that we often overlook. The "omni" relates not only to the places where God is, but also to how much of Him is in any given place. God is not only present in all places but God is fully present in every place. This is called His immensity. Believers living in New York enjoy the fullness of the presence of God while believers in Moscow enjoy that same presence. His immensity, then, does not refer to His size, but to His ability to be fully present everywhere.

The doctrine of God's omnipresence appropriately fills us with awe. In addition to the reverence it engenders, the doctrine also proves to be comforting. We can always be certain of God's undivided attention. We don't ever need to stand in line or make an appointment to be with God. When we are in God's presence, He is not preoccupied with events on the other side of the world. The doctrine is, of course, not at all comforting to the nonbeliever. There is no place to hide from God. There is no corner of the universe where God is not. The wicked in hell are not separated from God, only from His benevolence. His wrath is with them constantly.

David, who often extolled the glory of God's omnipresence in the Psalms, gives us a poetic summary of this doctrine:

Where can I go from Your Spirit? Or where can I flee from Your presence? If I ascend into heaven, You are there; if I make my bed in hell, behold, You are there. If I take the wings of the morning, and dwell in the uttermost parts of the sea, even there Your hand shall lead me, and Your right hand shall hold me. (Psalm 139:7-10)

Biblical passages for reflection:
1 Kings 8:27
Job 11:7-9
Jeremiah 23:23-24
Acts 17:22-31

Summary

1. Only an infinite Spirit can be omnipresent.
2. God is not bound by time or space. His Being transcends time and space.
3. God's omnipresence includes His immensity by which He is able to be present in His fullness at all times and in all places.
4. God's omnipresence is a comfort to the believer and a terror to the unbeliever.

THE OMNISCIENCE OF GOD

My first exposure to the concept of omniscience was linked to my childhood understanding of Santa Claus. I was told that he was "making a list and checking it twice." I also thought the Easter Bunny lived in our attic (in the off-season) where he could invisibly keep his eye on me.

The word *omniscience* means "to have all (*omni*) knowledge (*science*)." It is a term that is properly applied to God alone. Only a being that is infinite and eternal is capable of knowing everything. The knowledge of a finite creature is always limited by a finite being.

God, being infinite, is able to be aware of all things, to understand all things, and to comprehend all things. He never learns anything or acquires new knowledge. The future as well as the past and present are completely known by Him. He is surprised by nothing.

Because God's knowledge far exceeds our knowledge (it is of a higher sort), some Christians believe that His thinking differs radically *in kind* from ours. For example, it has become commonplace for Christians to assert that God operates with a different form of logic than ours. This concept is convenient when we run into snags in our theology. If we find ourselves affirming both poles of a contradiction, we can alleviate our tension by appealing to God's different order of logic. We can say with ease, "This may all be contradictory to us, but it isn't in the mind of God."

This kind of reasoning is fatal to Christianity. Why? If God in fact has a different order of logic whereby what is contradictory to us is logical to Him, then we have no reason to trust a single word of the Bible. Whatever the Bible says to us could then mean its exact opposite to God. In God's mind good and evil may not be opposites, and the Antichrist might really be Christ.

God's superior knowledge allows Him to be able to resolve mysteries that baffle us. But that points to a difference of *degree* in God's knowledge, not a difference in the *kind* of logic He uses. Because God is rational, even He cannot reconcile contradictions.

God's omniscience also grows out of His omnipotence. God is not all-knowing simply because He has applied His superior intellect to a sober study of the universe and all its contents. Rather, God knows all because He created all and He has willed all. As sovereign Ruler over the universe, God controls the universe. Though some theologians have tried to separate the two, it is impossible for God to know all without controlling all, and it is impossible for Him to control all without knowing all. Like all attributes of God, they are codependent, two necessary parts of the whole.

God's omniscience, like His omnipotence and omnipresence, also relates to time. God's knowledge is absolute in the sense that He is forever aware of all things. God's intellect is different from ours in that He does not have to "access" information, like a computer might retrieve a file. All knowledge is always directly before God.

God's knowledge of all things is a two-edged sword. For the believer the idea offers security—that God is in control, that He understands. God is not puzzled by those problems that puzzle us. For the unbeliever, however, the doctrine highlights the fact that people cannot hide from God. Their sins are exposed. Like Adam, they seek to hide. However, there is no corner of the universe that God's gaze, either in love or wrath, fails to reach.

The omniscience of God is also a crucial part of God's promise to bring about justice in the world. For a judge to render a perfectly just verdict he must first know all the facts. No evidence is hidden from the scrutiny of God. All mitigating circumstances are known to Him.

Biblical passages for reflection:

Psalm 147:5
Ezekiel 11:5
Acts 15:18
Romans 11:33-36
Hebrews 4:13

Summary

1. *Omniscience* means "all knowledge."
2. Only an infinite Being can possess infinite knowledge.
3. God has a higher degree of knowledge than His creatures, but it is of the same logical order.
4. To attribute a different kind of logic to God is fatal to Christianity.
5. God's omniscience is grounded in His infinity and His omnipotence.
6. God's omniscience is crucial to His role as the Judge of the world.

16 THE HOLINESS OF GOD

The first prayer I learned as a child was the simple table grace: "God is great; God is good. And we thank Him for this food." I suppose this prayer is supposed to rhyme. It did when my grandmother said it because she pronounced *food* as if it rhymed with *good* or *hood.*

The two virtues assigned to God in this prayer, greatness and goodness, may be captured by one biblical word, *holy.* When we speak of God's holiness, we are accustomed to associating it almost exclusively with the purity and righteousness of God. Surely the idea of holiness contains these virtues, but they are not the primary meaning of holiness.

The biblical word *holy* has two distinct meanings. The primary meaning is "apartness" or "otherness." When we say that God is holy, we call attention to the profound difference between Him and all creatures. It refers to God's transcendent majesty, His august superiority, by virtue of which He is worthy of our honor, reverence, adoration, and worship. He is "other" or different from us in His glory. When the Bible speaks of holy objects or holy people or holy time, it refers to things that have been set apart, consecrated, or made different by the touch of God upon them. The ground where Moses stood near the burning bush was holy ground because God was present there in a special way. It was the nearness of the divine that made the ordinary suddenly extraordinary and the common, uncommon.

The secondary meaning of *holy* refers to God's pure and righteous actions. God does what is right. He never does what is wrong. God always *acts* in a righteous manner because His *nature* is holy. Thus, we can distinguish between the *internal* righteousness of God (His holy nature) and the *external* righteousness of God (His actions).

Because God is holy, He is both great and good. There is no evil mixed in with His goodness. When we are called to be holy, it does not mean that we share in God's divine majesty, but that we are to be different from our normal fallen sinfulness. We are called to mirror and reflect the moral character and activity of God. We are to imitate His goodness.

Summary

Biblical passages for reflection:
Exodus 3:1-6
1 Samuel 2:2
Psalm 99:1-9
Isaiah 6:1-13
Revelation 4:1-11

1. *Holiness* has two distinct meanings: (1) "otherness"

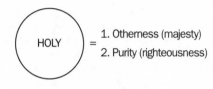

or being "set apart" and (2) "pure and righteous actions."
2. We are called to be holy—to reflect God's righteousness and purity.

17 THE GOODNESS OF GOD

One of life's amusing moments comes when we observe a puppy or a kitten chasing its own shadow. It tries in vain to catch it. When it moves, its shadow moves with it. Not so with God. James declares: "Every good gift and every perfect gift is from above, and comes down from the Father of lights, with whom there is no variation or shadow of turning" (James 1:17).

God never changes. With him there is "no shadow of turning." This suggests not only that God is immaterial and therefore incapable of casting a shadow, but also that there is no "shadow side," in a figurative or moral sense, to God. Shadows suggest darkness, and in spiritual terms darkness suggests evil. Since there is no evil in God, there is no hint of darkness in Him either. He is the Father of lights.

When James adds that there is no "shadow of turning" with God, it is not enough to understand this merely in terms of God's unchanging or immutable being. This reference is also to God's character. Not only is God altogether good, He is consistently good. God doesn't know how to be anything but good.

So closely linked is goodness to God that even pagan philosophers such as Plato equated ultimate goodness, the highest good, with God Himself. God's goodness refers both to His character and His behavior. His actions proceed from and flow out of His being. He acts according to what He is. Just as a corrupt tree cannot bear incorrupt fruit, neither can an incorrupt God produce corrupt fruit.

The law of God reflects His goodness. God is said to be good not because He obeys some cosmic law outside of Himself that judges Him or because God so defines goodness that He can act in a lawless manner and by the sheer power of His authority declare His actions good. God's goodness is neither arbitrary nor capricious. God does obey a law, but the law He obeys is the law of His own character. He always acts according to His own character, which is eternally, immutably, and intrinsically good. James teaches that every good and perfect gift comes from God. He is not only the ultimate standard of goodness; He is the Source of all goodness.

One of the most popular New Testament verses is Romans 8:28: "And we know that all things work together for good to those who love God, to those who are the called according to His purpose." This text on divine providence is as difficult to comprehend as it is popular. If God is able to make everything that happens to us work together for our good, then ultimately everything that happens to us is good. We must be careful to stress here the word *ultimately.* On the earthly plane things that happen to us may indeed be evil. (We must be careful not to call good, evil or evil, good.) We encounter affliction, misery, injustice, and a host of other evils. Yet God in His goodness transcends all of these things and works them to our good. For the Christian, *ultimately,* there are no tragedies. Ultimately, the providence of God works all these proximate evils for our final benefit.

Martin Luther understood this aspect of God's good providence when he said, "If God told me to eat the dung from off the streets, not only would I eat it, but I would know it was good for me."

Summary

1. Creatures have shadows cast by the darkness of sin.

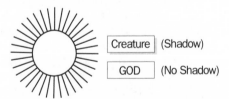

Creature (Shadow)

GOD (No Shadow)

2. There is no shadow side to God.
3. God is not under Law

Law

GOD

Biblical passages for reflection:
Exodus 34:6-7
Psalm 25:8-10
Psalm 100:1-5
Romans 8:28-39
James 1:17

4. God is not apart from Law

Law/GOD

5. God is a Law unto Himself

18 THE JUSTICE OF GOD

Justice is a word we hear every day. We use it in personal relationships, in social conventions, with respect to legislation, and to the verdicts rendered in court. As commonplace as the word is, it has perplexed philosophers who seek an adequate definition of it.

Sometimes we link or equate justice with what is earned or deserved. We speak of people getting their just deserts in terms of rewards or punishments. But rewards are not always based upon merit. Suppose we hold a beauty contest and declare that a prize will be awarded to the person deemed most beautiful. If the "beauty" wins the prize, it is not because there is something meritorious in being beautiful. Rather, justice is served when the most beautiful contestant is rightfully awarded the prize. If the judges vote for someone they do not deem the most beautiful (for political reasons or because they are bribed) then the outcome of the contest will be unjust.

For reasons such as the above, Aristotle defined justice as "giving a person what is his or her *due.*" What is "due" may be determined by ethical obligation or by some prior agreement. If a person is punished more severely than his crime deserves, the punishment is unjust. If a person receives a lesser reward than she has earned, then the reward is not just.

How then does mercy relate to justice? Mercy and justice are obviously different things, though they are sometimes confused. Mercy occurs when wrongdoers are given less punishment than deserved or greater rewards than they earned.

God tempers His justice with mercy. His grace is essentially a kind of mercy. God is gracious to us when He withholds the punishment we deserve and when He rewards our obedience despite the fact that we owe obedience to Him, and so we do not merit any reward. Mercy is always voluntary with God. He is never obligated to be merciful. He reserves the right to exercise

His grace according to the good pleasure of His will. For He says to Moses, "I will have mercy on whomever I will have mercy, and I will have compassion on whomever I will have compassion" (Romans 9:15).

People often complain that because God does not distribute His grace or mercy equally on all people, He is therefore not fair. We complain that if God pardons one person He is therefore obligated to pardon everybody.

Yet, we see clearly in Scripture that God does not treat everyone equally. He revealed Himself to Abraham in a way He did not to other pagans in the ancient world. He graciously appeared to Paul in a way He did not appear to Judas Iscariot.

Paul received grace from God; Judas Iscariot received justice. Mercy and grace are forms of nonjustice, but they are not acts of injustice. If Judas's punishment was more severe than he deserved, then he would have something about which to complain. Paul received grace, but this does not require that Judas also receive grace. If grace is *required* from God, if God is *obligated* to be gracious, then we are no longer speaking of grace, but of justice.

Biblically, justice is defined in terms of righteousness. When God is just, He is doing what is right. Abraham asked God a rhetorical question that can only have one obvious answer: "Shall not the Judge of all the earth do right?" (Genesis 18:25). Likewise, the apostle Paul raised a similar rhetorical question: "What shall we say then? Is there unrighteousness with God? Certainly not!" (Romans 9:14).

Biblical passages for reflection:
Genesis 18:25
Exodus 34:6-7
Nehemiah 9:32-33
Psalm 145:17
Romans 9:14-33

Summary

1. Justice is giving what is due.
2. Biblical justice is linked to righteousness, to doing what is right.
3. Injustice is outside the category of justice and is a violation of justice. Mercy is also outside the category of justice but is not a violation of justice.

Part

III

THE WORKS
AND DECREES
OF GOD

19

CREATION

Everything in time and space had a beginning. I had a beginning; you had a beginning. The houses we live in had a beginning. The clothes we wear had a beginning. There was a time when our houses, our clothes, cars, washing machines, and ourselves, did not exist. They were not. Nothing could be more obvious.

Because we are surrounded by things and by people that obviously had a beginning, we are tempted to jump to the conclusion that *everything* had a beginning. Such a conclusion, however, would be a fatal leap into the abyss of absurdity. It would be fatal to religion. It would also be fatal to science and to reason.

Why? Did I not say that everything in time and space had a beginning? Isn't that the same thing as saying simply that everything had a beginning? By no means. It is simply logically and scientifically impossible that everything had a beginning. Why? If everything that exits once had a beginning, then there had to be a time when nothing existed.

Stop for a moment to reflect. Try to imagine nothing existing. Absolutely nothing. We can't even conceive of absolute nothingness. The very concept is merely the negation of something.

Yet, if there ever was such a time when absolutely nothing existed, what would there be now? Right. Nothing! If ever there was nothing, then by resistless logic, there would always be nothing. There's not even an "always" during which there could be nothing.

Why can we be so sure, indeed, absolutely certain, that if ever there was nothing then there would be nothing now? The answer is astonishingly simple, despite the fact that extremely intelligent people often stumble over the obvious. The answer is simply that you can't get something *from* nothing. An absolute law of science and logic is *ex nihilo nihil fit,* (out of nothing, nothing comes). Nothing cannot produce anything. Nothing can't laugh, sing, cry, work, dance, or breathe. It certainly can't create. Nothing can't do anything because it isn't anything. It doesn't exist. It has no power whatsoever because it has no being.

For something to come out of nothing it would have to possess the power of self-creation. It would have to be able to create itself or bring itself into existence. But that is a manifest absurdity. For something to create or produce itself it would have to *be* before it *is.* But if something already is, it doesn't need to be created. To create itself, something would have to be and not be, exist and not exist, at the same time and in the same respect. That is a contradiction. It violates the most fundamental of all rational and scientific laws, the law of noncontradiction.

If we know anything, we know that if anything exists now, then somehow, somewhere, something did not have a beginning. I am aware that brilliant thinkers such as Bertrand Russell, in his famous debate with Frederick Copelston, argued that the present universe is the result of an "infinite series of finite causes." It poses an endless series, working backwards into eternity, of one caused thing causing another forever. This idea merely compounds the problem of self-creation infinitely. It is a fundamentally silly concept. The fact that it has been proposed by intelligent people makes it no less silly. It's worse than silly. Silly things can be real. But this concept is logically impossible.

Russell can deny the law that out of nothing, nothing comes, but he cannot refute it without committing mental suicide. We know (with logical certitude) that if anything exists now, then there must be something that did not have a beginning. Now the question becomes *what* or *who.*

Many serious scholars believe that the answer to the *what* is found within the universe itself. They argue (as Carl Sagan does) that there is no need to go above or beyond the universe to find something that had no beginning from which everything else comes. That is, we need not assume something like "God" who is transcendent to the universe. The universe or something in it can do the job quite well itself.

There is a subtle error lurking in the above scenario. It has to do with the meaning of the term *transcendent.*

In philosophy and theology the idea of transcendence means that God is "above and beyond" the universe in the sense that He is a higher order of being than other beings. We commonly refer to God as the supreme Being.

What makes the supreme Being different from a human being? Notice that both concepts share a common word, *being*. When we say that God is the supreme Being, we are saying that He is a being who differs in *kind* from other ordinary beings. What precisely is that difference? He is called *supreme* because He has no beginning. He is supreme because all other beings owe their existence to Him, and He owes His existence to none other than Himself. He is the eternal Creator. Everything else is the work of His creation.

When Carl Sagan and others say that in the universe, and not above it or beyond it, there is something that is not created, he is merely quibbling about the Creator's address. He is saying that what is uncreated lives here (within the universe), not "out there" (above or transcendent to the universe). But He still requires a supreme Being. His mysterious part of the universe from which all created things come is still beyond and above everything else in the creation in terms of *being*. In other words, there still must be a transcendent Being.

The more we probe this "within-the-universe Creator," the more it or He begins to sound like God. He is uncreated. He creates everything else. He, or it, has the power in itself of being.

What is crystal clear is that if something exists now, then there must be a supreme Being from which all other beings come. The first assertion of the Bible is "In the beginning God created the heavens and the earth." This text is foundational to all Christian thought. It is not only a religious statement, it is a rationally necessary concept.

Summary

1. Everything in time and space has a beginning.
2. Something cannot come from nothing. Nothing cannot do anything.
3. If ever there was nothing, then nothing could exist now.

Biblical passages for reflection:
Genesis 1
Psalm 33:1-9
Psalm 104:24-26
Jeremiah 10:1-16
Hebrews 11:3

4. Something exists now; therefore something must exist that has no beginning.

5. Things cannot create themselves because they would have to be before they are.

6. If some "part" of the universe is uncreated, then it is superior or transcendent to the parts that have a beginning.

7. An uncreated being is supreme (a higher order of being than created beings), regardless of where it lives.

8. *Transcendence* refers to a level of being, not to geography.

20
PROVIDENCE

In Rhode Island there is a major city named Providence. There is something extraordinary about its name. The name of the city calls attention to the wide gap in thinking that exists between former generations and our present society. Who would name a city "Providence" today? The word itself sounds old fashioned and archaic.

When I read the writings of Christians from earlier centuries I am struck by the multitude of references to God's providence. It seems as though prior to the twentieth century, Christians were more keenly in tune with the providence of God in their lives than we are. The spirit of naturalism that views all events in nature to be ruled by independent natural forces has made its impact on our generation.

The root meaning of the word *providence* is "to see in advance or beforehand," or "to provide for." As such, the word fails to convey the deep meaning of the doctrine of providence. The doctrine signifies far more than that God is a spectator of human events. It contains far more than a mere reference to His foreknowledge.

The Westminster divines in the seventeenth century defined providence in this manner:

God, the great Creator of all things, doth uphold, direct, dispose and govern all creatures, actions, and things, from the greatest even to the least, by his most wise and holy providence, according to his infallible foreknowledge, and the free and immutable counsel of his own will, to the praise of the glory of his wisdom, power, justice, goodness, and mercy.[1]

What God creates, He also sustains. The universe is not only dependent upon God for its origin, it depends upon God for its continuity of existence. The universe can neither exist nor operate by its own power. God upholds all things by His power. It is in Him that we live, and move, and have our being.

The central point of the doctrine of providence is the stress on God's government of the universe. He rules His creation with absolute sovereignty and authority. He governs everything that comes to pass, from the greatest to the least. Nothing ever happens beyond the scope of His sovereign providential government. He makes the rain to fall and the sun to shine. He raises up kingdoms and brings them down. He numbers the hairs on our head and the days of our life.

There is a crucial difference between the providence of God and fortune, fate, or luck. The key to this difference is found in the personal character of God. Fortune is blind while God is all-seeing. Fate is impersonal while God is a Father. Luck is dumb while God can speak. There are no blind, impersonal forces at work in human history. All is brought to pass by the invisible hand of Providence.

In a universe governed by God there are no chance events. Indeed, there is no such thing as chance. Chance does not exist. It is merely a word we use to describe mathematical possibilities. But chance itself has no power because it has no being. Chance is not an entity that can influence reality. Chance is not a thing. It is nothing.

Another aspect of providence is called *concurrence.* Concurrence refers to the coterminous actions of God and human beings. We are creatures with a will of our own. We make things happen. Yet the causal power we exert is secondary. God's sovereign providence stands over and above our actions. He works out His will through the actions of human wills, without violating the freedom of those human wills. The clearest example of concurrence that we find in Scripture is in the case of Joseph and his brothers. Though Joseph's brothers incurred true guilt through their treachery against him, the providence of God was working even through their sin. Joseph said to his brothers, "But as for you, you meant evil against me; but God meant it for good, in order to bring it about as it is this day, to save many people alive" (Genesis 50:20).

God's redemptive providence can work through the most diabolical actions. The worst offense ever committed by a human being was the betrayal of Christ by Judas. Yet the death of Christ was no accident of history. It was according to the determinate counsel of God. Judas's act of wickedness helped to bring about the best thing that ever happened in history, the Atonement. It is not fortuitous that we refer to that day in history as "Good" Friday.

Summary

Biblical passages for reflection:
Job 38:1–41:34
Daniel 4:34-35
Acts 2:22-24
Romans 11:33-36

1. The concept of divine providence is not generally believed in our day.
2. Providence includes God's work of sustaining His creation.
3. Providence refers chiefly to God's government of creation.
4. In light of divine providence there are no impersonal forces such as fortune, fate, or chance.
5. Providence includes concurrence by which God works His divine will through the wills of His creatures.

21

MIRACLES

Sometimes when I play golf with friends at my course (which is marked by a high number of water hazards), I will hit a poor shot that heads for a lake and then skips across the surface to land safely on the other side. Because I am a minister, such a feat is greeted by raised eyebrows and the expression, "It's a miracle!" As any child knows, it does not require a miracle to skip a stone across water. Nor does it require a miracle to skip a golf ball over water. As long as the ball has the proper spin and trajectory, it is a simple matter.

The term *miracle* tends to be used loosely today. A touchdown pass, a narrow escape, or the beauty of a sunset are routinely called miracles. But the word *miracle* can be used in three distinct ways. The first describes common, but nevertheless impressive, events. We speak of the birth of a baby, for instance, as a miracle. In so doing, we honor God for the intricacy and beauty of His creation. We stand in awe of the majesty of the cosmos as God works through the secondary means of natural laws, which are themselves creations of God. Here the term *miracle* refers to common things that point to an uncommon cause in the power of God.

A second way in which we use the term *miracle* is similar to the first. Often in Scripture we read of God's working through secondary means at a most opportune time or place. The star of Bethlehem, for instance, perhaps had a natural, scientific cause. The extraordinary alignment of a group of stars, or a supernova may explain its brightness. To concede this possibility, however, makes the event no less a miracle. The light radiated its brilliance at the time of Christ's birth. It pointed the magi to Bethlehem. The star is then a miracle of timing and placement. Such a miracle honors God as He weaves the tapestry of history in such a way that the event occurred in a miraculous way.

Thirdly, miracles refer to acts of God against nature.

This is the more technical usage of the term. Jesus' turning water into wine or raising Lazarus from the dead are examples of God working against His laws of nature. There can be no natural explanation for these events. They serve to validate Christ as the divine Son of God.

The Bible uses several words to capture the concept contained in the single word *miracle*. The Bible speaks of signs, wonders, and powers. In its narrowest sense, we link miracle to the biblical word for *sign*. Miracles are called signs because like all signs they point beyond themselves to something more significant. God used miracles to prove or attest His agents of divine revelation (Hebrews 2:3-4). God gave Moses the power to perform miracles in order to demonstrate that He had sent Moses. So also the Father authenticated the Son through the signs that He performed.

Today there are three distinct views of miracles. The first is the skeptical view that denies that miracles can ever happen. The second view argues that miracles happened in Bible times and continue to happen today. The third view is that true miracles happened in the Bible, but God ceased performing miracles once His revelation was established in Scripture. This view holds that God still works in the world in a supernatural way but no longer grants miracle-working power to human beings.

Biblical passages for reflection:
Exodus 4:1-9
1 Kings 17:21-24
John 2:11
Hebrews 2:1-4

Summary

1. The Bible speaks of signs, powers, and wonders.
2. The Bible records different types of miracles.
3. All miracles are supernatural events, but not all supernatural events are miracles.

THE WILL OF GOD

Doris Day sang a popular song entitled "Que Sera, Sera," "What will be, will be." At first glance this theme communicates a kind of fatalism that is depressing. Islamic theology frequently says of specific events, "It is the will of Allah."

The Bible is deeply concerned about the will of God—His sovereign authority over His creation and everything in it. When we speak about God's will we do so in at least three different ways. The broader concept is known as God's *decretive, sovereign,* or *hidden will.* By this, theologians refer to the will of God by which He sovereignly ordains everything that comes to pass. Because God is sovereign and His will can never be frustrated, we can be sure that nothing happens over which He is not in control. He at least must "permit" whatever happens to happen. Yet even when God passively permits things to happen, He *chooses* to permit them in that He always has the power and right to intervene and prevent the actions and events of this world. Insofar as He lets things happen, He has "willed" them in this certain sense.

Though God's sovereign will is often hidden from us until after it comes to pass, there is one aspect of His will that is plain to us—His *preceptive* will. Here God reveals His will through His holy law. For example, it is the will of God that we do not steal; that we love our enemies; that we repent; that we be holy. This aspect of God's will is revealed in His Word as well as in our conscience, by which God has written His moral law upon our heart.

His laws, whether they be found in the Scripture or in the heart, are binding. We have no authority to violate this will. We have the power or the ability to thwart the preceptive will of God, though never the right to do so. Nor can we excuse ourselves for sinning by saying, "Que sera, sera." It may be God's sovereign or hidden will that we be "permitted" to sin, as He brings His sovereign will to pass even through and by means of the sinful acts of people. God ordained that Jesus be betrayed by the instrument of Judas's treachery. Yet this makes Judas's sin no less evil or treacherous. When God "permits" us to break His preceptive will, it is not to be understood as permission in the moral sense of His granting us a moral right. His permission gives us the *power,* but not the *right* to sin.

The third way the Bible speaks of the will of God is with respect to God's *will of disposition.* This will describes God's attitude. It defines what is pleasing to Him. For example, God takes no delight in the death of the wicked, yet He most surely wills or decrees the death of the wicked. God's ultimate delight is in His own holiness and righteousness. When He judges the world, He delights in the vindication of His own righteousness and justice, yet He is not gleeful in a vindictive sense toward those who receive His judgment. God is pleased when we find our pleasure in obedience. He is sorely displeased when we are disobedient.

Many Christians become preoccupied or even obsessed with finding the "will" of God for their lives. If the will we are seeking is His secret, hidden, or decretive will, then our quest is a fool's errand. The secret counsel of God is His secret. He has not been pleased to make it known to us. Far from being a mark of spirituality, the quest for God's secret will is an unwarranted invasion of God's privacy. God's secret counsel is none of our business. This is partly why the Bible takes such a negative view of fortune-telling, necromancy, and other forms of prohibited practices.

We would be wise to follow the counsel of John Calvin when he said, "When God closes His holy mouth, I will desist from inquiry." The true mark of spirituality is seen in those seeking to know the will of God that is revealed in His preceptive will. It is the godly person who meditates on God's law day and night. While we seek to be "led" by the Holy Spirit, it is vital to remember that the Holy Spirit is primarily leading us into righteousness. We are called to live our lives by every word that proceeds from the mouth of God. It is His revealed will that is our business, indeed, the chief business of our lives.

Biblical passages for reflection:

John 19:11
Romans 9:14-18
Ephesians 1:11
Colossians 1:9-14
Hebrews 6:13-18
2 Peter 3:9

Summary

1. The three meanings of the will of God:
   (a) *Sovereign decretive will* is the will by which God brings to pass whatsoever He decrees. This is hidden to us until it happens.
   (b) *Preceptive will* is God's revealed law or commandments, which we have the power but not the right to break.
   (c) *Will of disposition* describes God's attitude or disposition. It reveals what is pleasing to Him.
2. God's sovereign "permission" of human sin is not His moral approval.

COVENANT

The basic structure of the relationship God has established with His people is the covenant. A covenant is usually thought of as a contract. While there surely are some similarities between covenants and contracts, there are also important differences. Both are binding agreements. Contracts are made from somewhat equal bargaining positions, and both parties are free not to sign the contract. A covenant is likewise an agreement. However, covenants in the Bible are not usually between equals. Rather, they follow a pattern common to the ancient Near East suzerain-vassal treaties. Suzerain-vassal treaties (as seen among the Hittite kings) were made between a conquering king and the conquered. There was no negotiation between the parties.

The first element of these covenants is the preamble, which lists the respective parties. Exodus 20:2 begins with "I am the LORD your God." God is the suzerain; the people of Israel are the vassals. The second element is the historical prologue. This section lists what the suzerain (or Lord) has done to deserve loyalty, such as bringing the Hebrews out of slavery in Egypt. In theological terms, this is the section of grace.

In the next section, the Lord lists what He will require of those He rules. In Exodus 20, these are the Ten Commandments. Each of the commandments were considered morally binding on the entire covenant community.

The final part of this type of covenant lists blessings and cursings. The Lord lists the benefits that He will bestow upon His vasssals if they follow the stipulations of the covenant. An example of this is found in the fifth commandment. God promises the Israelites that their days will be long in the Promised Land if they honor their parents. The covenant also presents curses should the people fail in their responsibilities. God warns Israel that He will not hold them guiltless if they fail to honor His name. This basic pattern is evident in God's covenants with Adam, Noah, Abraham, Moses, and the covenant between Jesus and His church.

In biblical times, covenants were ratified in blood. It was customary for both parties to the covenant to pass between dismembered animals, signifying their agreement to the terms of the covenant (see Jeremiah 34:18). We have an example of this kind of covenant in Genesis 15:7-21. Here, God made certain promises to Abraham, which were ratified by the sacrificing of animals. However in this case, God alone passes through the animals, indicating that He is binding Himself by a solemn oath to fulfill the covenant.

The new covenant, the covenant of grace, was ratified by the shed blood of Christ upon the cross. At the heart of this covenant is God's promise of redemption. God has not only promised to redeem all who put their trust in Christ, but has sealed and confirmed that promise with a most holy vow. We serve and worship a God who has pledged Himself to our full redemption.

Biblical passages for reflection:
Genesis 15
Exodus 20
Jeremiah 31:31-34
Luke 22:20
Hebrews 8
Hebrews 13:20-21

Summary

Elements of a covenant:
1. Preamble: identifies the sovereign.
2. Historical prologue: rehearses the history of the relationship between the parties.
3. Stipulations: outline the terms of the covenant.
4. Oaths/Vows: the promises that bind the parties to the terms.
5. Sanctions: the blessings and curses (rewards and punishments) to be enacted for keeping or breaking the covenant.
6. Ratification: the sealing of the covenant by blood, i.e., animal sacrifice or the death of Christ.

24 COVENANT OF WORKS

When Adam and Eve were created, they stood in a moral relationship with God, their Creator. They possessed a duty of obedience to Him without any inherent claim to reward or blessing for such obedience. In His love, mercy, and grace, however, God voluntarily entered into a covenant with His creatures by which He added a promise of blessing to His law. This was not a covenant of equal partners, but one that rested on God's initiative and His divine authority.

The original covenant between God and humankind was a covenant of works. In this covenant, God required perfect and total obedience to His rule. He promised eternal life as the blessing of obedience, but threatened mankind with death for disobeying God's law. All human beings from Adam to the present are inescapably members of this covenant. People may refuse to obey or even acknowledge the existence of such a covenant, but they can never escape it. All human beings are in a covenant relationship to God, either as covenant breakers or covenant keepers. The covenant of works is the basis of our need of redemption (because we have violated it) and our hope of redemption (because Christ has fulfilled its terms for us).

A single sin is enough to violate the covenant of works and make us debtors who cannot pay our own debt to God. That we, after even a single sin, have any hope of redemption is due to God's grace and God's grace alone.

The rewards we will receive from God in heaven are also acts of grace. They are God's crowning of His own gracious gifts. Had Adam been obedient to God's covenant of works, he would only have achieved the merit that comes by virtue of fulfilling the covenant agreement with God. Because Adam fell into sin, God, in His mercy, added a new covenant of grace by which salvation became possible and actual.

Only one human being has ever kept the covenant of works. That person was Jesus. His work as the second or new Adam fulfilled all the terms of our original covenant with God. His merit in achieving this is available to all who put their trust in Him.

Jesus is the first person to get into heaven by His good works. We also get into heaven by good works—the good works of Jesus. They become "our" good works when we receive Christ by faith. When we put our faith in Christ, God credits the good works of Christ to our account. The covenant of grace fulfills the covenant of works because God graciously applies the merit of Christ to our account. Thus by grace we meet the terms set forth in the covenant of works.

Biblical passages for reflection:
Genesis 2:17
Romans 3:20-26
Romans 10:5-13
Galatians 3:10-14

Summary

1. God entered into a covenant of works with Adam and Eve.
2. All humans are inescapably related to God's covenant of works.
3. All human beings are violators of the covenant of works.
4. Jesus fulfilled the covenant of works.
5. The covenant of grace provides us with the merits of Christ by which the terms of the covenant of works are satisfied.

Part
IV

JESUS CHRIST

25 THE DEITY OF CHRIST

Faith in the deity of Christ is necessary to being a Christian. It is an essential part of the New Testament gospel of Christ. Yet in every century the church has been forced to deal with people who claim to be Christians while denying or distorting the deity of Christ.

In church history there have been four centuries in which confession of the deity of Christ has been a crucial and stormy issue *inside* the church. Those centuries have been the fourth, fifth, nineteenth, and twentieth. Since we are living in one of the centuries where heresy assaults the church, it is urgent that we safeguard the church's confession of Christ's deity.

At the Council of Nicea in A.D. 325, the church, in opposition to the Arian heresy, declared that Jesus is begotten, not made, and that His divine nature is of the same essence (*homo ousios*) with the Father. This affirmation declared that the Second Person of the Trinity is one in essence with God the Father. That is, the "being" of Christ is the being of God. He is not merely similar to Deity, but He *is* Deity.

The confession of the deity of Christ is drawn from the manifold witness of the New Testament. As the Logos Incarnate, Christ is revealed as being not only preexistent to creation, but eternal. He is said to be in the beginning *with* God and also that He *is* God (John 1:1-3). That He is *with* God demands a personal distinction within the Godhead. That He *is* God demands inclusion in the Godhead.

Elsewhere, the New Testament ascribes terms and titles to Jesus that are clearly titles of deity. God bestows the preeminent divine title of *Lord* upon Him (Philippians 2:9-11). As the Son of Man, Jesus claims to be Lord of the Sabbath (Mark 2:28) and to have authority to forgive sins (Mark 2:1-12). He is called the *"Lord* of glory" (James 2:1) and willingly receives worship, as when Thomas confesses, "My Lord and my God!" (John 20:28).

Paul declares that the fullness of the Godhead dwells in Christ bodily (Colossians 1:19) and that Jesus is higher than angels, a theme reiterated in the book of Hebrews. To worship an angel or any other creature, no matter how exalted, is to violate the biblical prohibition against idolatry. The *I am*s of John's Gospel also bear witness to the identification of Christ with Deity.

In the fifth century, the Council of Chalcedon (A.D. 451) affirmed that Jesus was truly man and truly God. Jesus' two natures, human and divine, were said to be without mixture, confusion, separation, or division.

Biblical passages for reflection:

Mark 2:28
John 1:1-14
John 8:58
John 20:28
Philippians 2:9-11
Colossians 1:19

Summary

1. The deity of Christ is a doctrine essential to Christianity.
2. The church has had crises of heresy regarding Christ's deity in the fourth, fifth, nineteenth, and twentieth centuries.
3. The Council of Nicea (A.D. 325) affirmed the deity of Christ, declaring that He is of the same substance or essence as the Father and that He was not a created being.
4. The New Testament clearly affirms the deity of Christ.
5. The Council of Chalcedon (A.D. 451) declared that Jesus was truly God.

26 THE SUBORDINATION OF CHRIST

What is a subordinate? In our language it is clear that to be subordinate to someone is to be "under" that person's authority. A subordinate is not a peer; a subordinate is not on an equal level of authority with his or her super-ordinate. The prefix *sub-* means "under" and *super-* means "over" or "above."

When we speak of the subordination of Christ we must do so with great care. Our culture equates subordination with inequality. But in the Trinity all members are equal in nature, in honor, and in glory. All three members are eternal, self-existent; they partake of all aspects and attributes of deity.

In God's plan of redemption, however, the Son *voluntarily* takes on a subordinate role to the Father. It is the Father who sends the Son into the world. The Son obediently comes to earth to do the will of the Father. We must be careful to note, however, that there is no sense of begrudging obedience. As they are the same in glory, the Father and the Son are also of one will. The Father wishes for redemption equally as much as the Son. The Son is eager to perform the work of salvation, just as the Father is eager for Him to do so. Jesus declared that zeal for His Father's house consumed Him (John 2:17) and that His meat and His drink was to do the will of the Father.

Finally, it should be noted that Christ's subordination and obedience was not only unto suffering. The plan included all aspects of Christ's work for us and Christ's ultimate glorification. The Westminster Confession explains the interconnectedness of the Father's purpose and Christ's work:

It pleased God, in His eternal purpose, to choose and ordain the Lord Jesus, His only begotten Son, to be the Mediator between God and man, the Prophet, Priest and King, the Head and Savior of His Church, the heir of all things, and Judge of the world: unto whom He did from all eternity give a people, to be His seed, and to be by Him in time redeemed, called, justified, sanctified and glorified.[1]

By submitting Himself to the perfect will of His Father, Jesus did for us what we were unwilling and unable to do for ourselves. He obeyed the law of God perfectly. At His baptism Christ told John, "It is fitting for us to fulfill all righteousness" (Matthew 3:15). Jesus' entire life and ministry demonstrate this perfect obedience.

By obeying the law perfectly, Jesus accomplished two vitally important things. On the one hand He was qualified to be our Redeemer, the Lamb without blemish. Had Jesus sinned, He could not have atoned for His own sins, let alone for ours. Second, by His perfect obedience He earned the rewards God promised to all who keep His covenant. He merited the rewards of heaven that He bestows upon us. As the subordinate One, He saved a people who had been insubordinate.

Biblical passages for reflection:

John 4:34
John 5:30
Philippians 2:5-8
Hebrews 5:8-10
Hebrews 10:5-10

FATHER = SON

Equal in being
and eternal attributes

Summary

1. Although Christ is equal to the Father in terms of His divine nature, He is subordinate to the Father in His role in redemption.
2. *Subordination* does not mean "inferior."
3. Christ's subordination is voluntary.
4. Christ's perfect obedience qualified Him to be the sin bearer for His people and earned the rewards of heaven promised to the redeemed.

FATHER

Son subordinate in
economy of redemption

SON

27 THE HUMANITY OF CHRIST

That God the Son took upon Himself a real human nature is a crucial doctrine of historic Christianity. The great ecumenical Council of Chalcedon in A.D. 451 affirmed that Jesus is truly man and truly God and that the two natures of Christ are so united as to be without mixture, confusion, separation, or division, each nature retaining its own attributes.

The true humanity of Jesus has been assaulted chiefly in two ways. The early church had to combat the heresy of docetism, which taught that Jesus did not have a real physical body or a true human nature. They argued that Jesus only "seemed" to have a body but in reality was a phantom sort of being. Over against this, John strongly declared that those who denied that Jesus came truly in the flesh are of the Antichrist.

The other major heresy the church rejected was the monophysite heresy. This heresy argued that Jesus did not have two natures, but one. This single nature was neither truly divine nor truly human but a mixture of the two. It was called a "theanthropic" nature. The mono-physite heresy involves either a deified human nature or a humanized divine nature.

Subtle forms of the monophysite heresy threaten the church in every generation. The tendency is toward allowing the human nature to be swallowed up by the divine nature in such a way as to remove the real limita-tions of Jesus' humanity.

We must distinguish between the two natures of Jesus without separating them. When Jesus hungers, for exam-ple, we see that as a manifestation of the human nature, not the divine. What is said of the divine nature or of the human nature may be affirmed of the person. On the cross for example, Christ, the God-man, died. This, however, is not to say that God perished on the cross. Though the two natures remain united after Christ's ascension, we must still distinguish the natures regarding the mode of His presence with us. Concerning His human nature, Christ is no longer present with us. However, in His divine nature, Christ is never absent from us.

Christ's humanity was like ours. He became a man "for our sakes." He entered into our situation to act as our Redeemer. He became our substitute, taking upon Himself our sins in order to suffer in our place. He also became our champion, fulfilling the law of God on our behalf.

In redemption there is a twofold exchange. Our sins are imparted to Jesus. His righteousness is imparted to us. He receives the judgment due to our imperfect humanity, while we receive the blessing due to His perfect humanity. In His humanity Jesus had the same limitations common to all human beings, except that He was without sin. In His human nature He was not omniscient. His knowledge, though true and accurate as far as it went, was not infinite. There were things He did not know such as the day and the hour of His return to earth. Of course in His divine nature He is omniscient and His knowledge is without limit.

As a human being Jesus was restricted by time and space. Like all human beings He could not be in more than one place at the same time. He sweated. He hungered. He wept. He endured pain. He was mortal, capable of suffering death. In all these respects He was like us.

Biblical passages for reflection:
John 1:1-14
Galatians 4:4
Philippians 2:5-11
Hebrews 2:14-18
Hebrews 4:15

Summary

1. Jesus had a true human nature that was perfectly united with His divine nature.
2. Docetism said that Jesus did not have a real physical body.
3. The monophysite heresy involves the deification of the human nature by which His humanity is eclipsed by His deity.
4. Christ's humanity is the basis of His identification with us.
5. Jesus took our sins upon Himself and imparts His righteousness to us.
6. Jesus' human nature had the limitations of normal humanity, except that He was without sin.

28 THE SINLESSNESS OF CHRIST

When we speak of Christ's sinlessness we generally refer to His humanity. It is unnecessary to plead the sinlessness of Christ's deity, as deity by our definition cannot and does not sin. The doctrine of Christ's sinlessness has been free of any fundamental controversy. Even the most crass heretics in history have not denied this of Christ.

The sinlessness of Christ does not merely serve as an example to us. It is fundamental and necessary for our salvation. Had Christ not been the "lamb without blemish" He not only could not have secured anyone's salvation, but would have needed a savior Himself. The multiple sins Christ bore on the cross required a perfect sacrifice. That sacrifice had to be made by one who was sinless.

Christ's sinlessness had negative and positive aspects to it. Negatively, Christ was completely free of any transgression. He broke none of God's holy law. He scrupulously obeyed whatsoever God commanded. Despite His sinlessness, Christ even obeyed Jewish law, submitting to circumcision, baptism, and perhaps even the system of animal sacrifice. Positively, Christ was eager to obey the law; He was committed to doing the will of His Father. It was said of Him that zeal for His Father's house consumed Him (John 2:17) and that His meat was to do the will of His Father (John 4:34).

One difficulty concerning the sinlessness of Christ is related to Hebrews 4:15: "For we do not have a High Priest who cannot sympathize with our weaknesses, but was in all points tempted as we are, yet without sin." If Christ was tempted as we are, how could He have been sinless? The problem becomes even greater when we read James 1:14-15: "But each one is tempted when he is drawn away by his own desires and enticed. Then, when desire has conceived, it gives birth to sin; and sin, when it is full-grown, brings forth death."

James describes a kind of temptation that arises from sinful desires within us. These desires are already sinful in nature. If Jesus was tempted as we are tempted it would seem to suggest that He had sinful desires. Yet this is precisely the point of the qualifier "yet without sin" in the book of Hebrews. Jesus had desires. But he had no sinful desires. When He was tempted by Satan the assault came from the outside. It was an external temptation. Satan tried to entice Jesus to eat during His period of fasting. Jesus surely had physical hunger; He had a desire for food. Yet there was no sin in being hungry. All things being equal, Jesus wanted to eat. But all things were not equal. Jesus was committed to obeying the will of the Father. He had no desire to sin.

It was by His sinlessness that Jesus qualified Himself as the perfect sacrifice for our sins. However, our salvation requires two aspects of redemption. It was not only necessary for Jesus to be our substitute and receive the punishment due for our sins; He also had to fulfill the law of God perfectly to secure the merit necessary for us to receive the blessings of God's covenant. Jesus not only *died* as the perfect for the imperfect, the sinless for the sinful, but He *lived* the life of perfect obedience required for our salvation.

Biblical passages for reflection:
Matthew 3:15
Romans 5:18-21
2 Corinthians 5:21
Hebrews 7:26
1 Peter 3:18

Summary

1. The sinlessness of Christ is necessary for our salvation.
2. Jesus made atonement as the Lamb without blemish.
3. Christ was not tempted by sinful desires.
4. By His perfect obedience Jesus supplied the righteousness (merit) we require to be saved.

29
THE VIRGIN BIRTH

The doctrine of the Virgin Birth of Jesus holds that Jesus' birth was the result of a miraculous conception whereby the Virgin Mary conceived a baby in her womb by the power of the Holy Spirit, without a human father. Christ's miraculous birth tells us much about his nature. That He was born of woman demonstrates that He was indeed human and became one of us. Christ's humanity, however, was not precisely the same as our own. We are born with original sin, Christ was not.

The Virgin Birth also relates to the deity of Christ. While it is certainly possible for Deity to enter the world in a manner other than a virgin birth, the miracle of his birth points to Christ's divinity. The announcement of the angel Gabriel to Mary underscores this point. When he told Mary she would have a son, Mary was perplexed: "How can this be, since I do not know a man?" (Luke 1:34).

Gabriel's answer to Mary is of decisive significance for our understanding of the Virgin Birth: "The Holy Spirit will come upon you, and the power of the Highest will overshadow you; therefore, also, that Holy One who is to be born will be called the Son of God" (Luke 1:35). Moments later the angel added, "For with God nothing will be impossible" (Luke 1:37).

Aside from artificial insemination, which is a modern, non-miraculous variation on conception, nothing is more regular or commonplace in nature than the normal causal relationship for the conception of a baby. For a woman to become pregnant who has not had sexual intercourse with a man is not only biologically extraordinary, it is clearly against the laws of nature.

But Mary's child was not generated by Mary, herself. The "father" of the baby is the Holy Spirit. The language of the Spirit's coming upon Mary and

Biblical passages for reflection:
Isaiah 7:10-16
Matthew 1:23
Romans 1:3-4
1 Corinthians
   15:45-49
Galatians 4:4

"overshadowing" her echoes the descriptive account of the Holy Spirit's work in the original creation of the world. It reveals that this baby will be a special creation with His father being God Himself.

Those who do not believe in the Virgin Birth usually do not believe that Jesus is the true Son of God. Thus, the Virgin Birth is a watershed doctrine, separating orthodox Christians from those who do not believe in the Resurrection and Atonement.

Summary

1. The Bible plainly and unambiguously teaches the Virgin Birth.
2. The birth of Jesus from a woman points to His humanity and His appearance as the new or second Adam.
3. That Jesus was born apart from human fatherhood points to His divine nature as the Son of God.
4. The denial of the Virgin Birth is usually linked to the denial of the supernatural or miraculous elements of Scripture.

30 JESUS CHRIST AS THE ONLY BEGOTTEN

That the Bible refers to Jesus as "the only begotten of the Father" (John 1:14) has provoked great controversy in church history. Because Jesus is also called the "first-born over all creation" (Colossians 1:15), it has been argued that the Bible teaches that Jesus is not divine, but an exalted creature.

Both Jehovah's Witnesses and Mormons deny the deity of Christ by appealing to these concepts. It is chiefly because of their denial of the deity of Christ that these two groups are regarded as sects rather than as bona fide Christian denominations.

The deity of Christ was a crucial issue in the fourth century when the heretic Arius denied the Trinity. Arius's chief argument against the deity of Christ anticipated the arguments of modern Jehovah's Witnesses and Mormons. Arius was condemned as a heretic at the Council of Nicea in A.D. 325.

Arius argued that the Greek word translated *begotten* means "to happen," "to become," "to start to be." That which is begotten must have a beginning in time. It must be finite with respect to time, which is a sign of creatureliness. To be the "firstborn over all creation" suggests the supreme level of creatureliness, ranking higher than the angels, but it does not rise above the level of creature. To worship a creature is to commit idolatry. No angel or any other creature is worthy of worship. Arius saw the attributing of deity to Jesus as a blasphemous rejection of biblical monotheism. For Arius God must be regarded as "one," both in being and in person.

The Nicene Creed reflects the church's response to the Arian heresy. It confesses that Jesus was "begotten, not made." In this simple formula the church was zealous to guard against the idea of interpreting the term *begotten* to mean or to imply creatureliness.

Some historians have faulted the Council of Nicea

for engaging in special pleading or mental gymnastics to evade the plain and simple meaning of the Greek word *begotten* and the phrase "firstborn over all creation." The church, however, did not flee from the simple meaning of these terms in an arbitrary manner. There was justifiable grounds for fencing their term *begotten* with the qualifier "not made."

First, the church was seeking to understand these terms in the total context of the biblical teaching concerning the nature of Christ. Being persuaded that the New Testament clearly ascribes deity to Christ, the church was against setting one part of Scripture against another.

Second, although the New Testament was written in the Greek language, most of the thought forms and concepts are loaded with Hebrew meanings. The Hebrew concepts are expressed through the vehicle of the Greek language. This fact sounds a warning against leaning too heavily upon tight nuances of classical Greek. Just as John uses the loaded term *logos* to refer to Jesus, it would be a mistake to fill that term exclusively with the Greek ideas associated with the use of the word.

Third, the term *begotten* is used in a qualified way in the New Testament. In John 1:14 Jesus is referred to as the "only begotten." Again in John 1:18 He is called the "only begotten Son." There is significant manuscript evidence that suggests that the original Greek read "only begotten God." Had that text been accepted the debate would be over. However, if we treat the text as reading "only begotten Son," we still have a crucial qualifier. Jesus is called the *only* begotten (*monogenais*). The prefix *mono-* is stronger in Greek than the word *only* is in English. Jesus is absolutely singular in his begottenness. He is uniquely begotten. No one or nothing else is begotten in the sense Jesus is begotten. That the church can speak of Christ's eternal begottenness is an attempt to do justice to this. The Son proceeds eternally from the Father, not as a creature, but as the Second Person of the Trinity.

The book of Hebrews, which also refers to Jesus as "begotten" (Hebrews 1:5), is the epistle that gives us

Biblical passages for reflection:
John 1:1-18
Colossians 1:15-19
Hebrews 1:1-14

perhaps the highest Christology to be found in the New Testament. The only book in the New Testament that rivals Hebrews in this regard is the Gospel of John. It is John who clearly calls Jesus "God." It is also John who speaks of Christ as the "only begotten."

Finally, the phrase "firstborn over all creation" must be understood from the background of first-century Jewish culture. From this vantage point we can see that the term *firstborn* refers to Christ's exalted status as the heir of the Father. Just as the firstborn son usually received the patriarchal inheritance, so Jesus as the divine Son receives the Father's kingdom as His inheritance.

Summary

1. That Jesus is called "the only begotten of the Father" and "firstborn over all creation" has sparked controversy in church history over the deity of Christ.
2. Jehovah's Witnesses and Mormons use these passages to deny the deity of Christ.
3. The Nicene Creed clearly spelled out that Jesus was "begotten, not made." This careful distinction was a reflection of the New Testament's affirmation of Christ's deity.
4. Jesus is called "the *only begotten*" of the Father. Jesus is *uniquely* begotten of the Father, not as a creature, but as the eternal Son of God, the Second Person of the Trinity.
5. The term *firstborn* must be understood from a first-century Jewish background. Jesus is the "firstborn over all creation" in the sense that He is the heir of all that belongs to the Father.

31 THE BAPTISM OF CHRIST

The rite of water baptism performed by John the Baptist is closely linked to the sacrament of baptism instituted by Jesus as the sign of the new covenant. Though there is a continuity between the two baptisms, they must not be seen as identical.

Biblical passages for reflection:
Isaiah 40:3
Matthew 3:13-17
Mark 1:1-5
2 Corinthians 5:21

John's baptism, properly considered, belongs to the Old Testament. Although we read of it in the New Testament, the New Covenant did not begin until after John's ministry. It was a requirement God gave to His people, Israel. It was a baptism of *preparation.* John preached that the kingdom of God was at hand. He was the herald of the Messiah. The nearness of the coming kingdom of God was seen in the imminent appearance of Christ. The Messiah King was about to be made known, but the people of Israel were not ready for Him. They were unprepared. They were unclean.

John's baptism was a radical innovation. Prior to John, Gentiles converting to Judaism were required to undergo a purification rite of cleansing. With the appearance of John the Baptist, God commanded the Jews also to repent and be washed. The Jewish clergy regarded John's requirement as heretical and insulting. It meant that John was treating Jews as if they were as unclean as Gentiles.

Jesus willingly submitted to John's baptism, even insisting upon it (against John's protests) because in His role as Messiah it was necessary for Jesus to submit to every requirement of God's law for Israel. In His identification with His people, Jesus was baptized to fulfill all righteousness.

When Jesus entered the Jordan River to be baptized by John, this event marked the beginning of Jesus' earthly ministry. Here He not only identified Himself with the sin of His people, He was also anointed by the Holy Spirit for ministry. In a sense this was Jesus' ordination. Here He began His vocation as the Christ.

The term *Christ* means "anointed one." Jesus was anointed by the Holy Spirit at His baptism and began to fulfill the role of Messiah as described by Isaiah: "The Spirit of the Lord GOD is upon Me, because the LORD has anointed Me to preach good tidings to the poor" (Isaiah 61:1).

Summary

1. John's baptism was preparation for the coming of the Messiah.
2. John's baptism was insulting to the Jewish officials because it meant they were "unclean."
3. Jesus was baptized not for His own sins but to identify with the sinners He came to save.
4. Jesus was ordained or anointed at His baptism.

32 THE GLORY OF CHRIST

We tend to think of glory as something achieved by extraordinary athletic victories, business achievements, or personal fame. In the Bible, however, it has to do with the radiant shining forth of the transcendent majesty of God. At crucial moments the splendor of Jesus' deity burst through the cloak of His humanity.

The glory of Christ perhaps never became more evident than at His transfiguration. The Greek word for transfiguration is *metamorphoomai*, from which we get the word *metamorphosis*. It denotes a change in form as, for example, the transformation that occurs when
a caterpillar becomes a butterfly. The prefix *trans-* means literally "across." In the transfiguration a limit or barrier is crossed. We might call it a crossing of the line between the natural and the supernatural, between the human and the divine. It crosses a boundary of dimensions into the realm of God.

At the Transfiguration a brilliant light shone from Jesus. This light was the visible manifestation that the barrier had indeed been crossed. There are some similarities between this manifestation of glory and the shining face of Moses when he returned from Mount Sinai with the Ten Commandments. The differences, however, are significant. Moses' face shone with *reflected* glory. Christ did not merely reflect the brightness of divine glory, but His glory *is* the brightness of divine glory. In this respect, His glory clearly transcends the reflected glory on the face of Moses.

Christ, then, did not reflect light but was the source of light. The Transfiguration was akin to what the Christian will experience in the New Jerusalem. In Revelation 21:23, John explains that the heavenly city will have no need of the sun or of the moon to shine in it. God's glory will illumine it. The Lamb will be its

Biblical passages for reflection:
Matthew 17:1-9
Mark 13:24-27
Hebrews 1:1-3
Revelation 22:4-5

light. John writes, "They shall see His face, and His name shall be on their foreheads. There shall be no night there: They need no lamp nor light of the sun, for the Lord God gives them light" (Revelation 22:4-5).

That the glory of Christ shone forth at the Transfiguration should not surprise us. The surprise is that He willingly veiled His glory for the sake of His children.

Summary

1. The glory of Christ was revealed at His transfiguration.
2. The transfiguration of Christ was a change in form, a crossing of the natural into the supernatural.
3. Christ's glory is not merely a reflection of God's glory but the very glory of God Himself.

33 THE ASCENSION OF CHRIST

The significance of the Ascension is often overlooked in the modern church. We have special celebrations and holidays (holy days) to commemorate the birth (Christmas), the death (Good Friday), and the resurrection (Easter) of Christ. Most churches, however, make little or no mention of the Ascension. However, the Ascension is a redemptive event of profound importance. It marks the moment of Christ's highest point of exaltation prior to His return. It is in the Ascension that Christ entered into His glory.

Jesus described His departure from this earth as being better for us than His abiding presence. When He first announced His departure to the disciples, they were saddened by the news. However, they later came to realize the significance of this great event. Luke records the Ascension for us:

Now when He had spoken these things, while they watched, He was taken up, and a cloud received Him out of their sight. And while they looked steadfastly toward heaven as He went up, behold, two men stood by them in white apparel, who also said, "Men of Galilee, why do you stand gazing up into heaven? This same Jesus, who was taken up from you into heaven, will so come in like manner as you saw Him go into heaven." (Acts 1:9-11)

We notice that Jesus departed in a cloud. This is probably a reference to the Shekinah, the cloud of God's glory. The Shekinah exceeds in radiance any ordinary cloud. It is the visible manifestation of God's radiant glory. Therefore, the manner of Jesus' departure was not at all ordinary. It was a moment of remarkable splendor.

To ascend means "to go up" or "to rise." However, when the term *ascension* is used with respect to Christ, it has a deeper, richer, and more specific meaning. Jesus' ascension is unique. It goes beyond Enoch being taken directly into heaven or the departure of Elijah in a chariot of fire.

Jesus' ascension refers to His going to a special place for a special purpose. He goes to the Father, to the Father's right hand. He rises to the seat of cosmic authority. Jesus goes to heaven for His coronation, His confirmation as the King of Kings.

Jesus also ascended to enter the heavenly Holy of Holies to continue His work as our great High Priest. In heaven Jesus reigns as King and intercedes for us as our High Priest. From His position of ascended authority He poured out His Spirit upon the church. John Calvin remarked,

Being raised to heaven, he withdrew his bodily presence from our sight, not that he might cease to be with his followers, who are still pilgrims on the earth, but that he might rule both heaven and earth more immediately by his power.[1]

When Jesus ascended to heaven for His coronation as King of Kings, He was seated at the right hand of God. The right hand of God is the seat of authority. From this position Jesus rules, administrates His kingdom, and presides as the judge of heaven and earth.

At the right hand of the Father, Jesus is seated as the Head of His body, the church. Yet in this position, Jesus' authority and governmental jurisdiction and administration extend beyond the sphere of His church to embrace the whole world. Though church and state may be distinguished within Jesus' domain, they are never separated or divorced. His authority extends over both. All earthly rulers are accountable to Him and will be judged by Him in His office as King of Kings and Lord of Lords.

Everyone in heaven and on earth is called of God to reverence Jesus' majesty, to be ruled by His hand, to do Him proper homage, and to submit to His power. Everyone will ultimately stand before Him as He sits in final judgment.

Jesus has the authority to pour out His Holy Spirit upon the church. But Jesus did not pour out the Spirit until He was first seated at the right hand of God. The Spirit ministers in subordination to the Father and the

Son, who together sent Him to apply Christ's work of salvation to believers.

While seated at the right hand of God, Jesus not only exercises His role as King of Kings, He also fulfills the role of cosmic judge. He is judge over all nations and all people. Although Jesus rules as our judge, He has also been appointed by the Father to be our advocate. He is our defense attorney. At the last judgment our court-appointed defense lawyer will be the presiding judge. A foretaste of Jesus' intercession on behalf of saints can be seen in the martyrdom of Stephen:

Biblical passages for reflection:
Luke 24:50-53
Romans 8:34
Romans 14:9-10
Ephesians 4:7-8
Hebrews 9:23-28

But he [Stephen], being full of the Holy Spirit, gazed into heaven and saw the glory of God, and Jesus standing at the right hand of God, and said, "Look! I see the heavens opened and the Son of Man standing at the right hand of God!" (Acts 7:55-56)

Summary

1. The Ascension receives too little attention in the modern church.
2. The Ascension marks a critical point of Christ's exaltation in redemptive history.
3. Christ departed in a cloud of glory.
4. Christ ascended to a specific place for a specific purpose: His coronation as King of Kings.
5. In His ascension, Christ entered His role as our heavenly High Priest and was seated at the right hand of God, the seat of cosmic authority.
6. From His position at the right hand of God, Jesus authorized the outpouring of the Holy Spirit at Pentecost.
7. In His position of authority, Jesus is judge over all.
8. Jesus also serves as the advocate or defense attorney for His people.

34 JESUS CHRIST AS MEDIATOR

A mediator is a go-between. He is one who stands between two or more persons or groups who are in a dispute and tries to reconcile them. In biblical terms, human beings are described as being at enmity against God. We rebel, revolt, and refuse to obey the law of God. As a result, God's wrath is upon us. For this catastrophic situation to be changed or redeemed it is necessary that we become reconciled to God.

To effect our reconciliation, God the Father appointed and sent His Son to be our Mediator. Christ brings to us nothing less than the divine majesty of God Himself—He is God incarnate. Yet He took upon Himself a human nature and willingly submitted Himself to the demands of God's law.

Christ did not initiate reconciliation in an attempt to persuade the Father to put aside His wrath. Rather, in the eternal counsel of the Godhead there was complete agreement between the Father and the Son that the Son should come as our Mediator. No angel could adequately represent God to us; only God Himself could do that.

In the Incarnation, the Son took upon Himself human nature in order to accomplish the redemption of Adam's fallen seed. By His perfect obedience, Christ satisfied the demands of God's law and merited eternal life for us. By His submission to the atoning death on the cross, He satisfied the demands of God's wrath against us. Both positively and negatively Christ satisfied the divine requirements for reconciliation. He brought about a new covenant with God for us by His blood and continues daily to intercede for us as our High Priest.

An effective mediator is one who is able to make peace between parties who are in conflict or estranged from each other. This is the role Jesus performed as our perfect Mediator. Paul declared that we have peace with God through Christ's work of reconciliation: "Therefore, having been justified by faith, we have peace with God through our Lord Jesus Christ" (Romans 5:1).

The mediating work of Christ is superior to all other mediators. Moses was the mediator of the Old Covenant. He served as God's go-between, giving the Israelites the law. But Jesus is superior to Moses. The author of Hebrews declares,

Biblical passages for reflection:
Romans 8:33-34
1 Timothy 2:5
Hebrews 7:20-25
Hebrews 9:11-22

For this One has been counted worthy of more glory than Moses, inasmuch as He who built the house has more honor than the house. . . . And Moses indeed was faithful in all His house as a servant . . . but Christ [was faithful] as a Son over His own house, whose house we are." (Hebrews 3:3-6)

Summary

1. A mediator works to bring about reconciliation between estranged parties.
2. Christ as the God-man reconciles us to the Father.
3. Christ and the Father are agreed from eternity that Christ should be our Mediator.
4. Christ's work of mediation is superior to prophets, angels, and Moses.

35 THE THREEFOLD OFFICE OF CHRIST

One of the great contributions to a Christian understanding of the work of Christ is John Calvin's exposition of the threefold office of Christ as Prophet, Priest, and King.[1] As the prophet of God par excellence, Jesus was both the object and subject of prophecy. His person and His work are the focal point of Old Testament prophecy, yet He Himself was a prophet. In Jesus' own prophetic statements, the kingdom of God and His role within the coming kingdom are major themes. A principal activity of a prophet was to declare the Word of God. Jesus not only declared the Word of God, He is Himself the Word of God. Jesus was the supreme Prophet of God, being God's Word in the flesh.

The Old Testament prophet was a kind of mediator between God and the people of Israel. He spoke to the people on behalf of God. The priest spoke to God on behalf of the people. Jesus also fulfilled the role of the great High Priest. The Old Testament priests offered sacrifices regularly, but Jesus offered a sacrifice of everlasting value once for all time. Jesus' offering to the Father was the sacrifice of Himself. He was both the offering and the offerer.

Whereas in the Old Testament the mediating offices of prophet, priest, and king were held by separate individuals, all three offices are held supremely in the one person of Jesus. Jesus fulfilled the messianic prophecy of Psalm 110. He is the one who is both David's descendant and David's Lord. He is the Priest who is also the King. The Lamb who is slain is also the Lion of Judah. To gain a full understanding of the work of Christ we must not view Him merely as a prophet, or as a priest, or as a king. All three offices are perfectly fulfilled in Him.

Summary

1. Jesus was the fulfillment of Old Testament prophecy and was Himself a prophet.
2. Jesus was both Priest and sacrifice. As Priest, He offered Himself as the perfect sacrifice for sin.

Biblical passages for reflection:
Psalm 110
Isaiah 42:1-4
Luke 1:26-38
Acts 3:17-26
Hebrews 5:5-6

3. Jesus is the anointed King of all kings and Lord of all lords.

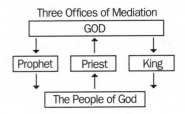

Three Offices of Mediation

36 THE TITLES OF JESUS

Jesus of Nazareth was given more titles than any other person in history. A brief sampling would include the following:

Christ
Lord
Son of Man
Savior
Son of David
Great High Priest
Son of God
Alpha & Omega
Master
Teacher
Righteousness
Prophet
Rose of Sharon
Lily of the Valley
Advocate
Lion of Judah
Lamb of God
Second Adam

The chief titles given to Jesus are:

1. *Christ.* The title *Christ* is so often given to Jesus that people often mistake it for his last name. It is, however, not a name, but a title that refers to his position and work as Messiah. The term *Christ* comes from the Greek *Christos,* which is used to translate the Hebrew word for *Messiah.* Both *Christ* and *Messiah* mean "Anointed One."

In the Old Testament the concept of the promised Messiah, who would be uniquely anointed by the Holy Spirit, was a many-sided and complex idea. The Jews did not all have the same idea about the Messiah.

One concept of the Messiah was that he would be a king. He would be the anointed Son of David, the Lion of Judah, who would restore the fallen kingdom of David. (This aspect greatly excited the Jews and fanned the flames of their hope for a political ruler who would free them from their bondage to Rome.)

But the Messiah was also called to be the Servant of God, indeed the Suffering Servant spoken of in Isaiah's prophecy. These two strands seemed virtually impossible to unite in one person, though in Jesus they obviously were.

The Messiah would also be a heavenly being (Son of Man) and would be uniquely related to God the Father (Son of God). He would be both priest and prophet as well. The more we realize how complex the concept of Messiah was, the more amazed we are at the intricate way in which all these strands were woven together in the person and work of Jesus.

2. *Lord.* The second most frequently used title for Jesus in the New Testament is the title *Lord.* This title is of supreme importance to understanding the New Testament portrait of Jesus. The term *lord* is used in three distinct ways in the New Testament. The first is as a common form of polite address, similar to the English word *sir.* The second usage refers to a slave owner or "master." Here it is applied in a figurative sense to Jesus. He is our master. The third usage is the imperial usage. Here it refers to one who is sovereign.

In the first century, the Roman emperors demanded a loyalty oath from their subjects by which they were required to confess the formula "Caesar is Lord." Christians were martyred for refusing to comply. Instead, they proclaimed the first Christian creed, "Jesus is Lord." To call Jesus "Lord" was radical not only from a Roman standpoint but especially from a Jewish standpoint, for it is the title given to God Himself in the Old Testament.

The title *Lord* was bestowed upon Jesus by God the Father. It is the "name which is above every name" that Paul speaks of in Philippians 2:9.

3. *Son of Man.* This title is one of the more fascinating titles given to Jesus and perhaps the one most frequently misunderstood. Because the church confesses the dual nature of Jesus, that He is truly man and truly God, and because the Bible describes Jesus as Son of Man and Son of God, it is tempting to assume that Son

of Man refers to Jesus' humanity and Son of God refers to His deity. This, however, is not exactly the case. Though the title *Son of Man* includes an element of humanity, its primary reference is to Jesus' divine nature. The title *Son of God* also includes a reference to deity but its primary focus is on Jesus' *obedience* as a son.

This title, *Son of Man,* takes on added importance when we realize that though it ranks third (well down the list) in terms of *frequency of usage* in the New Testament (behind *Christ* and *Lord*), it ranks *first* (by a wide margin) of Jesus' use of titles for Himself. *Son of Man* is far and away Jesus' favorite designation for Himself.

The importance of this title is drawn from its link to Daniel's use of it in the Old Testament (see Daniel 7). Here *Son of Man* clearly refers to a heavenly being who functions in the role of cosmic Judge. On Jesus' lips the title is not an exercise in false humility, but a bold claim to divine authority. Jesus claimed, for example, that the Son of Man had authority to forgive sins (Mark 2:10), a divine perogative, and was Lord of the Sabbath (Mark 2:28).

4. *The Logos*. No title for Jesus engendered more intense philosophical and theological interest in the first three centuries than the title *Logos*. *Logos* was central to the early church's development of Christology. The prologue of John's Gospel is crucial to this Christological understanding of the *Logos*. John writes, "In the beginning was the Word (*Logos*), and the Word (*Logos*) was with God, and the Word (*Logos*) was God" (John 1:1).

In this remarkable passage the *Logos* is both distinguished from God ("was with God") and identified with God ("was God"). This paradox had great influence on the development of the doctrine of the Trinity, whereby the *Logos* is seen as the Second Person of the Trinity. He differs in person from the Father, but is one in essence with the Father.

That Christian philosophies were drawn to the *logos* concept as a title for Jesus is easy to understand. Though the term *logos* can be translated simply "word," it had a history of technical philosophical usage which gave *logos* a rich meaning. The ancient Greeks were concerned about making sense of the universe and thus embarked on a quest for "ultimate reality" (metaphysics). Their philosophers sought the unifying factor or power that brought order and harmony to the wide diversity of the created realm (cosmology). They searched for a *nous* (mind) to which (or whom) they could attribute the order of all things. To this unifying ultimate reality the Greeks gave the name *logos*. It provided the coherence or "logic" of reality. The concept was used by Heraclitus and later by Stoic philosophy, where it was used as a cosmic, abstract law.

Though the term is thus loaded with pre-Christian Greek philosophical baggage, the biblical use of *logos* goes well beyond the Greek usage. In Genesis 1:3ff. we are told that "God said . . . and there was." Thus, it is by God's word that creation came into being. What sets the *logos* concept apart most significantly from Greek philosophy, however, is that the New Testament "logos" is *personal*—the Word became a man who lived and died in our world.

Biblical passages for reflection:
Genesis 1:1–2:3
Matthew 9:1-8
Matthew 16:13-21
John 1:1-18
Revelation
    19:11-16

Summary

1. *Messiah* means "anointed one" and is used as a title for Jesus to signify His role as both King and Suffering Servant. Messiah is the title most frequently used for Jesus.
2. *Lord* is the second most frequently used title for Jesus and refers to His supreme authority as Sovereign of the universe.
3. *Son of Man* is the title Jesus used most often in reference to Himself. This title primarily refers to Jesus' role as Judge of the whole cosmos.
4. The title *Logos* has a rich heritage in both Hebrew and Greek culture. Jesus is the *Logos*—the Creator of the universe, the ultimate reality behind the universe, and the One who is constantly sustaining the universe.

Part

V

THE HOLY SPIRIT

37 THE DEITY OF THE HOLY SPIRIT

In the liturgy of the church we frequently hear the words, "In the name of the Father, and of the Son, and of the Holy Ghost, amen." This expression is a trinitarian formula that ascribes deity to all three persons in the Godhead.

Likewise, we sing the *Gloria:*

Glory be to the Father, and to the Son, and to the Holy Ghost.
As it was in the beginning, is now, and ever shall be, world without end. Amen.

This song ascribes eternal glory to all three persons of the Trinity. The Holy Ghost is ascribed eternal glory along with the Father and the Son.

While the deity of Christ has been debated for centuries, and the debate continues today, the deity of the Holy Spirit is generally accepted in the church. Perhaps the reason the deity of the Holy Spirit has not been very controversial is because the Spirit never took on human form.

The Bible clearly represents the Holy Spirit as possessing divine attributes and exercising divine authority. Since the fourth century, nearly all who agree that the Spirit is a person also agree that He is divine.

In the Old Testament what is said of God is also often said of the Spirit of God. The expressions "God said" and "the Spirit said" are repeatedly interchanged. In the New Testament this pattern continues, perhaps no more forcefully than in Acts 5:3-4, where Peter said, "Ananias, why has Satan filled your heart to lie to the Holy Spirit and keep back part of the price of the land for yourself? . . . You have not lied to men but to God." Simply put, lying to the Holy Spirit is lying to God Himself.

Scripture also ascribes divine attributes to the Holy

Spirit. Paul writes of the Spirit's omniscience in 1 Corinthians 2:10-11, "The Spirit searches all things, yes, the deep things of God. For what man knows the things of a man except the spirit of the man which is in him? Even so no one knows the things of God except the Spirit of God." The psalmist attests to the omnipresence of the Spirit in Psalm 139:7-8: "Where can I go from Your Spirit? Or where can I flee from Your presence? If I ascend unto heaven, You are there; if I make my bed in hell, behold, You are there." The Spirit also works in creation, hovering over the face of the waters (Genesis 1:1-2).

As a concluding statement on the deity of the Holy Spirit, we have Paul's benediction in his second letter to the Corinthians, "The grace of the Lord Jesus Christ, and the love of God, and the communion of the Holy Spirit be with you all. Amen" (2 Corinthians 13:14).

Biblical passages for reflection:
Genesis 1:1-2
Acts 5:3-4
Romans 8:9-17
1 Corinthians
   6:19-20
Ephesians 2:19-22

Summary

1. The liturgy of the church ascribes deity to the Holy Spirit.
2. The Old Testament ascribed divine attributes and authority to the Holy Spirit.
3. The New Testament assigns divine attributes to the Holy Spirit.

38 THE PERSONALITY OF THE HOLY SPIRIT

The night my wife was converted to Christ she exclaimed, "Now I know who the Holy Spirit is." Prior to that time she had thought of the Holy Spirit as an "it" rather than a personal "who."

When we speak of the personality of the Holy Spirit, we mean that the Third Member of the Trinity is a person and not a force. This is clear from Scripture, where only personal pronouns are used when referring to the Spirit. In John 16:13, Jesus said, "When He, the Spirit of truth, has come, He will guide you into all truth; for He will not speak on His own authority, but whatever He hears He will speak; and He will tell you things to come."

Because the Holy Spirit is a real and distinct person and not an impersonal force, it is possible for us to enjoy a personal relationship with Him. Paul gives a benediction to the Corinthian church that highlights this, "The grace of the Lord Jesus Christ, and the love of God, and the communion of the Holy Spirit be with you all. Amen" (2 Corinthians 13:14). To have communion with someone is to enter a personal relationship with him. In addition, we are called not to sin against, resist, or grieve the Holy Spirit. Impersonal forces cannot be "grieved." Grief can only be experienced by a personal being.

Because the Holy Spirit is a person, it is appropriate to pray to Him. His role in prayer is to assist us in expressing ourselves adequately to the Father. As Jesus intercedes for us as our High Priest, so the Holy Spirit intercedes for us in prayer.

Finally, the Bible speaks of the Holy Spirit performing tasks that only persons can perform. The Spirit *comforts, guides,* and *teaches* the elect (see John 16). These activities are done in a manner that involves intelligence, will, feeling, and power. He searches, selects, reveals, comforts, convicts, and admonishes. Only a person could do these things. The response of the Christian, then, is not mere affirmation that such a being exists, but

Biblical passages for reflection:
John 16:13
2 Corinthians 13:14
1 Timothy 4:1
James 4:5
1 John 5:6

rather, to obey, love, and adore the Holy Spirit, the Third Person of the Trinity.

Summary

1. The Holy Spirit is a person, not an impersonal force.
2. Scripture uses personal pronouns when referring to the Holy Spirit.
3. The work of the Holy Spirit both requires and exhibits personality.
4. The Christian enjoys a personal relationship with the Holy Spirit.
5. The Holy Spirit is to be worshiped and obeyed.

39 THE INTERNAL TESTIMONY OF THE HOLY SPIRIT

In any courtroom drama that includes witnesses, the testimony that is given is crucial to the case. Testimony is important because it is designed to help us get at the truth of the matter. In some trials, the testimony of witnesses is challenged because their character is suspect. The testimony of a psychopathic liar has little value. For testimony to be credible, the witness must be credible.

When God testifies to the truth of something, His witness is sure. His testimony is altogether unimpeachable. Testimony that has God as its author cannot fail. It is, in fact, infallible testimony. It proceeds from the highest possible character, the deepest possible font of knowledge, and from the most supreme authority. The trustworthiness of God's testimony is what once prompted Luther to declare, "The Holy Spirit is no skeptic."[1] The truths that the Spirit reveals are more certain than life itself.

John Calvin taught that even though the Scriptures manifest clear and reasonable signs of their divine authority and exhibit sufficient evidence of their divine origin, these evidences do not fully persuade us until or unless they are sealed to our hearts by the inward testimony of the Holy Spirit.[2] Calvin recognized the difference between proof and persuasion. Even though we may be able to offer objective and compelling proofs of the truth of Scripture, that is no guarantee that people will believe, yield to, or embrace them. For us to be persuaded of their truth we need the help of the internal testimony of the Spirit. The Spirit causes us to acquiesce or yield to the compelling evidence of the truth of the Scriptures.

In His inner witness, the Holy Spirit offers no new secret information or clever argument otherwise unavailable to us. Rather, He operates upon our spirits to break down and overcome our resistance to

God's truth. He moves us to surrender to the clear teaching of God's Word and embrace it with full assurance.

The internal testimony of the Spirit is not a flight into mysticism or an escape into subjectivism, where personal feelings are elevated to the status of absolute authority. There is a crucial difference between the testimony of the Holy Spirit *to* our spirits and the human testimony *of* our own spirits. The testimony of the Holy Spirit is to the Word of God. It comes to us *with* the Word and *through* the Word. It does not come apart from or without the Word.

Just as the Holy Spirit bears witness to our spirits that we are the children of God, confirming His word to us (Romans 8:16), so the Holy Spirit inwardly assures us that the Bible is the Word of God.

Biblical passages for reflection:

John 15:13
Acts 5:32
Acts 15:28
Romans 8:16
Galatians 5:16-18

Summary

1. The testimony of God is completely trustworthy.
2. The Bible offers objective evidence that it is the Word of God.
3. We are not fully persuaded of the truth of Scripture without the testimony of the Holy Spirit.
4. The internal testimony of the Spirit offers no new argument to the mind, but works upon our hearts and spirits to yield to the evidence already there.
5. The doctrine of the internal testimony of the Holy Spirit is not a license for believing that whatever we feel to be true is true.

40 THE ILLUMINATION OF THE HOLY SPIRIT

One of the most useful modern inventions is the flashlight or, as the British call it, the "torch." When the power goes off and the house is plunged into darkness, the flashlight is a lifesaver. Its function is to shine light into darkness in order that we may see what is there. It works to *illumine* the scene.

The Bible is not a book of darkness. On the contrary, it is a source of much-needed light. The psalmist calls God's Word "a lamp to my feet and a light to my path" (Psalm 119:105).

Not every part of Scripture is equally clear to our understanding. Certain passages are difficult to grasp. We struggle at certain points to gain insight into the meaning of the text. The effect of sin upon us is to shroud our mind in darkness. In our fallen nature we are creatures of darkness who are in desperate need of light.

Though the Scriptures themselves are light for us, there is need for additional illumination so that we may clearly perceive the light. The same Holy Spirit who inspires the Scripture, works to illumine the Scriptures for our benefit. He sheds more light on the original light. Illumination is the work of the Holy Spirit. He helps us to hear, receive, and properly understand the message of God's Word. As the apostle Paul writes,

But as it is written: "Eye has not seen, nor ear heard, nor have entered into the heart of man the things which God has prepared for those who love Him." But God has revealed them to us through His Spirit. For the Spirit searches all things, yes, the deep things of God. For what man knows the things of a man except the spirit of the man which is in him? Even so no one knows the things of God except the Spirit of God. (1 Corinthians 2:9-11)

Here Paul draws an analogy from human experience. You may learn many things about me from observing me or from hearsay, but you cannot know what is going on inside my mind or my spirit unless I choose to reveal it. Only I know what I am thinking. (Though at times I'm sure my wife can read my mind!)

Likewise, it is the Holy Spirit who knows the innermost thoughts of God. Paul says that the Spirit "searches" the deep things of God. This does not mean that the Holy Spirit must investigate and inquire into the mind of God in order to be instructed. He is not seeking for information He otherwise lacks. He "searches" as a searchlight scans the night to bring into the light what otherwise would remain hidden.

Illumination is not to be confused with revelation. It is commonplace today to hear people speak about private revelations they claim to have received from the Holy Spirit. The work of the Holy Spirit in illumination is not the supplying of new information or fresh revelations beyond those found in sacred Scripture.

Reformed Christianity emphatically denies that God is giving new normative revelation today. The Spirit is still working to illumine what is revealed in Scripture. The Spirit helps us to understand the Bible, to convict us of the truth of the Bible, and to apply that truth to our lives. He works with the Word and through the Word. His task is never to teach against the Word. It is therefore always necessary to test what we hear by the teaching of Scripture. The Scripture is the Spirit's book.

Biblical passages for reflection:
John 16:13-15
1 Corinthians
   2:9-16
2 Peter 1:21

Summary

1. Illumination refers to the Holy Spirit's assistance in helping us understand and apply Scripture.
2. Illumination is not to be confused with revelation.

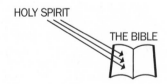

HOLY SPIRIT

THE BIBLE

41 THE BAPTISM OF THE HOLY SPIRIT

"Have you received the baptism of the Holy Spirit?" A person in our day who becomes a Christian will sooner or later be asked this question. The question is frequently posed by charismatic Christians who are enthusiastic about their experiences with the Holy Spirit.

A doctrine that was once largely confined to Pentecostal and Assembly of God churches has now become of central importance to a vast number of believers. The Neo-Pentecostal movement has reached into nearly every Christian denomination. A sense of excitement and spiritual renewal usually accompanies this fresh discovery of the presence and the power of the Holy Spirit in the church.

Neo-Pentecostalism has sought to define a doctrine of the baptism of the Holy Spirit based on people's experiences. The doctrine has been widely controversial.

Usually, but not always, the charismatic Christian considers the baptism of the Holy Spirit as a second work of grace, distinct from and subsequent to regeneration and conversion. It is a work of the Holy Spirit that is available to all Christians but not appropriated by all. Charismatics are divided among themselves on the issue of whether speaking in tongues is a necessary sign or manifestation of the "baptism."

Pentecostals point to the pattern in the book of Acts where believers (who obviously had the regenerating work of the Spirit prior to Pentecost) were filled by the Holy Spirit and spoke in tongues. This biblical pattern, which includes a time gap between conversion and baptism of the Spirit, is then seen as normative for all ages.

Pentecostals are correct in seeing a distinction between regeneration by the Holy Spirit and the baptism of the Holy Spirit. Regeneration refers to the Holy Spirit giving new life to the believer—making alive one who was dead in sin. The baptism of the Holy Spirit refers to God empowering His people for ministry.

Biblical passages for reflection:
Joel 2:28-29
John 7:37-39
Acts 2:1-11
1 Corinthians 12
1 Corinthians 14:26-33

While the distinction between regeneration and the baptism of the Holy Spirit is legitimate, making a time gap between the two normative for all subsequent ages is invalid. The normal pattern since the time of the apostles has been that Christians receive the empowering of the Holy Spirit along with regeneration. It is not necessary for believers to seek a specific second work of Spirit baptism following conversion. Every Christian is Spirit-filled to a greater or lesser degree, depending on the amount of yielding to the Spirit.

Another problem with the Pentecostal doctrine is that it has an inadequate view of Pentecost. Pentecost marks a watershed moment in New Testament history. In the Old Testament, only a select few believers were endowed by God with gifts for ministry (see Numbers 11). That pattern changed at Pentecost. At Pentecost all the believers present (all of whom were Jews) received the baptism. Likewise, in subsequent outpourings, the Samaritan converts (Acts 8), the believers at Cornelius's household (Acts 10), and the Gentile disciples of John living in Ephesus (Acts 19) all received the baptism of the Spirit.

The first believers did not think that the Samaritans, the God-fearers, and the Gentile disciples of John could be Christians. So the baptism of the Holy Spirit served as confirmation of their membership in the church. Since each of these groups experienced the baptism of the Holy Spirit in the same way that the Jews had at Pentecost, their inclusion in the church could not be denied. Peter himself experienced this firsthand. When Peter saw the Holy Spirit come upon the God-fearing Gentiles at Cornelius's house, he concluded that there was nothing to keep them from full membership in the church. Peter said, "Can anyone forbid water, that these should not be baptized who have received the Holy Spirit just as we have?" (Acts 10:47).

The subsequent episodes of Holy Spirit baptism beyond the day of Pentecost should be understood as an extension of Pentecost by which the whole body of Christ was gifted for ministry. In the New Testament church not every believer spoke in tongues, but every Christian was gifted by the Holy Spirit. The prophecy of Joel was thus fulfilled (Acts 2:16-21).

Summary

1. The baptism of the Holy Spirit is a distinct work in which the Spirit endows believers with gifts for ministry.
2. In Acts, the Holy Spirit is poured out on four groups (Jews, Samaritans, God-fearers, and Gentiles), indicating they all are included in the New Covenant church.
3. Pentecost fulfills the Old Testament prophecy that the Spirit would be poured out on all believers and not restricted to a few.

42 THE HOLY SPIRIT AS COMFORTER

In His teaching in the upper room on the eve of His death, Jesus spoke at length about the Holy Spirit. He said, "I will pray the Father, and He will give you another Helper" (John 14:16). The word *Helper* is sometimes translated "Comforter" or "Counselor" and comes from the Greek word *paraclete.*

The first thing we notice in this passage is that Jesus promises *another* "Paraclete" or "Helper." For Jesus to say that the Holy Spirit will be another Helper, there had to be a Helper before the Spirit. The New Testament clearly identifies the first Helper, or Paraclete, as Jesus Himself. John writes: "My little children, these things I write to you, so that you may not sin. And if anyone sins, we have an Advocate with the Father, Jesus Christ the righteous" (1 John 2:1).

The title *Advocate* given here to Jesus is another translation of the Greek word *paraclete.* We see then that Jesus is the first Paraclete, and upon His departure from this world, Jesus prays that the Father will supply another Paraclete in Jesus' absence. The Spirit is sent to be Christ's substitute; He is the supreme vicar of Christ on earth.

In the ancient world, a paraclete was someone summoned to give assistance in a court of law. The Holy Spirit, in fulfilling this role, performs more than one task. One such task is the Spirit's aiding the believer in addressing the Father. Paul writes to the Roman church:

Likewise the Spirit also helps in our weaknesses. For we do not know what we should pray for as we ought, but the Spirit Himself makes intercession for us with groanings which cannot be uttered. Now He who searches the hearts knows what the mind of the Spirit is, because He makes intercession for the saints according to the will of God. (Romans 8:26-27)

The Holy Spirit also aids the believer in addressing the world. He speaks on our behalf when we face conflict, as Jesus promises in Mark 13:11. The Spirit defends us against the world by convicting it of sin. The Holy Spirit works to vindicate the righteous against the attacks of the ungodly.

The concept of Paraclete also includes the role of Comforter. This has two aspects to it. He is a tender source of solace to the wounded, the defeated, and the grief-stricken. The second aspect is equally important. The word *Comforter* in its Latin derivation means "with strength." The Spirit comes to us when we are in need of strength. He empowers us with courage and boldness. As Comforter, He both consoles and emboldens that in Christ we may be more than conquerors (Romans 8:37).

Biblical passages for reflection:
John 14:16-18
Acts 19:1-7
Romans 8:26-27
Galatians 4:6

Summary

1. Jesus is our first Comforter in His role of Advocate before the Father.
2. The Holy Spirit is another Comforter who is a substitute for Jesus after His ascension.
3. The Spirit acts as our present Helper.

43 THE HOLY SPIRIT AS SANCTIFIER

God calls every person to mirror and reflect His holy character: "As He who called you is holy, you also be holy in all your conduct, because it is written, 'Be holy, for I am holy'" (1 Peter 1:15-16). Our problem is that in ourselves we are not holy; we are unholy. Yet the Bible refers to us as "saints." The term *saint* means "one who is holy." Since holiness is not found in ourselves, we must be made holy. The One who works to make us holy, to conform us to the image of Christ, is the Holy Spirit. As the Third Person of the Trinity, the Holy Spirit is no more holy than the Father and the Son. Yet we do not speak of the Holy Father, the Holy Son, and the Holy Spirit. That the Spirit of God is called the Holy Spirit is not so much because of His person (which is indeed holy) but because of His work, to make us holy.

It is the special work of the Holy Spirit to make us saints. He consecrates us. The Holy Spirit fulfills the role of the sanctifier. To be sanctified is to be made holy, or righteous. Sanctification is a process that begins the moment we become Christians. The process continues until death when the believer is made finally, fully, and forevermore righteous.

The Reformed faith is distinctive in its emphasis on the working of the Holy Spirit *alone* in regeneration. We do not assist the Holy Spirit in our rebirth. We reject outright any notion of cooperative effort in the rebirth of the believer. Sanctification, however, is a different matter. Our sanctification is a cooperative venture. We must work with the Holy Spirit to grow in sanctification. The apostle Paul expressed this idea in his letter to the church at Phillipi:

Therefore, my beloved, as you have always obeyed, not as in my presence only, but now much more in my absence, work out your own salvation with fear and trembling; for it is God who works in you both to will and to do for His good pleasure. (Philippians 2:12-13)

The call to cooperation is one that involves work. We are to work in earnest. To work with fear and trembling does not suggest a spirit of terror but of reverence coupled with effort. We are consoled by the knowledge that we are not left to do this work alone or by our own efforts. God is working within us to accomplish our sanctification.

The Holy Spirit indwells the believer, working to bring about a more righteous life and heart. We must be careful, however, not to confuse the indwelling Spirit with any deification of the individual. The Spirit is in the believer and works with the believer, but does not become the believer. The Spirit works to produce sanctified human beings, not deified creatures. When the Spirit indwells us, He does not become human and we do not become gods. The Holy Spirit does not destroy our personal identities as human beings. In our sanctification we are to become godlike in character, but not in being.

Biblical passages for reflection:
John 15:26
2 Corinthians 3:17-18
Galatians 4:6
Philippians 2:12-13
1 Peter 1:15-16

Summary

1. God calls us to reflect His holiness.
2. To become holy requires that we receive holiness from outside of ourselves.
3. The Holy Spirit is called holy because of His work as our sanctifier.
4. Sanctification is a lifelong process.
5. Sanctification is a cooperative work, involving both the believer and the Holy Spirit.
6. The indwelling Holy Spirit does not work to deify us.

Part
VI

HUMAN BEINGS
AND THE FALL

KNOWLEDGE OF SELF AND KNOWLEDGE OF GOD

When a baby is born, its entrance into the world is customarily accompanied by a sharp slap to its bottom. The normal response of the infant is a wail of screeching protest. Why does the baby cry? Is the cry a response to pain? To fear? To anger?

Perhaps the cry is provoked by all of the above. Our entrance into the world is marked by sound and fury. This initial protest is regarded by some as a summation not only of the meaning of birth but of the meaning of the entirety of life. Macbeth mused:

Life's but a walking shadow, a poor player
That struts and frets his hour upon the stage,
And then is heard no more; 'tis a tale
Told by an idiot, full of sound and fury,
Signifying nothing.[1]

To signify nothing is to be utterly and completely insignificant. To be insignificant is to be meaningless. To be meaningless is to be without value or worth.

My significance and yours is tied to the questions *who are we?* and *what are we?* It is a question of identity. My identity is ultimately connected with my relationship to God. I cannot understand who or what I am without understanding who or what God is.

There is a mutual dependence between our knowledge of ourselves and our knowledge of God. As soon as I am aware of myself as a self, I realize that I am not God; I am a creature. I have a birth date, a time when my life began on earth. My tombstone at my death will not engrave eternity as my starting point. I don't now know the final date on my tombstone, but the first date will be 1939.

My sense of creatureliness drives my thinking back to my Creator or "up" to my Creator. I cannot contemplate God or anything else outside of myself until I am first aware of myself. Yet I cannot grasp the meaning of myself fully until I understand myself in relationship to

God. Ultimately then, anthropology, the study of man-kind, is a subdivision of theology, the study of God.

The crisis of modern humanity is found in the rupture between anthropology and theology, between the study of human beings and the study of God. When our story is told in isolation or divorced from the story of God, then it indeed becomes "a tale / Told by an idiot, full of sound and fury, / Signifying nothing." If we are considered without reference to God, we become a "useless passion," as philosopher Jean-Paul Sartre declared.

What is a "useless passion"? A passion is an intense feeling. Human life is marked by intense feelings. They include such passions as love, hate, fear, guilt, ambition, lust, envy, jealousy, and a host of others. As creatures we have deep feelings about our lives. The question haunts us: Are all these feelings useless? Is all our striving and caring merely an exercise in futility, an excursion of vanity?

The meaning of our lives is at stake. Our dignity is on the line. If human beings are considered alone, apart from relationship to God, then they remain alone and insignificant. If we are not creatures made by and related to God, we are cosmic accidents. Our origin is insignificant and our destiny is equally insignificant. If we emerge from the slime by accident and finally disentegrate into a void or abyss of nothingness, then we live our lives between two poles of absolute meaninglessness. We are peeled zeroes, stripped naked of dignity and worth.

To assign dignity to a human being temporarily, that is, between the poles of a meaningless origin and a meaningless destiny, is to indulge ourselves in pure unvarnished sentiment. We tease ourselves with self-delusion.

Our origin and our destiny are tied to God. The only ultimate meaning we can have must be theological. The question we ask was asked by the psalmist:

When I consider Your heavens, the work of Your fingers, the moon and the stars, which You have ordained, what is man that You are mindful of him, and the son of man that You visit him? For You have made him a little lower than the angels, and You have crowned him with glory and honor. (Psalm 8:3-5)

To be *created by* God is to be *related to* God. This inescapable relationship insures that we are not useless noise or feeling. In creation we receive a crown of glory. A crown of glory is a tiara of dignity. With God we have dignity; without God we are nothing.

Summary

Biblical passages for reflection:
Genesis 1:27
Psalm 51
Acts 14:8-18
Acts 17:22-31
Romans 1:18-23

1. We cannot know God without first being aware of ourselves.
2. We cannot accurately know ourselves without first knowing God.

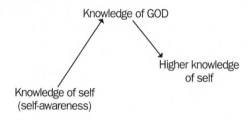

Self-knowledge leads us to knowledge of God, which in turn gives us a higher and fuller understanding of ourselves.

3. Human beings in relationship to God: Purposive origin + Purposive destiny = Meaningful life.
4. Human beings without relationship to God: Meaningless origin + Meaningless destiny = Meaningless life.

45 HUMAN BEINGS CREATED IN THE IMAGE OF GOD

In art, the making of images is an exercise of beauty. Painting, sculpture, and the like are often imitative. Through our craft we depict objects drawn from real life.

The ultimate artist is God. When He fashioned the universe, He left His own mark upon it in such a way that the heavens declare His glory and the firmament shows forth His handiwork.

When God made the creatures that filled the earth and the sea, He created one creature to be uniquely made in His own image. Genesis 1:26-27 declares:

Then God said, "Let Us make man in Our image, according to Our likeness; let them have dominion over the fish of the sea, over the birds of the air, and over the cattle, over all the earth and over every creeping thing that creeps on the earth." So God created man in His own image; in the image of God He created him; male and female He created them.

That the Bible says we are created in the image *and* likeness of God has led some (notably Roman Catholics) to conclude that there is a difference between being in the *image* and being in the *likeness* of God. But the structure of the biblical language indicates that image and likeness refer to the same thing. We are the icons of God, creatures made with a unique capacity to mirror and reflect the character of God.

Being made in the image of God is usually understood to point to the sense in which we are like God. Though He is the Creator and we are creatures, and though God transcends us in being, power, and glory, nevertheless there is some sense in which we are like Him. There is some analogy between God and us. God is an intelligent and moral being. We are also moral agents equipped with a mind, a heart, and a will. These faculties make it possible for us to mirror God's holiness, which was our original vocation.

The term *man,* when used in such Scripture passages as "God created man in His own image" (Genesis 1:27), means "humankind." Both male and female of the human species are made in the image of God. Part of the image includes mankind's call to rule the earth, to have dominion over it. We are called to dress, fill, and keep the earth as God's vice-regents. Here we are called to reflect the character of God's righteous rule over the universe. He never ravages or exploits what He rules, but rather reigns in justice and kindness.

In the fall of mankind, something ghastly happened. The image of God was severely tarnished. Our ability to mirror His holiness has been greatly affected so that now the mirror is fogged.

The Fall, however, did not destroy our humanity. Though our ability to reflect God's holiness was lost in the Fall, we are still human. We still have a mind, a heart, and a will. We still bear the mark of our Creator upon ourselves. The restoration of the fullness of the image of God in human beings is accomplished by Christ. He is, as the author of Hebrews declares, "the brightness of His glory and the express image of His person" (Hebrews 1:3).

Biblical passages for reflection:
Genesis 9:6
Romans 8:29
1 Corinthians 15:42-57
Colossians 1:15

Summary

1. God created human beings—both male and female—in His image and likeness.
2. There is some analogy between God and human beings that makes communication between them possible.
3. Human beings, like God, are moral agents with the faculties of mind and will.
4. Human beings are called to have dominion over the earth.
5. In the Fall, the image of God in human beings was marred.
6. Christ is the perfect image of God. He is restoring us to the fullness of the image of God.

46 HUMAN BEINGS AS BODY AND SOUL

Three days a week I suffer torture under the tutelage of my personal trainer at Gold's Gym. He is my private Pharaoh, my singular Simon Legree. Cardiovascular exercise, the pumping of iron, and the wretched contortions of stretch routines are part of my regimen. All of this despite the knowledge Scripture yields: "For bodily exercise profits a little" (1 Timothy 4:8)!

As I worry about my body, its weight, appearance, and health, I am reminded of the words of Jesus, "And do not fear those who kill the body but cannot kill the soul. But rather fear Him who is able to destroy both soul and body in hell" (Matthew 10:28).

Human beings, created in the image and likeness of God, are creatures made out of a material body and a nonmaterial soul. The soul is sometimes referred to as spirit.

Both body and soul are created by God and are distinct aspects of our personal makeup. The biblical view of human beings differs sharply from early Greek views. Our body and soul make up a *duality,* not a *dualism.* In Greek dualistic theories the body and soul are seen as incompatible substances that coexist in constant tension. They are fundamentally incompatible. Usually dualism asserts that there is something inherently evil or imperfect about anything physical and therefore sees the body as an evil container for the pure soul. For the Greek, salvation ultimately meant redemption *from* the body when the soul is finally released from the prison house of the flesh.

The biblical view of the body is that it is created good and has no inherent evil in its physical substance. Yet it suffers from moral corruption just like the soul. Human beings are sinful in both body and soul. Christianity, far from teaching redemption *from* the body, teaches redemption *of* the body.

As a duality, human beings are one entity with two distinct parts united by God's act of creation. There is no necessity, either philosophically or exegetically, to add a third part or substance (such as spirit) to bridge a dualistic tension. Orthodox theology rejects the trichotomous view of human beings, by which we are conceived of in three distinct parts: body, soul, and spirit.

Though many theologians have argued for the natural or essential immortality of the human soul, it is important to remember that the human soul is: (1) created by God and is not inherently eternal; (2) though not composed of matter and open to dissolution by physical forces, it is nevertheless capable of being destroyed by God. The soul cannot exist for a moment apart from the sustaining power of God. "In Him we live and move and have our being" (Acts 17:28).

At death, though the body dies, the soul of both the believer and unbeliever continues to live. Believers await the consummation of their redemption with the resurrection and glorification of their bodies, while the impenitent await the eternal judgment of God. Because God preserves the soul from death, human beings have a continuity of conscious personal existence beyond the grave. The whole person is fallen; both body and soul are the objects of God's saving grace.

Summary

1. Human beings have a material body and an immaterial soul.
2. Human beings are a unity-in-duality. Christianity rejects the Greek notion of dualism.

Human Being = Unity in duality

Greek view = Unified dualism

Biblical passages for reflection:
Genesis 1:1–2:25
Ecclesiastes 12:7
Matthew 10:28
Romans 8:18-23
1 Corinthians
    15:35-55

Trichotomy = The tension of body and soul buffered by the spirit

3. The human body is part of God's good creation. Though it is fallen, as is the soul, neither are inherently evil.
4. The human soul is not naturally eternal. It must be created and sustained by God.

47 HUMAN BEINGS AS FLESH AND SPIRIT

In the modern church there is much confusion about the biblical meaning of flesh and spirit. On the one hand, the church still struggles with the ancient Greek idea that anything physical must be evil to some degree. Some assume therefore that the Christian life is something entirely spiritual that has nothing to do with our bodily existence. Some take this to require that all bodily functions are necessarily evil, including eating, drinking, and sexual fulfillment. Others, thinking the body doesn't matter, deceive themselves into thinking that it doesn't matter how they use their bodies as long as their soul is healthy. Both positions reflect a serious distortion of biblical teaching that body and spirit alike are important and must be properly nourished and cared for.

A second problem emerges when too sharp of a distinction is made between "carnal" Christians and "Spirit-filled" Christians. Here, three types of people are considered: (1) carnal non-Christians, (2) carnal Christians, and (3) Spirit-filled Christians. If we think of a carnal Christian as one who is totally empty of the Holy Spirit and is given over to a completely carnal life-style, we are not speaking of a carnal Christian, we are speaking of one who is not a Christian at all. A person may profess to be a Christian and still be utterly carnal, making a lie of his profession. A totally carnal Christian is a contradiction in terms.

Every Christian is Spirit-filled. The "filling" of the Spirit may be to a lesser or greater degree as Christians vary from one another in yielding to the Spirit. But the Spirit dwells within all Christians.

The apostle Paul speaks of a warfare or conflict that the believer experiences between the flesh and the spirit. In doing so, Paul does not teach a dualism or inherent disharmony between the body and the soul. The conflict he describes is not one that may be reduced to a struggle between physical desires or appetites and spiritual virtue. The conflict goes deeper than that.

The word *flesh* (*sarx*) is sometimes used in the New Testament as a virtual synonym for *body* (*soma*). However, when this word is used in clear contrast with *spirit* (*pneuma*), it most often refers to something other than a physical body. Here, *flesh* usually refers to the corrupt nature of fallen human beings. When we are regenerated by the Holy Spirit and become new creatures in Christ, the power of our fallen nature (flesh) is conquered but not destroyed. Because sanctification is a lifelong process, Christians are daily engaged in warfare with their old nature as they seek to grow in the Spirit and in grace. The old person dies daily as the new person in Christ is strengthened by the indwelling Holy Spirit. The Spirit, who is given to us as a pledge and by whom we are sealed, will prevail in this warfare in the end. In the meantime, however, the struggle can be intense. Christians continue to struggle with sin and temptation. Conversion liberates us from the total control of the flesh, but it does not perfect us.

The struggle between the old person (the flesh) and the Spirit continues until we die. After death we are glorified: the flesh is completely put to death, and the new person is completely purified.

Biblical passages for reflection:
Matthew 26:36-41
John 3:6
Romans 7:13–8:17
Ephesians 2:1-3
1 Peter 2:11

Summary

1. The Bible rejects the Greek idea that the body is intrinsically evil.
2. Christians are neither to despise nor exalt the body. The body *and* the soul are in need of sanctification.
3. No Christian is completely carnal or completely free of carnality.
4. Every Christian is indwelt by the Holy Spirit.
5. The warfare between flesh and spirit is not a conflict between body and soul but a conflict between our fallen sin nature (old person) and our regenerated nature (new person).
6. The struggle between the flesh and the Spirit continues in the Christian life until glorification.

48
SATAN

The figure of Satan is often perceived as a fugitive from a Halloween party. He is portrayed as wearing a silly red suit. He has cloven hoofs, horns, a tail, and carries a trident. Such a figure is a point of ridicule among those who deny biblical Christianity. I once asked a college class of about thirty students, "How many of you believe in God?" The majority of the students raised their hand. Then I asked, "How many of you believe in the devil?" Only a couple raised their hand.

One student blurted out, "How can any intelligent person believe in the devil in this day and age? The devil belongs to superstition along with ghosts, goblins, and things that go bump in the night."

I replied, "There is a far more credible source for believing in Satan than for believing in goblins. You may not be persuaded of the trustworthiness of the Bible, but it is surely a more credible source than Mother Goose."

To lump Satan with witches and goblins is to do violence to serious and sober thought. I followed my discussion with the college class with another question: "If you believe that God is an invisible, personal being who has the capacity to influence people for good, why do you find it hard or incredible to imagine that there is an invisible, personal being who has the capacity to influence people for evil?"

Perhaps our problem with Satan rests on the fact that we react to a caricature instead of the biblical view of him. In Scripture, the term *Satan* means "adversary." We know him as the devil. He is a high angelic creature who, before the creation of the human race, rebelled against God and has since battled with human beings and God. He is called the prince of darkness, the father of lies, the accuser, and the beguiling serpent. The real portrait is nothing like the horned, triad-bearing, comedic adversary to which we have become accustomed.

That image, at least in part, arose out of the medieval church. The silly picture of Satan was intentionally created by the church in order to poke fun at him. The church was convinced that an effective ploy to withstand Satan was to insult him. His most vulnerable part was seen as his pride. To attack his pride was seen as an effective way to repel him.

The biblical view of Satan is far more sophisticated. He appears as an "angel of light." That image points to Satan's clever ability to manifest himself under the appearance of good. Satan is subtle, beguiling, and crafty. He speaks with eloquence; his appearance is stunning. The prince of darkness wears a cloak of light. Scripture also speaks of Satan as a roaring lion, seeking whom he may devour. Christ is also referred to as a lion, the Lion of Judah. He is a redeemer, the anti-lion and devourer. Both images speak of strength.

How, then, should the believer react to Satan? On the one hand Satan is indeed fearsome. In 1 Peter 5:8 we are told that "your adversary the devil walks about like a roaring lion, seeking whom he may devour." The believer is not to respond, however, in sheer terror. Satan may be stronger than we are, but Christ is stronger than Satan. The Bible declares, "He who is in you is greater than he who is in the world" (1 John 4:4). Satan is, after all, a creature. He is finite and limited. He is limited in space and time. He cannot be in more than one place at a time. He is never to be regarded in any way as an equal with God. Satan is a higher order of being than humans; he is a fallen angel. But he is not divine. He has more power than earthly creatures but infinitely less power than almighty God.

Biblical passages for reflection:
Job 1:6-12
Matthew 4:1-11
Luke 22:31
2 Thessalonians
2:5-10
1 Peter 5:8-11

Summary

1. Satan is not to be compared to mythical creatures.
2. Satan is a fallen angel with sophisticated powers to delude, tempt, and accuse people.
3. Satan is a finite creature without divine powers or attributes.

DEMONS

Demons are supernatural beings who are subservient to Satan. They, like Satan, were once angels. They joined Satan in his rebellion and were cast out of heaven with him. When they are mentioned in Scripture, the primary focus is on demon possession of human beings.

The apostle Paul points out that while the idolatrous gods pagans worship do not actually exist, there are demons who do exist, instigating and propagating such pagan worship. Those who participate in these pagan rituals are actually offering worship to demons and are thus operating under demonic direction.

The New Testament reveals several characteristics of demons. There is often a physical or mental ailment associated with them, such as blindness or self-torture. Demons often recognized Christ as the Holy One of God. They feared and were subject to the authority of Jesus. In addition, demons had superior or supernatural knowledge, superior strength, and the ability to foretell the future.

The Reformers reacted strongly against the excess practices and superstitions surrounding demons in the Middle Ages. By the end of the sixteenth century, the practice of expelling demons had been abolished in the Lutheran church.

While demons still continue to act, the level and severity of activity expressed in the New Testament is unique. It was the "fullness of time," the last great defense of this world against the Redeemer of mankind. Satan, as it were, pulled out all the stops. With the Resurrection and the coming of the Holy Spirit at Pentecost, Satan's reign, and that of his fellow demons, was severely restricted. However, both Paul and John warn believers that in the end times the activities of Satan and his demons will be on the increase.

If we take the Bible seriously, we must take the demonic world seriously. There can be no biblical theology without a corresponding demonology.

Though demons are real and powerful, there is no reason to believe that they can ever possess a Christian. We may be harassed, tempted, or accused by demons, but never controlled by them. Every Christian is indwelt by the Holy Spirit. His presence guarantees liberty from demonic possession. He is stronger than any demon that might attack us.

Summary

1. Demons are fallen angels under the rule of Satan.
2. Demons appeared in unusual force when Jesus was on earth.
3. Demons cannot possess a Christian.

SIN

Sin can be pictured as an archer releasing an arrow from his bow and missing the target. It is not, of course, that failure to hit the bull's-eye in target shooting is a grave moral matter. Rather, the simplest biblical definition of sin is "to miss the mark." In biblical terms, the mark that is missed is not a target filled with straw; it is the mark or "norm" of God's law. God's law expresses His own righteousness and is the ultimate standard for our behavior. When we miss achieving this standard, we sin.

The Bible speaks of the universality of sin in terms of missing the mark of God's glory. "For all have sinned and fall short of the glory of God" (Romans 3:23). To say that "nobody's perfect" or "to err is human" is to acknowledge the universality of sin. We are all sinners in need of redemption.

Sin has been defined as "any want of conformity unto, or transgression of, any law of God, given as a rule to the reasonable creature"[1] In this definition there are three crucial dimensions. First, sin is a lack or want of conformity. It is nonconformity to the law of God. A sin of *omission* is a failure to do what God commands. If God commands us to love our neighbor and we fail to do so, that is sin.

Second, sin is defined as a transgression of the law. To transgress the law is to cross its boundaries, to overstep its limits. Hence, we sometimes describe sin as a "trespass." We walk where we are not permitted to walk. Here we speak of sins of *commission* whereby we commit actions prohibited by God. When God's law is pronounced in negative terms, "You shall not," and we do what is disallowed, we commit sin.

Third, sin is an action performed by reasonable creatures. As creatures made in the image of God, we are free moral agents. Because we have a mind and a will, we are capable of moral action. When we do what we know is wrong, we choose to disobey God's law and sin.

Protestantism rejects the classic distinction in Roman

Catholic theology between venial and mortal sin. Traditional Catholic theology defines a mortal sin as a sin that "kills" grace in the soul and requires renewed justification through the sacrament of penance. A venial sin is sin of a less serious sort. It does not destroy saving grace.

John Calvin declared that all sin against God is mortal sin in that it *deserves* death, but no sin is mortal in the sense that it destroys our justification by faith.[2] Protestantism affirms that all sin is serious. Even the smallest sin is an act of rebellion against God. Every sin is an act of cosmic treason, a futile attempt to dethrone God in His sovereign authority.

However, the Bible still regards some sins as more heinous than others. There are degrees of wickedness even as there will be degrees of punishment rendered at the bar of God's justice. Jesus rebuked the Pharisees for omitting the weightier matters of the law and warned the towns of Bethsaida and Chorazin that their sin was worse than that of Sodom and Gomorrah (Matthew 11:20-24).

The Bible also warns us about the guilt incurred from multiple sins. Though James teaches that to sin against one part of the law is to sin against the whole law (James 2:10), nevertheless there is added guilt with each particular transgression. Paul admonishes us against heaping up or treasuring up wrath against the day of wrath (Romans 2:1-11). With each sin we commit we add to our guilt and exposure to the wrath of God. Nevertheless, the grace of God is greater than all our guilt combined.

The Bible takes sin seriously because it takes God seriously and it takes human beings seriously. When we sin against God, we do violence to His holiness. When we sin against our neighbor, we violate his or her humanity.

Biblical passages for reflection:

Romans 2:1-11
Romans 3:10-26
Romans 5:12-19
James 1:12-15
1 John 1:8-10

Summary

1. The biblical meaning of sin is to miss the mark of God's righteousness.
2. All human beings are sinners.
3. Sin involves a failure to conform to (omission) and a transgression of (commission) the law of God.
4. Only moral agents can be guilty of sin.
5. Protestantism rejects the distinction between mortal and venial sin but affirms the gradation of sin.
6. Each sin committed incurs greater guilt.
7. Sin violates God and people.

51

ORIGINAL SIN

It is commonplace to hear the statement, "people are basically good." Though it is admitted that no one is perfect, human wickedness is minimized. Yet if people are basically good, why is sin so universal?

It is often suggested that everybody sins because society has such a negative influence upon us. The problem is seen with our environment, not with our nature. This explanation for the universality of sin begs the question, how did society become corrupt in the first place? If people are born good or innocent, we would expect at least a percentage of them to remain good and sinless. We should be able to find societies that are not corrupt, where the environment has been conditioned by sinlessness rather than sinfulness. Yet the most dedicated-to-righteousness communes we can find still have provisions for dealing with the guilt of sin.

Since the fruit is universally corrupt we look for the root of the problem in the tree. Jesus indicated that a good tree does not produce corrupt fruit. The Bible clearly teaches that our original parents, Adam and Eve, fell in sin. Subsequently, every human being has been born with a sinful and corrupt nature. If the Bible didn't explicitly teach this, we would have to deduce it rationally from the bare fact of the universality of sin.

Yet the Fall is not simply a question of rational deduction. It is a point of divine revelation. It refers to what we call *original sin*. Original sin does not refer primarily to the *first* or original sin committed by Adam and Eve. Original sin refers to the *result* of the first sin—the corruption of the human race. Original sin refers to the fallen condition in which we are born.

That the Fall occurred is clear in Scripture. The Fall was devastating. How it came to pass is open to dispute even among Reformed thinkers. The Westminster Confession explains the event simply, much in the manner that Scripture explains it:

Our first parents, being seduced by the subtlety and temptation of Satan, sinned, in eating the forbidden fruit. This their sin, God was pleased, according to His wise and holy counsel, to permit, having purposed to order it to His own glory.[1]

Biblical passages for reflection:
Genesis 3:1-24
Jeremiah 17:9
Romans 3:10-26
Romans 5:12-19
Titus 1:15

Thus, the Fall occurred. The results, however, reached far beyond Adam and Eve. They not only touched all mankind, but decimated all mankind. We are sinners in Adam. We cannot ask, "When does the individual *become* a sinner?" For the truth is that human beings come into existence in a state of sinfulness. They are seen by God as sinful because of their solidarity with Adam.

The Westminster Confession again elegantly expresses the results of the Fall, particularly as it relates to human beings:

By this sin they fell from their original righteousness and communion with God, and so became dead in sin, and wholly defiled in all the parts and faculties of soul and body. They being the root of all mankind, the guilt of this sin was imputed, and the same death in sin, and corrupted nature, conveyed to all their posterity descending from them by ordinary generation. From this original corruption, whereby we are utterly indisposed, disabled, and made opposite to all good, and wholly inclined to all evil, do proceed all actual transgressions.[2]

That last phrase is crucial. We are sinners not because we sin. Rather, we sin because we are sinners. Thus David laments, "Surely I was sinful at birth, sinful from the time my mother conceived me" (Psalm 51:5, NIV).

Summary

1. The universality of sin cannot be accounted for by pointing to societal or environmental factors.
2. The universality of sin is explained by the Fall of mankind.
3. *Original sin* does not refer to the first sin, but to the result of that sin.
4. All people are born with a sinful nature or "original sin."
5. We all sin because we are sinners by nature.

52 HUMAN DEPRAVITY

As we said in the previous chapter, a common point of debate among theologians focuses on the question, are human beings basically good or basically evil? The hinge upon which the argument turns is the word *basically*. It is a virtual universal consensus that nobody is perfect. We accept the maxim "To err is human."

The Bible says that "all have sinned and fall short of the glory of God" (Romans 3:23). Despite this verdict on human shortcomings, the idea persists in our humanistically dominated culture that sin is something peripheral or tangential to our nature. Indeed, we are flawed by sin. Our moral records exhibit blemishes. But somehow we think that our evil deeds reside at the rim or edge of our character and never penetrate to the core. Basically, it is assumed, people are inherently good.

After being rescued from captivity in Iraq and experiencing firsthand the corrupt methods of Saddam Hussein, one American hostage remarked, "Despite all that I endured I never lost my confidence in the basic goodness of people." Perhaps this view rests in part on a sliding scale of the relative goodness or wickedness of people. Obviously some people are far more wicked than others. Next to Saddam Hussein or Adolf Hitler the ordinary run-of-the-mill sinner looks like a saint. But if we lift our gaze to the ultimate standard of goodness—the holy character of God—we realize that what appears to be a basic goodness on an earthly level is corrupt to the core.

The Bible teaches the total depravity of the human race. Total depravity means radical corruption. We must be careful to note the difference between *total* depravity and *utter* depravity. To be utterly depraved is to be as wicked as one could possibly be. Hitler was extremely depraved, but he could have been worse than he was. I am a sinner. Yet I could sin more often and more severely than I actually do. I am not utterly depraved, but I am totally depraved. For total depravity means that I and everyone else are depraved or corrupt in the totality of our being. There is no part of us that is left untouched by sin. Our minds, our wills, and our bodies are affected by evil. We speak sinful words, do sinful deeds, have impure thoughts. Our very bodies suffer from the ravages of sin.

Perhaps *radical corruption* is a better term to describe our fallen condition than "total depravity." I am using the word *radical* not so much to mean "extreme," but to lean more heavily on its original meaning. *Radical* comes from the Latin word for "root" or "core." Our problem with sin is that it is rooted in the core of our being. It permeates our hearts. It is because sin is at our core and not merely at the exterior of our lives that the Bible says:

There is none righteous, no, not one; there is none who understands; there is none who seeks after God. They have all turned aside; they have together become unprofitable; there is none who does good, no, not one. (Romans 3:10-12)

It is because of this condition that the verdict of Scripture is heard: we are "dead in trespasses and sins" (Ephesians 2:1); we are "sold under sin" (Romans 7:14); we are in "captivity to the law of sin" (Romans 7:23) and are "by nature children of wrath" (Ephesians 2:3). Only by the quickening power of the Holy Spirit may we be brought out of this state of spiritual death. It is God who makes us alive as we become His craftsmanship (Ephesians 2:1-10).

Summary

1. Humanism sees sin at the edge or periphery of human life. It considers human beings to be basically good.

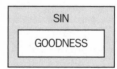

2. Biblical Christianity teaches that sin permeates the core of our life.

3. Total depravity is not utter depravity. We are not as wicked as we possibly could be.
4. Radical corruption points to the core sinfulness of our hearts.

53 HUMAN CONSCIENCE

It was Jiminy Cricket who said, "Always let your conscience be your guide." This is good advice if our conscience is informed and ruled by the Word of God. However, if our conscience is ignorant of Scripture or has been seared or hardened by repeated sin, then Jiminy Cricket theology is disastrous.

Biblical passages for reflection:
Luke 11:39-44
Romans 2:12-16
Romans 14:23
Titus 1:15

There is an important role for the conscience to play in the Christian life. It is vital, however, that we have a proper understanding of it.

Conscience has often been described as an inner voice of God through which our mind either accuses or excuses us from sins. It includes two basic elements: (1) an inner awareness or consciousness of right and wrong and (2) a mental ability to apply laws, norms, and rules to concrete situations.

In Romans 2:15, Paul teaches that God has written His law on the human heart. The human conscience is informed by the revelation of God's law, which He has implanted in the human heart.

People have a moral responsibility to follow their conscience. It is sinful to act against one's conscience. At the Diet of Worms, Luther declared, "My conscience is captive to the Word of God . . . to go against conscience is neither right nor safe."[1]

Luther's reply displays two important biblical principles. First, the conscience is to be informed or "captured" by the Word of God. It is possible for the conscience to be misinformed or to become seared or dulled by repeated sin. We can become so hardened by habitual sin or societal acceptance of sin that we stifle the voice of conscience and sin without remorse.

On the other hand, if our conscience persuades us that something is unlawful or sinful, though, in fact, it isn't sinful, then it is still wrong for us to do it. To do what we deem to be evil, even if it is not in fact evil, is to sin. Paul teaches that whatever is not of faith is sin (Romans 14:23). In this instance to act against conscience is neither right nor safe.

Summary

1. The conscience is a good guide only when it is informed and ruled by God.
2. The conscience is a moral voice within us that accuses or excuses us of our actions.
3. It is a sin to act against the conscience.

54 THE UNFORGIVABLE SIN

That the Bible describes one sin as "unforgiveable" sparks fear in the hearts of those who worry that perhaps they have committed it. Although the gospel freely offers forgiveness to all who repent of their sins, there is a limit reached at the door of this one crime. The unforgiveable or unpardonable sin of which Jesus warned is identified as blasphemy against the Holy Spirit. Jesus declared that this sin cannot be forgiven either in the present or in the future:

Therefore I say to you, every sin and blasphemy will be forgiven men, but the blasphemy against the Spirit will not be forgiven men. Anyone who speaks a word against the Son of Man, it will be forgiven him; but whoever speaks against the Holy Spirit, it will not be forgiven him, either in this age or in the age to come. (Matthew 12:31-32)

Various attempts have been made to identify the specific crime that is unforgiveable. It has been assigned to such grievous crimes as murder or adultery. However, though both of these sins are clearly heinous sins against God, the Scripture makes it clear that they may be forgiven if earnest repentance is made. David, for example, was guilty of both of them, yet he was restored to grace.

Frequently the unforgiveable sin is identified with persistent and final unbelief in Christ. Since death brings the end of a person's opportunity to repent of sin and embrace Christ, the finality of unbelief brings the consequence of the termination of hope of forgiveness.

Though persistent and final unbelief does bring about such consequences it does not adequately explain Jesus' warning concerning blasphemy against the Holy Spirit. Blasphemy is something one does with the mouth or the pen. It involves words.

Though any form of blasphemy is a serious assault on the character of God, it is usually regarded as forgiveable.

When Jesus warned of the unforgiveable sin, it was in the context of His accusers declaring that He was in league with Satan. His warning was sober and frightening. Yet, on the cross Jesus prayed for the forgiveness of those who blasphemed against Him on the grounds of their ignorance, "Father, forgive them, for they do not know what they do" (Luke 23:34).

If, however, people are *enlightened* by the Holy Spirit to the degree that they know Jesus is truly the Christ, and then they accuse Him of being satanic, they have committed a sin for which there is no pardon. Christians left to their own devices are capable of committing the unpardonable sin, but we are confident that God in His preserving grace will restrain His elect from ever committing such a sin. When earnest Christians are fearful that perhaps they have actually committed this sin, it is probably an indication that they haven't. Those who do commit such a sin would be so hardened of heart and abandoned in their sin as to feel no remorse for it.

Even in a pagan, secularized culture like our own, people seem to be reluctant to go too far in their blasphemy against God and Christ. Though the name of Christ is dragged through the mud as a common curse word and the gospel is ridiculed by irreverent jokes and comments, people still seem constrained to avoid linking Jesus with Satan.

Though the occult and Satanism provide a context of perilous danger for the commission of the unpardonable sin, if radical blasphemy occurs here it may still be forgiven because it is committed in ignorance by those unenlightened by the Holy Spirit.

Biblical passages for reflection:
Matthew 12:22-32
Luke 23:34
1 John 5:16

Summary

1. Blasphemy against the Holy Spirit is not to be equated with murder or adultery.
2. Blasphemy is an offense against God involving words.
3. Christ's original warning was against attributing the works of God the Holy Spirit to Satan.
4. Jesus prayed for the forgiveness of blasphemers who were ignorant of His true identity.
5. Christians will never commit this sin because of the restraining grace of God.

SYNCRETISM

Syncretism is the process by which aspects of one religion are assimilated into, or blended with, another religion. This leads to fundamental changes in both religions.

In the Old Testament, God was deeply concerned with the pressure and temptation toward syncretism. As the people of God moved into the Promised Land they were confronted with pagan religions. The Canaanite gods, Baal and Asherah, became objects of Israelite devotion. Later, God's people worshiped the national gods of Assyria and Babylon. The law of God clearly warned Israel not only against abandoning Yahweh for other gods, but against worshiping other gods in addition to the true God. The prophets warned of coming judgments as the people modified their faith to accommodate foreign doctrines and practices.

The New Testament period was one of widespread syncretism. As the Greek Empire expanded, her gods mingled with the indigenous gods of conquered nations. The Roman Empire also welcomed all manner of cults and mystery religions. Christianity was not left untouched. The church fathers not only spread the gospel but labored to protect its integrity. Manichaeism (a dualistic philosophy that saw the physical as evil) crept into some doctrines. Docetism (a teaching that denied Jesus had a physical body) was a problem even as the New Testament was being written. Many forms of Neoplatonism made a conscious effort to combine elements of Christian religion with Platonic philosophy and oriental dualism. The history of the Christian creeds is the history of God's people seeking to separate themselves from the snares of foreign religions and philosophies.

The problem is still with the church today. Non-Christian philosophies such as Marxism or existentialism seek the power of Christianity while giving up

Biblical passages for reflection:
1 Kings 16:29-34
1 Corinthians 10:14-23
2 Corinthians 6:14-18
Galatians 3:1-14
Colossians 2:8
1 John 5:19-21

what is uniquely Christian. Syncretism continues to be a powerful tool to separate God from His people.

Every generation of Christians faces the temptation of syncretism. In our desire to be "with it" or contemporary in our practices and beliefs, we yield to the temptation of being conformed to the patterns of this world. We accept pagan practices and ideas and seek to "baptize them." Even when we confront and engage alien religions and philosophies we have a tendency to be influenced by them. Every foreign element that creeps into Christian faith and practice is an element that weakens the purity of faith.

Summary

1. Syncretism is the blending or mixing of alien religions or philosophies into one.
2. One of the constant problems of Israelite religion in the Old Testament was the intrusion of pagan religions.
3. The New Testament church struggled against the influence of Greek and Roman religion and culture.
4. Modern Christianity is threatened by attempts to combine Christian thought with pagan religion and secular philosophy.

Part
VII

SALVATION

56

SALVATION

I was once confronted by a young man in Philadelphia who asked me, "Are you saved?" My reply to him was, "Saved from what?" He was taken aback by my question. He obviously hadn't thought much about the meaning of the question he was asking people. I was certainly not saved from people interrupting me on the street and buttonholing me with the question "Are you saved?"

The question of being saved is the supreme question of the Bible. The subject matter of the sacred Scriptures is the subject of salvation. Jesus, at His conception in the womb of Mary, is announced as the Savior. Saviorhood and salvation go together. It is the role of the Savior to save.

Yet again we ask, saved from what? The biblical meaning of salvation is broad and varied. In its simplest form the verb *to save* means "to be rescued from a dangerous or threatening situation." When Israel escapes defeat at the hands of her enemies in battle, she is said to be saved. When people recover from a life-threatening illness, they experience salvation. When the harvest is rescued from blight or drought, the result is salvation.

We use the word *salvation* in a similar way. A boxer is said to be "saved by the bell" if the round ends before the referee counts him out. *Salvation* means to be rescued from some calamity. However, the Bible also uses the term *salvation* in a specific sense to refer to our ultimate redemption from sin and reconciliation to God. In this sense, salvation is from the ultimate calamity—the judgment of God. The ultimate salvation is accomplished by Christ who "delivers us from the wrath to come" (1 Thessalonians 1:10).

The Bible clearly announces that there will be a day of judgment in which all human beings will be held accountable before the tribunal of God. For many this "day of the Lord" will be a day of darkness with no light in it. It will be the day when God will pour out His wrath against the wicked and impenitent. It will be the ultimate holocaust, the darkest hour, the worst calamity in human history. To be delivered from God's wrath, which most assuredly will come upon the world, is ultimate salvation. This is the rescue operation Christ performs for His people as their Savior.

The Bible uses the term *salvation* not only in many senses, but in many tenses. The verb *to save* appears in virtually every possible tense of the Greek language. There is a sense in which we *were* saved (from the foundation of the world); we *were being* saved (by the work of God in history); we *are saved* (by being in a justified state); we *are being* saved (by being sanctified or made holy); and we *will be* saved (experience the consummation of our redemption in heaven). The Bible speaks of salvation in terms of the past, present, and future.

Sometimes we equate present salvation in terms of our justification, which is present. At other times, we see justification as one specific step in the whole order or plan of salvation.

Finally, it is important to note another central aspect of the biblical concept of salvation. Salvation is of the Lord. Salvation is not a human enterprise. Human beings cannot save themselves. Salvation is a divine work; it is accomplished and applied by God. Salvation is both *of* the Lord and *from* the Lord. It is the Lord who saves us from the wrath of the Lord.

Biblical passages for reflection:
Ezekiel 36:26-27
Zephaniah 1
John 3:16-17
Romans 1:16-17
1 Corinthians 1:26-31
1 Thessalonians 1:6-10

Summary

1. The broad meaning of *salvation* is "to be rescued from a threatening situation."
2. Ultimate salvation means to be delivered from the ultimate calamity of God's wrath.
3. The Bible uses *salvation* in several tenses, referring to God's past, present, and future work of redemption.
4. *Justification* is sometimes used as a synonym for *salvation;* at other times it is seen as one aspect in the whole scheme of redemption.
5. Salvation is *of* the Lord and *from* the Lord.

PREDESTINATION

Few doctrines spark as much controversy or provoke as much consternation as the doctrine of predestination. It is a difficult doctrine that demands to be handled with great care and caution. Yet it is a biblical doctrine and therefore demands to be handled. We dare not ignore it.

Virtually all Christian churches have some doctrine of predestination. This is unavoidable since the concept is clearly found in Holy Scripture. Those churches however disagree, sometimes strongly, over its meaning. The Methodist view differs from the Lutheran view, which disagrees with the Presbyterian view. Though their views differ, each is trying to come to grips with this difficult matter.

What predestination means, in its most elementary form, is that our final destination, heaven or hell, is decided by God not only before we get there, but before we are even born. It teaches that our ultimate destiny is in the hands of God. Another way of saying it is this: From all eternity, before we even existed, God decided to save some members of the human race and to let the rest of the human race perish. God made a choice—He chose some individuals to be saved into everlasting blessedness in heaven and others He chose to pass over, to allow them to follow the consequences of their sins into eternal torment in hell.

Accepting this definition is common to many churches. To get to the heart of the matter one must ask, how does God choose? The non-Reformed view, held by the vast majority of Christians, is that God makes that choice on the basis of His foreknowledge. God chooses for eternal life those whom He knows will choose Him. This is called the *prescient* view of predestination because it rests on God's foreknowledge of human decisions or acts.

The Reformed view differs in that it sees the ultimate

decision for salvation resting with God and not with us. In this view, God's election is sovereign. It does not rest upon the foreseen decisions or responses of human beings. Indeed, it sees those decisions as flowing from the sovereign grace of God.

The Reformed view holds that, left to himself, no fallen person would ever choose God. Fallen people still have a free will and are able to choose what they desire. But the problem is that we have no desire for God and will not choose Christ unless first regenerated. Faith is a gift that comes out of rebirth. Only those who are elect will ever respond to the gospel in faith.

The elect do choose Christ, but only because they were first chosen by God. As in the case of Jacob and Esau, the elect are chosen solely on the basis of the sovereign good pleasure of God and not on the basis of anything they have done or will do. Paul declares:

And not only this, but when Rebecca also had conceived by one man, even by our father Isaac (for the children not yet being born, nor having done any good or evil, that the purpose of God according to election might stand, not of works, but of Him who calls), it was said to her, "The older shall serve the younger." . . . So then it is not of him who wills, nor of him who runs, but of God who shows mercy. (Romans 9:10-12, 16)

A vexing problem with predestination is that God does not choose or elect to save everybody. He reserves the right to have mercy upon whom He will have mercy. Some of fallen humanity receive the grace and mercy of election. The rest God passes over, leaving them in their sin. The nonelect receive justice. The elect receive mercy. No one receives injustice. God is not obligated to be merciful to any or to all alike. It is His decision how merciful He chooses to be. Yet He is never guilty of being unrighteous toward anyone (see Romans 9:14-15).

Summary

1. Predestination is a difficult doctrine and must be handled with care.
2. The Bible teaches the doctrine of predestination.
3. Many Christians define predestination in terms of God's foreknowledge.

Biblical passages for reflection:
Proverbs 16:4
John 13:18
Romans 8:30
Ephesians 1:3-14
2 Thessalonians
    2:13-15

4. The Reformed view does not consider foreknowledge to be an explanation of biblical predestination.
5. Predestination is based upon God's choice, not the choice of human beings.
6. Unregenerate people have no desire to choose Christ.
7. God does not elect everybody. He reserves the right to have mercy upon whom He pleases.
8. God treats no one unjustly.

58 PREDESTINATION AND REPROBATION

Every coin has a flip side. There is also a flip side to the doctrine of election. Election refers to only one aspect of the broader question of predestination. The other side of the coin is the question of reprobation. God declared that He loved Jacob but hated Esau. How are we to understand this reference to divine hatred?

Predestination is double. The only way to avoid the doctrine of double predestination is to either affirm that God predestinates everybody to election or that He predestinates no one to either election or reprobation. Since the Bible clearly teaches predestination to election and denies universal salvation, we must conclude that predestination is double. It includes both election and reprobation. Double predestination is unavoidable if we take Scripture seriously. What is crucial, however, is how double predestination is understood.

Some have viewed double predestination as a matter of equal causation, where God is equally responsible for causing the reprobate not to believe as He is for causing the elect to believe. We call this a *positive-positive* view of predestination.

The positive-positive view of predestination teaches that God positively and actively intervenes in the lives of the elect to work grace in their hearts and bring them to faith. Likewise, in the case of the reprobates, He works evil in the hearts of the reprobate and actively prevents them from coming to faith. This view has often been called "hyper-Calvinism" because it goes beyond the view of Calvin, Luther, and the other Reformers.

The Reformed view of double predestination follows a *positive-negative* schema. In the case of the elect, God intervenes to positively and actively work grace in their souls and bring them to saving faith. He unilaterally regenerates the elect and insures their salvation. In the case of the reprobate He does not work evil in them or

Biblical passages for reflection:
Exodus 7:1-5
Proverbs 16:4
Romans 9
Ephesians 1:3-6
Jude 1:4

prevent them from coming to faith. Rather, He passes over them, leaving them to their own sinful devices. In this view there is no symmetry of divine action. God's activity is asymmetrical between the elect and the reprobate. There is, however, a kind of equal ultimacy. The reprobate, who are passed over by God, are ultimately doomed, and their damnation is as certain and sure as the ultimate salvation of the elect.

The problem is linked to biblical statements such as those regarding God's hardening of Pharaoh's heart. That the Bible says God hardened Pharaoh's heart is beyond dispute. The question remains, how did God harden Pharaoh? Luther argued for a passive rather than an active hardening. That is, God did not create fresh evil in Pharaoh's heart. There was already enough evil present in Pharaoh's heart to incline him to resist the will of God at every turn. All God ever has to do to harden anybody is to remove His restraining grace from them and give them over to their own evil impulses. This is precisely what God does to the damned in hell. He abandons them to their own wickedness.

In what sense did God "hate" Esau? Two different explanations are offered to solve this problem. The first explains it by defining hate not as a negative passion directed toward Esau but as simply the absence of redemptive love. That God "loved" Jacob simply means that He made Jacob the recipient of His unmerited grace. He gave Jacob a benefit that Jacob did not deserve. Esau did not receive the same benefit and in that sense was hated by God.

The first explanation sounds a bit like special pleading to get God off the hook for hating somebody. The second explanation gives more strength to the word *hate*. It says simply that God did in fact hate Esau. Esau was odious in the sight of God. There was nothing in Esau for God to love. Esau was a vessel fit for destruction and altogether worthy of God's wrath and holy hatred. Let the reader decide.

Summary

1. Predestination is double; it has two sides to it.
2. Some teach that God is equally responsible for election and reprobation. This is characteristic of hyper-Calvinism.

3. The Reformed view of double predestination reflects a positive-negative schema.
4. God passively, not actively, hardened Pharaoh's heart.
5. God hated Esau in the sense of failing to give him a blessing of grace or in the sense of abhorring him as a vessel fit for destruction.

59 EFFECTUAL CALLING

When I was a boy my mother used to stand at the window and call me into the house for dinner. Usually I came at the first summons, but not always. If I delayed, she would call a second time, usually with greater volume. Her first call was not always effective; it failed to gain the desired effect. Her second call usually was effective; I hurried into the house.

There is a call of God that is effective. When God called the world into being, the universe did not hesitate to comply with the command. God's desired effect in creation came to pass. Likewise, when Jesus called the dead Lazarus from his grave, Lazarus responded with life.

There is also an effectual call of God in the life of the believer. It is a call that brings about its desired effect. Effectual calling is related to the power of God in regenerating the sinner from spiritual death. It is sometimes referred to as "irresistible grace."

Effectual calling refers to a call of God that by His sovereign power and authority brings about His designed and ordained effect, or result. When Paul teaches that those whom He predestines, He calls, and those whom He calls, He justifies, the call to which he is referring is the effectual call of God.

The effectual call of God is an inward call. It is the secret work of quickening or regeneration accomplished in the souls of the elect by the immediate supernatural operation of the Holy Spirit. It effects or works the inward change of the disposition, inclination, and desire of the soul. Before the inward effectual call of God is received, no person is inclined to come to Him. Everyone who is effectually called is now disposed to God and responds in faith. We see, then, that faith itself is a gift from God, having been given in the effectual call of the Holy Spirit.

The preaching of the gospel represents the outward

**Biblical passages
for reflection:**
Ezekiel 36:26-27
Romans 8:30
Ephesians 1:7-12
2 Thessalonians
  2:13-14
2 Timothy 1:8-12

call of God. This call is heard audibly by both the elect and the nonelect. Human beings have the ability to resist and refuse the outward call. He will not respond to the outward call in faith unless or until the outward call is accompanied by the effectual inward call of the Holy Spirit. Effectual calling is irresistible in the sense that God sovereignly brings about its desired result. This sovereign work of grace is resistible in the sense that we can and do resist it in our fallen nature, but irresistible in the sense that God's grace prevails over our natural resistance to it.

Effectual calling refers to the creative power of God by which we are brought to spiritual life. The apostle Paul writes:

And you He made alive, who were dead in trespasses and sins, in which you once walked according to the course of this world, according to the prince of the power of the air, the spirit who now works in the sons of disobedience, among whom also we all once conducted ourselves in the lusts of our flesh, fulfilling the desires of the flesh and of the mind, and were by nature children of wrath, just as the others. (Ephesians 2:1-3)

We who were once children of wrath and were spiritually dead have become the "called out ones" by virtue of the power and efficacy of the inward call of God. In His grace, the Holy Spirit gives us eyes to see what we would not see and ears to hear what we would not hear.

Summary

1. Human calls may be effectual or ineffectual.
2. God has the power to effectually call worlds into being, corpses from the grave, and people from spiritual death to spiritual life.
3. People may hear God's outer call of the gospel and reject it. But His inward call is always effective. It produces the desired results.

60

REBIRTH

When Jimmy Carter was elected president of the United States he described himself as a "born-again Christian." Then Charles Colson, former hatchet man in the Nixon White House, wrote a best-selling book by the title *Born Again.*[1] In it, he chronicled his own experience of conversion to Christianity. Since these two famous personalities popularized the phrase *born again,* it has become part of the currency of modern speech.

To describe someone as a born-again Christian is, technically speaking, to be guilty of redundancy. There is no such thing as a non-born-again Christian. An unregenerate (non-born-again) Christian is a contradiction in terms. Likewise, a born-again non-Christian is a contradiction.

It was Jesus who first declared that spiritual rebirth was an absolute necessity for entering the kingdom of God. He declared to Nicodemus, "Most assuredly, I say to you, unless one is born again, he cannot see the kingdom of God" (John 3:3). The word *unless* in Jesus' teaching signals a universally necessary condition for seeing and entering the kingdom of God. Rebirth, then, is an essential part of Christianity; without it, entrance into God's kingdom is impossible.

Regeneration is the theological term used to describe rebirth. It refers to a new generating, a new genesis, a new beginning. It is more than "turning over a new leaf"; it marks the beginning of a new life in a radically renewed person. Peter speaks of believers "having been born again, not of corruptible seed but incorruptible, through the word of God which lives and abides forever" (1 Peter 1:23).

Regeneration is the work of the Holy Spirit upon those who are spiritually dead (see Ephesians 2:1-10). The Spirit recreates the human heart, quickening it from spiritual death to spiritual life. Regenerate people are new creations. Where formerly they had no disposition, inclination, or desire for the things of God, now they are disposed and inclined toward God. In regeneration, God plants a desire for Himself in the human heart that otherwise would not be there.

Regeneration is not to be confused with the full experience of conversion. Just as birth is our initiation, our first entrance into life outside the womb, so our spiritual rebirth is the starting point of our spiritual life. It occurs by God's divine initiative and is an act that is sovereign, immediate, and instantaneous. An awareness of our conversion may be gradual. Yet rebirth itself is instantaneous. No one can be partially reborn any more than a woman can be partially pregnant.

Regeneration is not the fruit or result of faith. Rather, *regeneration precedes faith* as the necessary condition for faith. We also do not in any way dispose ourselves toward regeneration or cooperate as coworkers with the Holy Spirit to bring it to pass. We do not decide or choose to be regenerated. God chooses to regenerate us before we will ever choose to embrace Him. To be sure, *after* we have been regenerated by the sovereign grace of God, we do choose, act, cooperate, and believe in Christ. God does not have faith for us. It is our own faith by which we are justified. What God does is quicken us to spiritual life, rescuing us from darkness, bondage, and spiritual death. God makes faith possible and actual for us. He quickens faith within us.

Biblical passages for reflection:
Deuteronomy 30:6
Ezekiel 36:26-27
Romans 8:30
Titus 3:4-7

Summary

1. All who are truly Christians are born again.
2. All who are truly born again are Christians.
3. Rebirth is a necessary precondition to entering the kingdom of God.
4. Regeneration is the sovereign, gracious work of the Holy Spirit.
5. Regeneration precedes faith. It is God's divine initiative in salvation.

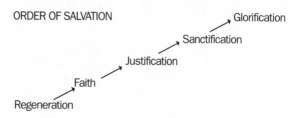

ORDER OF SALVATION

Glorification
Sanctification
Justification
Faith
Regeneration

61 ATONEMENT

The apostle Paul declared that he was determined to know nothing save Christ and Him crucified. This was the apostle's way of emphasizing the extreme importance of the Cross to Christianity. The doctrine of the Atonement is central to all Christian theology. Luther called Christianity a theology of the Cross. The figure of a cross is the universal symbol of Christianity. The concept of atonement reaches back to the Old Testament where God set up a system by which the people of Israel could make atonement for their sins. To atone is to make amends, to set things right.

Both the Old and New Testaments make it clear that all human beings are sinners. As our sins are against an infinite, holy God who cannot even look upon sin, atonement must be made in order for us to have fellowship with God. Because sin touches even our best acts, we are incapable of making a sufficient sacrifice. Even our sacrifices are tainted and would require a further sacrifice to cover that blemish, *ad infinitum.* We have no gift valuable enough, no work righteous enough to atone for our own sins. We are debtors who cannot pay their debts.

In receiving the wrath of the Father on the cross, Christ was able to make atonement for His people. Christ carried, or bore, the punishment for the sins of human beings. He atoned for them by accepting the just punishment due for those sins. The Old Testament covenant pronounced a curse upon any person who broke the law of God. On the cross, Jesus not only took that curse upon Himself, but He became "a curse for us" (Galatians 3:13). He was forsaken by the Father and experienced the full measure of hell on the cross.

Orthodox Christianity has insisted that the Atonement involves *substitution* and *satisfaction.* In taking God's curse upon Himself, Jesus satisfied the demands of God's holy justice. He received God's wrath for us, saving us from the wrath that is to come (1 Thessalonians 1:10).

A key phrase in the Bible regarding the Atonement is the phrase, "in behalf of." Jesus did not die for Himself, but for us. His suffering was vicarious; He was our substitute. He took our place in fulfilling the role of the Lamb of God who takes away the sin of the world.

While the Father's wrath is real, it should be noted that the atonement Christ made was not a case of the Son working against the Father's will. It is not as if Christ were snatching His people out of the Father's hand. The Son did not persuade the Father to save those whom the Father was loathe to save. On the contrary, both Father and Son willed the salvation of the elect and worked together to bring it to pass. As the apostle Paul wrote, "God was in Christ, reconciling the world to Himself" (2 Corinthians 5:19).

Biblical passages for reflection:
Romans 3:21-28
Romans 5:17-19
Ephesians 1:7
Philippians 3:8-9
Titus 3:1-7

Summary

1. Atonement involves a payment to make amends for a debt.
2. Human beings cannot atone for their own sins.
3. Jesus' perfection qualified Him to make atonement.
4. Christ fulfilled the curse of the Old Covenant.
5. Christ's atonement was both a work of substitution and satisfaction.
6. The Father and Son worked in harmony to effect our reconciliation.

62 DEFINITE ATONEMENT

Sometimes the distinctive doctrines of Reformed theology are summarized by the use of the acrostic T-U-L-I-P. The acrostic spells out the following:

T = Total depravity
U = Unconditional election
L = Limited atonement
I = Irresistible grace
P = Perseverance of the saints

Though the acrostic is helpful for aiding the memory, it can also cast confusion on the doctrines because of the way they are worded to fit the acrostic. This is especially true of the third point, limited atonement. Many, who style themselves "four-point" Calvinists, are willing to affirm all but limited atonement. They knock the *L* out of TULIP.

I prefer the term *definite* atonement to the term *limited* atonement (though it turns *tulip* into *tudip*). The doctrine of definite atonement focuses on the question of the *design* of Christ's atonement. It is concerned with God's intent in sending Jesus to the cross.

Anyone who is not a universalist is willing to agree that the effect of Christ's work on the cross is limited to those who believe. That is, Christ's atonement does not avail for unbelievers. Not everyone is saved through His death. Everyone also agrees that the merit of Christ's death is sufficient to pay for the sins of all human beings. Some put it this way: Christ's atonement is sufficient for all, but efficient only for some.

This, however, does not really get at the heart of the question of definite atonement. Those who deny definite atonement insist that Christ's work of atonement was designed by God to atone for the sins of everyone in the world. It made *possible* the salvation of everyone, but made *certain* the salvation of no one. Its design is therefore both unlimited and indefinite.

The Reformed view holds that Christ's atonement was designed and intended only for the elect. Christ laid down His life for His sheep and only for His sheep. Furthermore, the Atonement insured salvation for all the elect. The Atonement was an *actual,* not merely *potential,* work of redemption. In this view there is no possibility that God's design and intent for the Atonement could be frustrated. God's purpose in salvation is sure.

Reformed theologians differ over the question of the *offer* of the Atonement to the human race. Some insist that the offer of the gospel is universal. The Cross and its benefits are offered to anyone who believes. Others insist that this concept of a universal offer is misleading and involves a kind of play on words. Since only the elect will in fact believe, in reality the offer goes out only to them. The benefit of Christ's atonement is never offered by God to the impenitent or the unbelieving. Since belief and repentance are conditions met only by the elect, then ultimately the Atonement is offered only to them.

John writes that: "He Himself is the propitiation for our sins, and not for ours only but also for the whole world" (1 John 2:2). This text, more than any other, is cited as scriptural proof against definite atonement. At first glance it seems to argue that Christ's death was intended for everybody (the whole world). However, if it is taken in that sense the text proves more than non-Reformed people want it to prove. It becomes a proof-text for universalism. If Christ indeed propitiated or satisfied God's demands for the punishment of the sins of everybody, then clearly everybody would be saved. If God punished sins that were already propitiated then He would be unjust. If the text is understood to mean that everyone's sins have been conditionally propitiated (contingent upon faith and repentance) then we are back to the original question of only the elect satisfying the conditions.

The other way to view this text is to see the contrast in it between *our* sins and those of the *whole world.* Who are the people included in the word *our?* If John is speaking only of fellow believers, then the previous interpretation of the text would apply. But is that the only possible meaning of *our?*

In the New Testament a frequent contrast is made between the salvation enjoyed by Jews and that enjoyed by non-Jews. A crucial point of the gospel is that it is not limited to Jews but is extended to people all over the world, to people from every tribe and nation. God loves the whole world, but He does not save the whole world; He saves people from all parts of the world. In this text, John may merely be saying that Christ is not only a propitiation for our sins (Jewish believers) but for the elect found also throughout the whole world.

In any case, the plan of God was decided before anybody was in the world at all. The atonement of Christ was not a divine afterthought. The purpose of God in Christ's death was determined at the foundation of the world. The design was not guesswork but according to a specific plan and purpose, which God is sovereignly bringing to pass. All for whom Christ died are redeemed by His sacrificial act.

Biblical passages for reflection:
Matthew 1:21
John 3:16
John 10:27-30
John 17:9-12
Acts 20:28
Romans 8:30

Summary

1. Definite atonement replaces the term *limited atonement* in the acrostic TULIP.
2. Definite atonement refers to the scope of God's design for redemption and the intent of the Cross.
3. All who are not universalists agree that Christ's atonement is sufficient for all, but effective only for those who believe.
4. Christ's atonement was an actual propitiation for sin, not a potential or conditional propitiation.
5. The Atonement in a broad sense is offered to all; in a narrow sense, it is only offered to the elect.
6. John's teaching that Christ died for the sins of the whole world means that the elect are not limited to Israel but are found throughout the world.

63

FREE WILL

At this very moment you are reading these words because you choose of your own free will to read them. You may protest and say, "No! I didn't choose to read them. I was given an assignment to read this book. I really don't want to be reading it." Perhaps that is the case. Nevertheless you are reading it. Maybe there are other things you would rather be doing at the moment, but you have made a choice to read it nevertheless. You decided to read it instead of not reading it.

I don't know why you are reading this. But I do know that you must have a reason for reading it. If you had no reason to read it, you simply would not have chosen to read it.

Every choice that we make in life we make for some reason. Our decisions are based upon what seems good for us at the moment, all things considered. We do some things out of intense desire. We do other things with no awareness of desire at all. Yet the desire is there or we wouldn't choose to do them. This is the very essence of free will—to choose according to our desires.

Jonathan Edwards, in his work *The Freedom of the Will,* defines the will as "that by which the mind chooses."[1] There can be no doubt that human beings do indeed make choices. I am choosing to write, you are choosing to read. I will to write, and writing is set in motion. When the idea of freedom is added, however, the issue becomes terribly complicated. We have to ask, freedom to do what? Even the most ardent Calvinist would not deny that the will is free to choose *whatever it desires.* Even the most ardent Arminian would agree that the will is not free to choose what it does not desire.

With regard to salvation, the question then becomes, what do human beings desire? The Arminian believes that some desire to repent and be saved. Others desire to flee from God and thus reap eternal damnation. Why different people have different desires is never made clear by the Arminian. The Calvinist holds that all human beings desire to flee from God unless and until the Holy Spirit performs a work of regeneration. That regeneration changes our desires so that we will freely repent and be saved.

It is important to note that even the unregenerate are never forced against their will. Their wills are changed without their permission, but they are always free to choose as they will. Thus we are indeed free to do as we will. We are not free, however, to choose or select our nature. One cannot simply declare, "Henceforth I will desire only the good" anymore than Christ could have declared, "Henceforth I will desire only evil." This is where our freedom stops.

The Fall left the human will intact insofar as we still have the faculty of choosing. Our minds have been darkened by sin and our desires bound by wicked impulses. But we can still think, choose, and act. Yet something terrible has happened to us. We have lost all desire for God. The thoughts and desires of our heart are only evil continuously. The freedom of our will is a curse. Because we can still choose according to our desires, we choose to sin and thus we become accountable to the judgment of God.

Augustine said that we still have free will, but we have lost our liberty. The royal liberty of which the Bible speaks is the freedom or power to choose Christ as our own. But until our heart is changed by the Holy Spirit, we have no desire for Christ. Without that desire we never will choose Him. God must awaken our soul and give us a desire for Christ before we will ever be inclined to choose Him.

Edwards said that as fallen human beings we retain our *natural freedom* (the power to act according to our desires) but lose *moral freedom.*[2] Moral freedom includes the disposition, inclination, and desire of the soul toward righteousness. It is this inclination that was lost in the Fall.

Every choice I make is determined by something. There is a reason for it, a desire behind it. This sounds like determinism. By no means! Determinism teaches that our actions are completely controlled by something

Biblical passages for reflection:

Deuteronomy
   30:19-20
John 6:44, 65
John 8:34-36
John 15:5
Romans 8:5-8
James 1:13-15

external to us, making us do what we don't want to do. That is coercion and is opposed to freedom.

How can our choices be determined but not coerced? Because they are determined by something within—by what we are and by what we desire. They are determined by *ourselves.* This is *self-determination,* which is the very essence of freedom.

To be sure, for us to choose Christ, God must change our heart. That is precisely what He does. He changes our heart for us. He gives us a desire for Himself that we otherwise would not have. Then we choose Him out of the desire that is within us. We freely choose Him because we want to choose Him. That is the wonder of His grace.

Summary

1. Every choice we make is for a reason.
2. We always choose according to our strongest inclination at the moment of choice.
3. The will is the choosing faculty.
4. Fallen human beings have free will but lack liberty. We have natural freedom but not moral freedom.
5. Freedom is self-determination.
6. In regeneration, God changes the disposition of our heart and plants a desire for Himself within us.

64
FAITH

Christianity is often called a religion. More properly it is called a "faith." We often speak of the Christian *faith.* It is called a faith because there is a body of knowledge that is affirmed or believed by its adherents. It is also called a faith because the virtue of faith is central to its understanding of redemption.

What does faith mean? In our culture it is often mistaken for a blind belief in something that is unreasonable. To call the Christian faith a "blind faith," however, is not only demeaning to Christians, but an outrage to God. When the Bible speaks of blindness it uses this image for people who, by their sin, walk in darkness. Christianity calls people out of the darkness, not into the darkness. Faith is the antidote to blindness, not the cause of it.

At its root, the term *faith* means "trust." To trust God is not an act of unreasonable belief. God demonstrates Himself to be eminently trustworthy. He gives ample reason for us to trust Him. He proves that He Himself is faithful and worthy of our trust.

There is a huge difference between faith and credulity. To be credulous is to believe something for no sound reason. It is the stuff of which superstition is made and thrives on. Faith is established upon coherent and consistent reasoning and upon sound empirical evidence. Peter writes, "For we did not follow cunningly devised fables when we made known to you the power and coming of our Lord Jesus Christ, but were eyewitnesses of His majesty" (2 Peter 1:16).

Christianity does not rest upon myths and fables but on the testimony of those who saw with their eyes and heard with their ears. The truth of the gospel is based on historical events. If the account of those events is not trustworthy, then indeed our faith would be in vain. But God does not ask us to believe anything on the basis of myth.

The book of Hebrews gives us a definition of faith:

"Now faith is the substance of things hoped for, the evidence of things not seen" (Hebrews 11:1). Faith comprises the essence of our hope for the future. In simple terms this means that we trust God for the future based on our faith in what He has accomplished in the past. To believe that God will continue to be trustworthy is not a gratuitous faith. There is every reason to believe that God will be as faithful to His promises in the future as He has been in the past. There is a reason, a substantive reason, for the hope that is within us.

Biblical passages for reflection:
Romans 1:16-32
Romans 5:1-11
Romans 10:14-17
Galatians 3:1-14
Ephesians 2:8-9
James 2:14-26

The faith that is the evidence of things unseen has primary but not exclusive reference to the future. Nobody has a crystal ball that works. We all walk into the future by faith and not by sight. We may plan and make projections, but even the best foresight we have is based upon our educated guesses. None of us has experiential knowledge of tomorrow. We view the present and can recall the past. We are experts in hindsight. The only solid evidence we have for our own future is drawn from the promises of God. Here faith offers evidence for things unseen. We trust God for tomorrow.

We also trust or believe that God exists. And although God Himself is unseen, the Scriptures make it clear that the invisible God is made manifest through the things that are visible (Romans 1:20). Though God is not visible to us, we believe that He is there because He has manifested Himself so clearly in creation and in history.

Faith includes believing *in* God. Yet that kind of faith is not particularly praiseworthy. James writes, "You believe that there is one God. You do well. Even the demons believe—and tremble!" (James 2:19). Here sarcasm drips from James's pen. To believe in the existence of God merely qualifies us to be demons. It is one thing to believe *in* God; it is another thing to believe God. To believe God, to trust in Him for our very life, is the essence of the Christian faith.

Summary

1. Christianity is a faith because it is based on a body of knowledge revealed by God.
2. Faith is not a blind leap into darkness, but a trust in God that moves us out of darkness into light.
3. Faith is simple, but not simplistic.

4. Faith is not credulity. It is based on sound reason and historical evidence.
5. Faith provides the substance for our future hope.
6. Faith involves trusting in what is not seen.
7. Faith means more than believing *in* God; it means believing God.

65

SAVING FAITH

Jesus once remarked that unless we have the faith of a child we will by no means enter the kingdom of heaven. A childlike faith is a prerequisite for membership in God's kingdom. There is a difference, however, between a childlike faith and a childish faith. The Bible calls us to be babes in evil but mature in our understanding. Saving faith is simple, but not simplistic.

Since the Bible teaches that justification is by faith alone, and that faith is a necessary condition for salvation, it is imperative that we understand what comprises saving faith. James explains clearly what saving faith is not: "What does it profit, my brethren, if someone says he has faith but does not have works? Can faith save him?" (James 2:14). Here James distinguishes between a profession of faith and the reality of faith. Anyone can say that he has faith. Though we are certainly called to profess our faith, the bare profession itself saves no one. The Bible makes it clear that people are capable of honoring Christ with their lips while their hearts are far from Him. Lip service, with no manifestation of the fruit of faith, is not saving faith.

James goes on to say, "Thus also faith by itself, if it does not have works, is dead" (James 2:17). Dead faith is described by James as a faith that does not profit. It is futile and vain and doesn't justify anyone.

When Luther and the Reformers declared that justification is by faith alone, they realized that it was necessary to give careful definition to saving faith. They defined saving faith as including necessary constituent elements. Saving faith is composed of information, intellectual assent, and personal trust.

Saving faith involves content. We are not justified by believing just anything. Some have said, "It doesn't matter what you believe as long as you are sincere." That sentiment is radically opposed to the teaching of the Bible. The Bible teaches that it matters profoundly what we believe. Justification is not by sincerity alone. We may be sincerely wrong. Right doctrine, at least in the essential truths of the gospel, is a necessary ingredient of saving faith. We believe in the gospel, in the person and work of Christ. That is integral to saving faith. If our doctrine is heretical in the essentials, we will not be saved. If, for example, we say we believe in Christ but deny His deity, we do not possess the faith that justifies.

Though it is necessary to have a correct understanding of the essential truths of the gospel in order to be saved, a correct understanding of them is not enough to be saved. A student can earn an *A* on a Christian theology exam, grasping the truths of Christianity, without himself affirming that they are true. Saving faith includes the mind's assent to the truth of the gospel.

Even if people understand the gospel and affirm or assent to its truth, they may still fall short of saving faith. The devil knows the gospel is true, but he hates it with every fiber of his being. There is an element of trust in saving faith. It involves personal reliance and dependence upon the gospel. We can believe that a chair will bear our weight, but we do not exhibit personal trust in the chair until we sit on it.

Trust involves the will as well as the mind. To have saving faith requires that we love the truth of the gospel and desire to live it out. We embrace with our hearts the sweetness and loveliness of Christ.

Technically considered, personal trust could be made a subpoint or further delineation under intellectual assent. The devil may give assent to the truth of certain facts about Jesus, but he does not assent to all of them. He does not assent to the loveliness or the desirability of Christ. But whether we distinguish or combine intellectual assent and personal trust, the fact remains that saving faith requires what Luther called a living faith—a vital and personal trust in Christ as Savior and Lord.

Biblical passages for reflection:
Matthew 18:3
Romans 10:5-13
Ephesians 2:4-10
1 Thessalonians
    2:13
James 2:14-26

Summary

1. Saving faith is childlike but not childish.
2. A person is not justified by a mere profession of faith.
3. Saving faith requires intellectual assent to the truth of the gospel.
4. Saving faith involves a personal trust in and love for Christ.

66 JUSTIFICATION BY FAITH

Martin Luther declared that justification by faith alone is the article upon which the church stands or falls. This cardinal doctrine of the Protestant Reformation was seen as the battleground for nothing less than the gospel itself.

Justification may be defined as that act by which unjust sinners are made right in the sight of a just and holy God. The supreme need of unjust persons is righteousness. It is this lack of righteousness that is supplied by Christ on behalf of the believing sinner. Justification by faith alone means justification by the righteousness or merit of Christ alone, not by our goodness or good deeds.

The issue of justification focuses on the question of merit and grace. Justification by faith means that the works we do are not good enough to merit justification. As Paul puts it, "By the deeds of the law no flesh will be justified in His sight" (Romans 3:20). Justification is forensic. That is, we are declared, counted, or reckoned to be righteous when God imputes the righteousness of Christ to our account. The necessary condition for this is faith.

Protestant theology affirms that faith is the instrumental cause of justification in that faith is the means by which the merits of Christ are appropriated to us. Roman Catholic theology teaches that baptism is the primary instrumental cause of justification and that the sacrament of penance is the secondary, restorative cause. (Roman Catholic theology views penance as the second plank of justification for those who have made shipwreck of their souls—those who have lost the grace of justification by committing mortal sin.) The sacrament of penance requires works of satisfaction by which human beings achieve congruous merit for justification. The Roman Catholic view affirms that justification is by faith, but denies that it is by faith alone, adding good works as a necessary condition.

The faith that justifies is a living faith, not an empty

Biblical passages for reflection:
Romans 3:21-28
Romans 5:12-19
2 Corinthians 5:16-21
Galatians 2:11-21
Ephesians 2:1-10
Philippians 3:7-11

profession of faith. Faith is a personal trust that clings to Christ alone for salvation. Saving faith is also a penitent faith that embraces Christ as both Savior and Lord.

The Bible says that we are not justified by our own good works, but by what is added to us by faith, namely the righteousness of Christ. In a synthesis, something new is added to something basic. Our justification is a synthesis because we have the righteousness of Christ added to us. Our justification is by imputation. God transfers to us, by faith, the righteousness of Christ. This is not a "legal fiction" because God ascribes to us the real merit of Christ, to whom we now belong. It is a real imputation.

Summary

1. Justification is an act of God whereby He declares unjust sinners to be just after He has imputed to them the righteousness of Christ.
2. No one can earn justification by good works.
3. Faith is the necessary condition to receive the imputation of the merits of Christ.
4. Justification requires a living and real faith, not a mere profession of faith.

67 FAITH AND WORKS

Many people assume that by trying to live a good life, they have done all that is necessary to get to heaven. They rest their confidence on the good works they have performed to satisfy the demands of God's justice.

This is a futile hope. God's law requires perfection. Since we are not perfect, we lack the necessary goodness to enter heaven. Thus goodness can never be achieved by living a good life. We can only receive it by trusting in the righteousness of Christ. His merit is perfect and is made available to us through faith.

To believe that we are justified by our good works apart from faith is to embrace the heresy of legalism. To believe that we are justified by a kind of faith that produces no works is to embrace the heresy of antinomianism.

The relationship of faith and good works is one that may be distinguished but never separated. Though our good works add no merit to our faith before God, and though the sole condition of our justification is our faith in Christ, if good works do not follow from our profession of faith, it is a clear indication that we do not possess justifying faith. The Reformed formula is "We are justified by faith alone, but not by a faith that is alone." True justification always results in the process of sanctification. If there is justification, sanctification will inevitably follow. If sanctification does not follow, it is certain that justification was not really present. This does not mean that justification depends or rests upon sanctification. Justification depends on true faith, which in turn will inevitably lead to works of obedience.

When James declared that faith without works is dead, he asserted that such "faith" cannot justify anyone because it is not alive. Living faith produces good works, but these good works are not the basis for justification. Only the merit achieved by Jesus Christ can justify the sinner.

It is a grievous error, indeed a modern form of the antinomian heresy, to suggest that a person can be justified by embracing Jesus as Savior but not as Lord. True faith accepts Christ as both Savior *and* Lord. To rely on Christ alone for salvation is to acknowledge one's total dependence upon Him and to repent of one's sin. To repent of sin is to submit to Christ's authority over us. To deny His lordship is to seek justification with an impenitent faith, which is no faith.

Though our good works do not merit salvation, they are the basis upon which God promises to distribute rewards in heaven. Our entrance into the kingdom of God is by faith alone. Our reward in the kingdom will be *according* to our good works, which is, as Augustine noted, a case of God's gracious crowning of His own gifts.

Biblical passages for reflection:
Romans 3:9–4:8
Philippians
   2:12-13
James 2:18-24
2 Peter 1:5-11
1 John 2:3-6
1 John 4:7-11

Summary

1. No one can be justified by good works. Only through faith in Christ can we be justified.
2. Faith and good deeds must be distinguished but never separated. True faith always produces works of obedience.
3. Justification is by faith alone, but not by a faith that is alone.
4. Dead faith cannot justify.
5. Faith in Christ means trusting in Him as Savior *and* submitting to Him as Lord.
6. We are rewarded in heaven according to our good works, though this reward is one of grace.

Works = Justification	False
Faith + Works = Justification	False
Faith = Justification – Works	False
Faith = Justification + Works	True

REPENTANCE

The opening message of John the Baptist, who served as a herald for Jesus, was, "Repent, for the kingdom of heaven is at hand." This call to repentance was an urgent appeal to sinners. No one who refuses to repent can ever enter the kingdom of God. Repentance is a prerequisite, a necessary condition for salvation.

In Scripture, *repentance* means "to undergo a change of one's mind." This change of mind is not a mere switching of minor opinions, but of the entire direction of one's life. It involves a radical turning *from* sin and *to* Christ.

Repentance is not the cause of new birth or regeneration; it is the result or fruit of regeneration. Though repentance begins with regeneration, it is an attitude and action that must be repeated throughout the Christian life. As we continue to sin, we are called upon to repent as we are convicted of our sin by the Holy Spirit.

Theologians make a distinction between two kinds of repentance. The first is called *attrition.* Attrition is a false or spurious kind of repentance. It involves remorse caused by a fear of punishment or a loss of blessing. Every parent has witnessed attrition in a child when he is caught with his hand in the cookie jar. The child, fearing the paddle, cries, "I'm sorry, please don't spank me!" These pleas coupled with crocodile tears are usually not signs of genuine remorse for wrongdoing. This was the kind of repentance Esau exhibited (Genesis 27:30-46). He was sorry not because he had sinned, but because he had lost his birthright. Attrition, then, is repentance motivated by an attempt to get a ticket out of hell or to otherwise avoid punishment.

Contrition, on the other hand, is true and godly repentance. It is genuine. It includes a deep remorse for having offended God. The contrite person openly and fully confesses his sin with no attempt to excuse it or justify it. This acknowledgment of sin is coupled with a willingness to make restitution whenever possible and a resolve to turn away from sin. This is the spirit of repentance that David exhibited in Psalm 51. "Create in me a clean heart, O God, and renew a steadfast spirit within me. . . . The sacrifices of God are a broken spirit, a broken and a contrite heart—these, O God, You will not despise" (Psalm 51:10, 17).

When repentance is offered to God in a spirit of true contrition, He promises to forgive us and to restore us to fellowship with Him: "If we confess our sins, He is faithful and just to forgive us our sins and to cleanse us from all unrighteousness" (1 John 1:9).

Biblical passages for reflection:
Ezekiel 18:30-32
Luke 24:46-47
Acts 20:17-21
Romans 2:4
2 Corinthians 7:8-12

Summary

1. Repentance is a necessary condition for salvation.
2. Repentance is the fruit of regeneration.
3. Attrition is false repentance motivated by fear.
4. Contrition is true repentance motivated by godly remorse.
5. True repentance includes full confession, restitution, and resolve to turn from sin.
6. God promises forgiveness and restoration to all who truly repent.

69

MERIT AND GRACE

The issue of merit and grace is at the heart of the historic debate between Roman Catholic theology and Protestantism. A major declaration of the Reformation was *sola gratia*—salvation is by the grace of God alone. Believers bring no merit of their own before the judgment seat of God, but rest solely on God's mercy and grace.

Merit is defined as that which is earned or deserved. Justice demands that merit be given where it is deserved. Merit is something due a person for a performance. If it is not received, an injustice is committed.

Roman Catholic theology speaks of merit in three distinct ways. It speaks of *condign* merit, which is so meritorious as to impose an obligation for reward. It also speaks of *congruous* merit, which, though it is not as high as condign merit, nevertheless is "fitting or congruous" for God to reward it. Congruous merit is achieved by performing good works in conjunction with the sacrament of penance. A third type of merit is *supererogatory* merit, which is merit above and beyond the call of duty. It is the excess merit achieved by saints. This merit is deposited into the treasury of merit from which the church can draw to apply to the account of those lacking sufficient merit to progress from purgatory to heaven.

Protestant theology denies and "protests" against all three forms of merit, declaring that the only merit we have at our disposal is the merit of Christ. The merit of Christ comes to us by grace through faith. Grace is the *unmerited* favor of God. It is an action or disposition of God toward us. Grace is not a substance that can inhabit our souls. We grow in grace, not by a quantative measure of some substance in us, but by the merciful assistance of the Holy Spirit who dwells within us, acting graciously toward us and upon us. The means of grace God gives to assist us in the Christian life include Scripture, the sacraments, prayer, fellowship, and the nurture of the church.

Biblical passages for reflection:
John 15:1-8
Romans 4:1-8
Romans 5:1-5
2 Corinthians 5:17-19
Ephesians 2:8-9
Titus 3:4-7

Summary

1. Our salvation is *sola gratia,* by grace alone.
2. We have no merit of our own by which God is obligated to save us.
3. Roman Catholic theology distinguishes among *condign, congruous,* and *supererogatory* merit. All three are rejected by Protestantism.
4. Grace is the undeserved favor or mercy of God toward us.

70 PERSEVERANCE OF THE SAINTS

Most of us know people who have made a profession of faith in Christ and who have perhaps even made a strong display of faith, involving themselves deeply in the life and ministry of the church, only to later repudiate that faith and become spiritual dropouts. Such evidence always raises the question, can a person once saved lose his salvation? Is apostasy a clear and present danger for the believer?

The Roman Catholic church teaches that people can and do lose their salvation. If a person commits a mortal sin, such sin kills the grace of justification that inhabits his soul. If he dies before being restored to a state of grace via the sacrament of penance, he will go to hell.

Many Protestants also believe that it is possible to lose one's salvation. The warnings of Hebrews 6 and Paul's concern about becoming "disqualified" (1 Corinthians 9:27), as well as the examples of King Saul and others, have led some to conclude that people can fall fully and finally from grace. On the other hand, Reformed theology teaches the doctrine of the perseverance of the saints. This doctrine is sometimes called "eternal security." In essence the doctrine teaches that if you have saving faith you will never lose it, and if you lose it, you never had it. As John writes, "They went out from us, but they were not of us; for if they had been of us, they would have continued with us; but they went out that they might be made manifest, that none of them were of us" (1 John 2:19).

We know it is possible for people to be enamored by certain elements of Christianity without ever embracing Christ Himself. Perhaps a young person is attracted to a fun and stimulating youth group that has an appealing program. The person may be "converted" to the program without being converted to Christ. Such a person may be like those pictured in the parable of the sower:

A sower went out to sow his seed. And as he sowed, some fell by the wayside; and it was trampled down, and the birds of the air devoured it. Some fell on rock; and as soon as it sprang up, it withered away because it lacked moisture. And some fell among thorns, and the thorns sprang up with it and choked it. But others fell on good ground, sprang up, and yielded a crop a hundredfold. (Luke 8:5-8)

The parable may refer to those who believed at first, but afterwards fell away, or it may mean that those who "believed" had a false or spurious faith, as Reformed theology maintains. Only the seed that falls on the good ground yields the fruit of obedience. Jesus describes these as ones who hear the word "with a noble and good heart" (Luke 8:15). Their faith proceeds from a truly regenerate heart.

The doctrine of perseverance does not rest on our ability to persevere, even if we are regenerate. Rather, it rests on the promise of God to preserve us. Paul writes to the Philippians, "Being confident of this very thing, that He who has begun a good work in you will complete it until the day of Jesus Christ" (Philippians 1:6). It is by grace and grace alone that Christians persevere. God finishes what He begins. He insures that His purposes in election are not frustrated.

The golden chain of Romans 8 gives further testimony to this hope. "Moreover whom He predestined, these He also called; whom He called, these He also justified; and whom He justified, these He also glorified" (Romans 8:30). Paul goes on to declare that nothing "shall be able to separate us from the love of God which is in Christ Jesus our Lord" (Romans 8:39).

We have security because salvation is of the Lord and we are His craftsmanship. He gives the Holy Spirit to every believer as a promise that He will fulfill what He begins. He has likewise sealed every believer by the Holy Spirit. He has marked us with an indelible mark and given His personal down payment that guarantees He will finish the transaction.

A final basis of confidence is found in the high-priestly work of Christ, who intercedes for us. Just as

Biblical passages for reflection:
John 6:35-40
Romans 8:31-39
Philippians 1:6
2 Timothy 2:14-19
Hebrews 9:11-15

Jesus prayed for the restoration of Peter (and not for Judas), so He prays for our restoration when we stumble and fall. We may fall for a season but never fully or finally fall away. Jesus prayed in the upper room, "While I was with them in the world, I kept them in Your name. Those whom You gave Me I have kept; and none of them is lost except the son of perdition, that the Scripture might be fulfilled" (John 17:12). Only Judas, who was a son of perdition from the beginning, whose profession of faith was spurious, was lost. Those who are truly believers cannot be snatched from God's hand (John 10:27-30).

Summary

1. Many people make a profession of faith in Christ and later repudiate Him.
2. Perseverance of the saints rests on the promises of God to preserve the saints.
3. God will bring to completion the salvation of the elect.
4. Those who depart from the faith were never really believers.
5. We can have confidence in our salvation because we have been sealed with the Holy Spirit. He is God's pledge to bring our salvation to completion.
6. The intercession of Christ is for our preservation.

71 THE ASSURANCE OF SALVATION

Can anyone know for sure that he is saved? For someone to declare that he is certain of his salvation may seem to be an act of unspeakable arrogance. Yet the Bible calls us to make our salvation a matter of certainty. Peter commands, "Therefore, brethren, be even more diligent to make your call and election sure" (2 Peter 1:10).

It is our duty to seek assurance of our salvation with diligence. This is not done out of idle curiosity about the state of our soul, but to enhance our growth in sanctification. Christians who remain uncertain about the state of their salvation are subject to all sorts of questions that paralyze their walk with Christ. They stumble in doubt and are vulnerable to the assaults of Satan. So we must seek to be assured of our salvation. There are four possible positions with respect to one's assurance of salvation.

Position One: There are people who are unsaved and know that they are unsaved. These people are aware of the enmity they have in their hearts toward God and clearly want nothing to do with Christ as their Savior. They are bold to proclaim that they do not need Christ. Such people are often openly hostile to the gospel.

Position Two: There are people who are saved but do not know they are saved. These people are actually in a state of grace but are uncertain of it. Perhaps they are wrestling with sin in their lives and doubt their own salvation because of a troubled conscience. In this group are those who have not yet made certain that they are among the elect.

Position Three: There are people who are saved and know that they are saved. This is the group who are certain of their election and calling. They have a clear and sound understanding of what salvation requires and know they have met the requirements. They have believed the testimony of the Holy Spirit when He witnessed to their spirits that they are the children of God (Romans 8:16).

Position Four: There are people who are not saved but confidently believe that they are saved. These people have assurance of salvation without salvation. Their assurance is a false assurance.

Because it is possible to have a false assurance of salvation, how do we know if we are in group three or group four? To answer that we must look more closely at group four and ask how it is possible to have a false sense of assurance.

The easiest way to have a false assurance of salvation is to have a false doctrine of salvation. For example, if a person holds to a universalist view of salvation they may reason as follows:

Every person is saved.
I am a person.
Therefore, I am saved.

Because their doctrine is faulty, their assurance has no firm basis.

Another way that people falsely assure themselves of salvation is by believing that they will get to heaven by trying to live a good life. Those who think they are living a good enough life to satisfy the demands of a holy God are only deluding themselves into thinking they are saved.

But what if a person has a sound doctrine of salvation? Is it still possible to have false assurance? We must answer yes. A person might think he has saving faith but not really possess it. The test for authentic assurance is twofold. On the one hand, we must examine our own hearts to see if we have true faith in Christ. We must see whether or not we have any genuine love for the biblical Christ. For we know such love for Him would be impossible without regeneration.

Second, we must examine the fruit of our faith. We do not need perfect fruit to have assurance, but there must be some evidence of the fruit of obedience for our profession of faith to be credible. If no fruit is present, then no faith is present. Where saving faith is found, fruit of that faith is also found.

Finally, we seek our assurance from the Word of God through which the Holy Spirit bears witness to our spirit that we are His children.

Summary

1. It is our duty to diligently pursue assurance of salvation.
2. Assurance of salvation enhances our sanctification.
3. There are four possible groups or positions regarding assurance:
   (a) Those who are unsaved and know they are unsaved
   (b) Those who are saved but don't have assurance that they are are saved
   (c) Those who are saved and know they are saved
   (d) Those who are unsaved but believe they are saved
4. False assurance is primarily based on a false doctrine of salvation.
5. To gain authentic assurance we must search our own hearts and examine the fruit of our faith.
6. Full assurance comes from the Word of God coupled with the testimony of the Holy Spirit.

Biblical passages for reflection:
Matthew 7:21-23
John 3:1-21
Romans 8:15-17
2 Corinthians 1:12
1 John 2:3-6
1 John 5:13

72 THE INTERMEDIATE STATE

"She is not dead, but sleeping" (Luke 8:52). Jesus made this comment about Jairus's daughter when He was about to raise her from the dead. Frequently the Bible refers to death by the figure of "sleep." Because of this image, some have concluded that the New Testament teaches the doctrine of soul sleep.

Soul sleep is usually described as a kind of temporary suspended animation of the soul between the moment of personal death and the time when our bodies will be resurrected. When our bodies are raised from the dead, the soul is awakened to begin conscious personal continuity in heaven. Though centuries may pass between death and final resurrection, the "sleeping" soul will have no conscious awareness of the passing of time. Our transition from death to heaven will seem to be instantaneous.

Soul sleep represents a departure from orthodox Christianity. It remains, however, as a firmly entrenched minority report among Christians. The traditional view is called the intermediate state. This view holds that at death, the believer's soul goes immediately to be with Christ to enjoy a continuous, conscious, personal existence while awaiting the final resurrection of the body. When the Apostles' Creed speaks of the "resurrection of the body," it is not referring to the resurrection of Christ's human body (which is also affirmed in the Creed) but to the resurrection of our bodies at the last day.

But what happens in the meantime? The classical view is that at death the souls of believers are immediately glorified. They are made perfect in holiness and enter immediately into glory. Their bodies, however, remain in the grave, awaiting final resurrection.

Jesus promised the thief on the cross that "today you will be with Me in Paradise" (Luke 23:43). Those who support the concept of soul sleep argue that Jesus could not have meant that He would meet the thief in paradise that very day because Jesus would be dead for three days and He had not yet ascended. Although Christ's ascension had indeed not yet occurred and His body certainly was in the grave, He had commended His spirit to the Father. We are assured that at the moment of His death, the soul of Jesus went to Paradise as He declared. Soul sleep advocates argue that most English editions of the Bible have misplaced the comma. They read it this way: "I say to you today, you will be with Me in Paradise."

With this change in punctuation the "today" then refers to the time Jesus is speaking rather than the time Jesus will meet the thief in Paradise. This punctuation is unlikely, however. It was perfectly obvious to the thief on what day Jesus was conversing with him. It was hardly necessary for Jesus to say He was speaking "today." This waste of words for a man gasping for breath in the throes of crucifixion is highly unlikely. Rather, consistent with the rest of the biblical evidence to the intermediate state (see especially Philippians 1:19-26 and 2 Corinthians 5:1-10), the promise to the thief is that he would be reunited with Christ in Paradise that very day.

The state of the believer after death is both different and better than what we experience in this life, though not as different or as blessed as it will be in the final resurrection. In the intermediate state we will enjoy the continuity of conscious personal existence in the presence of Christ.

Mankind's probation ends at death. Our ultimate destiny is decided when we die. There is no hope of a second chance of repentance after death, and there is no place of purging such as purgatory to improve our future condition. For the believer, death is immediate emancipation from the conflict and turmoil of this life as we enter into our state of blessedness.

Though death brings rest to the soul and the Bible often refers to death by the euphemism of sleep, it is not proper to assume that in the intermediate state the soul sleeps or that we remain unconscious or in a state of suspended animation until the final resurrection.

Biblical passages for reflection:

Luke 8:49-56
Luke 23:43
2 Corinthians
   5:1-10
Philippians 1:19-26
1 Thessalonians
   4:13-18

Summary

1. Soul sleep affirms a period of unconscious "suspended animation" of the soul between death and the final resurrection. It is a departure from orthodox Christianity.

2. The intermediate state refers to our conscious presence with Christ in heaven as disembodied souls, between death and the resurrection of our bodies.
3. The intermediate state is *better* than our present state but not as wonderful as our final state.
4. There is no second chance of repentance after death.

73 THE LAST RESURRECTION

A question that every believer has contemplated is the question of what we will look like in heaven. Will we be able to recognize our loved ones? Will our resurrected bodies have the characteristics of age or of youth?

Many of these matters remain mysterious to us. The Bible only hints at these answers. We know that whatever our resurrected state will be like, it will far exceed our highest present expectations. The Bible says, "Eye has not seen, nor ear heard, nor have entered into the heart of man the things which God has prepared for those who love Him" (1 Corinthians 2:9). Paul tells us that at present we "see in a mirror, dimly, but then face to face. Now I know in part, but then I shall know just as I also am known" (1 Corinthians 13:12).

The Bible clearly teaches a final resurrection of the bodies of the saints. The resurrection of Jesus is declared to be the firstfruits of those who will also participate in this resurrection.

There is continuity between the earthly body that dies and the resurrected body we will be given. Our present bodies are corruptible and will indeed decay or, in some instances be torn asunder or fragmented in death. However, just as Jesus returned from the grave with His body, albeit changed, so shall our present bodies be resurrected though changed. A body may change its state without thereby destroying its identity.

Every resurrected body will be complete both in quantity and quality. Nothing will be lacking though much will be gained. We will be recognizeable in our resurrected bodies. We do not yet know how this will be accomplished by God's power, only that it will be so.

Our new bodies will be especially suited for eternal life in the kingdom of God. Our present bodies are not so adapted. Whatever changes are necessary will be

**Biblical passages
for reflection:**
Romans 8:11
1 Corinthians 2:9
1 Corinthians
  15:1-58
Philippians
  3:20-21
1 Thessalonians
  4:13-18

made by the power of God. We know that our resurrected bodies will still be human and finite. We will not be deified. Our new bodies will be incorruptible—without decay, illness, pain, or death. There will be added power to our present bodies as they will be raised in honor, power, and glory. Our bodies will be fashioned to be like the glorified body of Jesus.

The new body of the saint will be a spiritual and a heavenly body. It will be adapted to a higher order of living, perhaps glowing and radiant in countenance not unlike Christ in His transfiguration.

Summary

1. Our future state in the bodily resurrection is shrouded in mystery.
2. There will be a continuity between our present bodies and our resurrected bodies.
3. We will be able to recognize each other in heaven.
4. Our new bodies will be adapted and suited for life in heaven.

74

GLORIFICATION

I remember a crucial moment before a championship basketball game in high school when I huddled with my teammates for last minute instructions from our coach. Trying to inspire us to victory the coach said, "Boys, this is the moment we've all been working for. Now go out and cover yourselves with glory!" We did. We won the coveted championship and basked in the glory of it. But that kind of glory is fleeting. A new quest for it begins with the initiation of each new season or each new contest.

There is a greater glory, a permanent and far more satisfying glory that awaits every saint at the end of his or her spiritual pilgrimage. It is what the Bible calls "glorification." Glorification is the terminus of Paul's "golden chain" of redemption:

For whom He foreknew, He also predestined to be conformed to the image of His Son, that He might be the firstborn among many brethren. Moreover whom He predestined, these He also called; whom He called, these He also justified; and whom He justified, these He also glorified" (Romans 8:29-30).

The doctrine of glorification refers to that time when, at Christ's second coming, the true believers, both living and dead, will have full and final redemption of their bodies and reach their final state. The salvation of the elect will be complete. As Paul wrote to the Corinthians, "This corruptible must put on incorruption, and this mortal must put on immortality" (1 Corinthians 15:53). Finally, death, the last enemy will be swallowed up in victory. The process of sanctification will reach its goal.

Glorification, then, is the believer's great hope for the future. God will make all things right and keep it that way throughout all eternity. But glorification is a present comfort as well. In this fallen world where we experience sin both within and without, there is comfort in knowing that God is working even now to purify his saints in preparation for their future glory. The believer is in one sense already glorified, sealed for eternity, evermore a child of God.

Summary

1. Glorification is the endpoint of our salvation.
2. Glorification will complete our sanctification.
3. The promise of future glorification gives comfort and inspiration to us in the present.

Part
VIII

THE CHURCH
AND
SACRAMENTS

75

THE APOSTLES

Since twelve of those who were disciples of Christ later became His apostles, the two terms *disciple* and *apostle* are often confused. Although the terms are used interchangeably, they are not exact synonyms. A disciple is defined in the Bible as a "learner," one who entered into the fellowship of Jesus' rabbinic instruction. Though the apostles were disciples, not all disciples became apostles.

An apostle enjoyed a special office in the New Testament church. The term *apostle* means "one who is sent." Technically, however, an apostle was more than a messenger. He was commissioned with the authority to speak for and represent the One who sent him. The chief Apostle in the New Testament is Jesus Himself. He was sent by the Father and spoke with the authority invested in Him by the Father. To reject Jesus was to reject the Father, who sent Him.

Likewise, the apostles were called and commissioned directly by Christ and spoke with His authority. To reject apostolic authority was to reject the authority of Christ, who sent them.

In the New Testament, twelve disciples were commissioned as apostles. After Judas's death, the church replaced the vacancy by selecting Matthias, as Acts records. To this number Jesus added the apostle Paul as the special apostle to the Gentiles. Paul's apostleship was a matter of some debate because he did not meet all of the requirements for apostleship set forth in Acts. The criteria for apostleship included being: (1) a disciple of Jesus during His earthly ministry, (2) an eyewitness of the Resurrection, and (3) called and commissioned directly by Christ. Paul was not a former disciple, and his vision of the resurrected Christ occurred after Jesus' ascension. Paul was not an eyewitness of the Resurrection in the same way the other apostles were. Nevertheless, Paul was directly

Biblical passages for reflection:
Romans 1:1-6
Romans 11:13
1 Corinthians 9:2
1 Corinthians 15:9
Hebrews 3:1

called to the office by Christ. His call was confirmed by the other apostles, whose apostleship was not in doubt and was authenticated by the miracles God performed through him, attesting his authority as an apostolic agent of revelation.

By the late first century, the postapostolic fathers clearly recognized that their authority was subordinate to the original apostles. There are no official apostles alive today as no one can meet the biblical criteria for the office or be confirmed by the original apostles, as Paul was. The Bible is the only apostolic authority for us today.

Summary

1. The terms *disciple* and *apostle* are not synonyms.
   Disciple = learner
   Apostle = one who is sent with authority to speak for the one who commissioned him
2. Jesus was the "Apostle of the Father."
3. Biblical criteria for apostleship included being:
   (a) a disciple of Jesus
   (b) an eyewitness of Jesus' resurrection
   (c) called directly by Christ
4. Paul's apostleship was unique, and it was necessary for him to be confirmed by the other apostles.
5. There are no apostles today in the biblical sense.
6. Apostolic authority today is found in the Bible.

76

THE CHURCH

The church refers to all the people who belong to the Lord, those who have been purchased by the blood of Christ. Various other images and expressions are also used to define or describe the church. The church is called the body of Christ, the family of God, the people of God, the elect, the bride of Christ, the company of the redeemed, the communion of saints, the new Israel, among others.

The New Testament word for church, from which we get the word *ecclesiastical,* means "those called out." The church is viewed as an assembly or gathering of the elect, those whom God calls out of the world, away from sin and into a state of grace.

Because the church on earth is always what St. Augustine called "a mixed body," it is necessary to distinguish between the visible church and the invisible church. In the visible church (consisting of those who make a profession of faith, are baptized, and enrolled in membership of the institutional church), Jesus indicated there would be tares growing along with the wheat. Though the church is "holy," it always, in this age, has an unholy mixture within it. Not all of those who honor Christ with their lips honor Him with their heart as well. Since God alone can read the human heart, the true elect are visible to Him, but in some measure invisible to us. The invisible church is transparent but completely visible to God. It is the task of the elect to make the invisible church visible.

The church is one, holy, catholic, and apostolic. The church is one. Though fragmented by denominations, the elect are united by one Lord, one faith, and one baptism. The church is holy because it is sanctified by God and indwelt by the Holy Spirit. The church is catholic (the word *catholic* means "universal") in that its membership extends across the earth including people from all nations. The church is apostolic in that the teaching of

Biblical passages for reflection:
Matthew 13:24-43
1 Corinthians
   12:12-14
Ephesians 2:19-22
Ephesians 4:1-6
Colossians 1:18
Revelation 7:9-10

the apostles as contained in sacred Scripture is the foundation of the church and the authority by which the church is governed.

It is the duty and privilege of every Christian to be united to the church of Christ. It is our solemn responsibility not to neglect the gathering together of the saints in corporate worship, to be under the nurture and discipline of the church, and to be actively involved as witnesses in the mission of the church.

The church is not so much an organization as it is an organism. It is made up of living parts. It is called the body of Christ. Just as a human body is organized to function in unity by the coworking and codependence of many parts, so the church as a body displays unity and diversity. Though ruled by one "head"—Christ—the body has many members, each gifted and endowed by God to contribute to the work of the whole body.

Summary

1. The church is made up of those who belong to the Lord.
2. The biblical word for church means "those who are called out."
3. The church on earth is always a mixed body of believers and unbelievers.
4. The invisible church is visible only to God.
5. The church is one, holy, catholic, and apostolic.
6. The church is an organism likened to the human body.

77 THE MARKS OF A TRUE CHURCH

Since the world is dotted with thousands of distinct institutions called churches, and since it is possible for institutions as well as individuals to become apostate, it is important to be able to discern the essential marks of a true and legitimate visible church. No church is free from error or sin. Only in heaven will the church be perfect. But there is a significant difference between corruption, which affects all institutions, and apostasy. Therefore, to protect the care and nurture of the people of God, it is important to define the marks of a true church.

Historically the marks of a true church have been defined as: (1) the true preaching of God's Word, (2) the use of the sacraments in accordance with their institution, and (3) the practice of church discipline.

(1) *The Preaching of God's Word.* Though churches differ in details of theology and in levels of purity of doctrine, a true church affirms all that is essential to the Christian faith. Likewise, a church is false or apostate when it officially denies an essential tenet of the Christian faith such as the deity of Christ, the Trinity, justification by faith, the Atonement, or other doctrines essential to salvation. The Reformation, for example, was not a struggle over trifles but over a cardinal doctrine of salvation.

(2) *Administration of Sacraments.* To deny or defame the sacraments instituted by Christ is to falsify the church. The profanation of the Lord's Supper or the willful offering of the sacraments to professed unbelievers would disqualify a church from being recognized as a true church.

(3) *Church Discipline.* Though the exercise of church discipline may at times err in the direction of either severity or latitude, it can become so perverted as to no longer be recognized as legitimate. For example, if a church openly and impenitently endorses, practices, or refuses to

Biblical passages for reflection:
Matthew 18:15-17
Romans 11:13-24
1 Corinthians
  1:10-31
Ephesians 1:22-23
1 Peter 2:9-10

discipline gross and heinous sin, it fails to exhibit this mark of a true church.

Though Christians should be solemnly warned not to be schismatic in spirit or given to divisive or quarrelsome spirits, they must also be warned of the obligation to separate themselves from false or apostate communions. Every true church exhibits the true marks of a church to a greater or lesser degree. The reformation of the church is a never-ending task. We seek more and more to be faithful to the biblical call to preaching, the sacraments, and church discipline.

Summary

1. A true church has visible marks that distinguish it from a false or apostate church.
2. The preaching of the gospel is necessary for a church to be legitimate.
3. The proper administration of the sacraments, without profanation, is a mark of the church.
4. Discipline against heresy and gross sin is a necessary task of the church.
5. The church is always in need of being reformed in accordance with the Word of God.

78

EXCOMMUNICATION

To be excommunicated from the church of Christ is a dreadful thing. Yet there is only one sin so serious that it warrants dismissal from the body of Christ. That sin is the sin of *impenitence.* There are a multitude of sins serious enough to require church discipline. However, since church discipline is a multistep process with excommunication being the final step, the only sin that can bring us to that step is the refusal to repent of the sin that initiated the process in the first place.

Excommunication is the most extreme disciplinary measure of the church. It entails excluding the unrepentant sinner from communion with the faithful. The doctrine derives from Jesus' teaching on binding and loosing (Matthew 16:19; 18:15-20; John 20:23). The responsibility for discipline was given to the church. The passage in Matthew 18, however, lists three steps that are to be taken prior to excommunication. The sinner is first to be corrected privately. If such a procedure should fail, he is to be corrected by witnesses. This insures that the accuser in the first step is not at fault or bringing slanderous charges. Thirdly, the sinner is to be brought before the entire community of believers. Should this fail, the church is to cease communion with the offender.

It should be noted that excommunication is never to be performed with a sense of retribution. The entire process, up to and including excommunication, is a form of discipline designed to bring the unrepentant person back into the fold. At the point of excommunication, the guilty party is handed over to the devil. The intent is not to punish but to awaken the guilty party to his sin. John Calvin held that church discipline is the "best help" to sound doctrine, order, and unity.[1]

The Westminster Confession enumerates five purposes for excommunication:

Church censures are necessary, for the reclaiming and gaining of offending brethren, for deterring of others from like offenses, for purging out of that leaven which might infect the whole lump, for vindicating the honor of Christ, and the holy profession of the Gospel, and for preventing the wrath of God, which might justly fall upon the Church, if they should suffer His covenant, and the seals thereof, to be profaned by notorious and obstinate offenders.[2]

This list could perhaps be accurately reduced to two primary reasons: concern for the soul of the sinner and concern for the health of the church.

Church discipline is commanded by Christ, and it is a matter that requires great prudence. The church can fall into errors of two sorts. It can become too lax and fail to discipline those who scandalize the faith, or it can become too severe and lack the charity God commands.

Church discipline should not be invoked over trivial or minor matters. Pettiness can be a source of ruin among the people of God. We are called to a spirit of patience and forbearance with each other as God is patient with us. The Scripture calls us to a kind of love that will "cover a multitude of sins."

Biblical passages for reflection:
Matthew 7:1-5
1 Corinthians 5
1 Corinthians 11:27-32
1 Timothy 1:18-20
1 Timothy 5:19-20
1 Peter 4:8

Summary

1. Excommunication is the final step of church discipline.
2. The only sin that ultimately results in excommunication is impenitence.
3. Christ instituted the process of church discipline.
4. The goal of excommunication is the restoration of the offender and the protection of the church.
5. Church discipline must not be either lax or harsh.
6. Christians must exercise a love that is patient and forbearing.

79

THE SACRAMENTS

The word *sacrament* historically was used for something sacred. The Latin term *sacramentum* was used to translate the New Testament word for mystery. In a broad sense all religious rites and ceremonies were called sacraments. In time, the term *sacrament* took on a more precise and narrow meaning. A sacrament became defined as a *visible sign* by which God offers His promise of grace in an outward form. Outward signs seal and confirm the covenant promises of God. The sacraments consist of some visible element such as water, bread, or wine; a definite activity ordained by God in association with the sign; and a redeeming benefit given to the believer.

The Roman Catholic church set the number of sacraments (in the special sense) at seven. They are Baptism, Confirmation, Holy Communion (the Lord's Supper), Penance, Matrimony, Holy Orders, and Extreme Unction. Historic Protestantism limited the sacraments to two: Baptism and the Lord's Supper. Though Protestants recognize other rites such as marriage as special ordinances, they are not recognized as attaining the level of sacraments. Sacraments are limited to: (1) those ordinances directly instituted by Christ, (2) ordinances that are by their very nature significant, (3) ordinances designed to be perpetual, and (4) ordinances designed to signify, instruct, and seal the believers who receive them in faith.

The sacraments are real means of grace that convey the promises of God. Their power does not reside in the elements themselves, but in God, whose signs they are. Nor does their power depend upon the character or the faith of those who administer them, but on the integrity of God.

The sacraments are nonverbal forms of communication. They were never intended to stand alone without reference to the Word of God. Sacraments confirm the

Biblical passages for reflection:
Matthew 28:19-20
Acts 2:40-47
Romans 6:1-4
1 Corinthians
    11:23-34
Galatians 3:26-29

Word of God so that the administering of the sacraments and the preaching of the Word go together.

Salvation is not through the sacraments. Salvation is by faith in Christ. Yet where faith is present the sacraments are not ignored or neglected. They are a vital part of the worship of God and the nurture of the Christian life.

Though sacraments involve the use of outward forms, they are not to be despised as empty formalism or ritualism. Though they can be corrupted into empty rituals, they are not to be rejected. They are indeed rituals, but they are God-ordained rituals and therefore to be joyfully and solemnly partaken of.

Summary

1. A sacrament is a visible sign of God's promise of grace to believers.
2. The Roman Catholic church includes seven sacraments while most of Protestantism has two: Baptism and the Lord's Supper.
3. Sacraments do not automatically convey the things they signify. The content of the sacraments is received by faith.
4. Sacraments are not empty rituals, but are ordained by Christ.
5. Sacraments are to be connected with the preaching of the Word.

80

BAPTISM

Baptism is the sacramental sign of the New Covenant. It is a sign by which God seals His pledge to the elect that they are included in the covenant of grace.

Baptism signifies several things. In the first instance, it is a sign of cleansing and the remission of our sins. It also signifies being regenerated by the Holy Spirit, being buried and raised together with Christ, being indwelt by the Holy Spirit, being adopted into the family of God, and being sanctified by the Holy Spirit.

Baptism was instituted by Christ and is to be administered in the name of the Father, Son, and Holy Spirit. The outward sign does not automatically or magically convey the realities that are signified. For example, though baptism signifies regeneration, or rebirth, it does not automatically convey rebirth. The power of baptism is not in the water but in the power of God.

The reality to which sacrament points may be present before or after the sign of baptism is given. In the Old Testament the sign of the covenant was circumcision. Circumcision was, among other things, a sign of faith. In the case of adults, such as Abraham, faith came prior to the sign of circumcision. With the children of believers, however, the sign of circumcision was given prior to their possession of faith, as was the case with Isaac. Likewise, in the New Covenant, Reformed theology requires adult converts to be baptized after making a profession of faith, while their children receive baptism before they profess faith.

Baptism signifies a washing with water. The command to baptize may be fulfilled by immersion, dipping, or sprinkling. The Greek word *to baptize* includes all three possibilities.

The validity of baptism does not rest upon the character of the minister who performs it or the character of the person who receives it. Baptism is a sign of the promise of God of salvation to all who believe in Christ.

Biblical passages for reflection:
Romans 4:11-12
Romans 6:3-4
1 Corinthians 12:12-14
Colossians 2:11-15
Titus 3:3-7

Since it is God's promise, the validity of the promise rests on the trustworthiness of the character of God.

Because baptism is the sign of God's promise, it is not to be administered to a person more than once. To be baptized more than once is to cast a shadow of doubt on the integrity and sincerity of God's promise. Surely those who have been baptized two or more times do not intend to cast doubt on God's integrity, but the action, if properly understood, would communicate such doubt. It is every Christian's duty, however, to be baptized. It is not an empty ritual, but a sacrament commanded by our Lord.

Summary

1. Baptism is the sacramental sign of the New Covenant.
2. Baptism has multiple significance.
3. Baptism was instituted by Christ and is to be administered with water in the name of the Father, Son, and Holy Spirit.
4. Baptism does not automatically convey rebirth.
5. Baptism may be administered by immersion, sprinkling, or dipping in water.
6. The validity of baptism rests upon the integrity of God's promise and should only be administered to a person once.

81 INFANT BAPTISM

Though infant baptism has been the majority practice of historic Christianity, its propriety has been solemnly challenged by godly Christians of various denominations. The question surrounding infant baptism rests upon several concerns. The New Testament neither explicitly commands infants to be baptized nor explicitly prohibits them from being baptized. The debate centers on questions surrounding the meaning of baptism and the degree of continuity between the Old Covenant and New Covenant.

The most crucial objection from those who oppose infant baptism is that the sacrament of baptism belongs to members of the church and the church is a company of believers. Since infants are incapable of exercising faith, they ought not to be baptized. It is also stressed that of the baptisms recorded in the New Testament there are no specific references to infants. A further objection is that the Old Covenant, though not conveying salvation via biological blood lines, nevertheless did involve an ethnic emphasis on the nation of Israel. The covenant was passed through family and national ties. In the New Testament the covenant is more inclusive, allowing Gentiles into the community of faith. This point of discontinuity makes a difference between circumcision and baptism.

On the other hand, those who favor infant baptism stress its parallels with circumcision. Though baptism and circumcision are not identical, they have crucial points in common. Both are signs of the covenant, and both are signs of faith. In the case of Abraham, he came to faith as an adult. He made a profession of faith before he was circumcised. He had faith before he received the sign of that faith. Abraham's son Isaac, on the other hand, received the sign of his faith before he had the faith that the sign signified (as was the case with all future children of the covenant).

The crucial point is that in the Old Testament, God ordered that a sign of faith be given *before* faith was present. Since that was clearly the case, it is erroneous to argue *in principle* that it is wrong to administer a sign of faith before faith is present.

It is also important to notice that the narrative record of baptisms in the New Testament are of adults who were previously unbelievers. They were first generation Christians. Again, it has always been the rule that adult converts (who were not children of believers at the time of their infancy) must first make a profession of faith before receiving baptism, which is the sign of their faith.

About one fourth of the baptisms mentioned in the New Testament indicate that entire households were baptized. This strongly suggests, though it does not prove, that infants were included among those baptized. Since the New Testament does not explicitly exclude infants from the covenant sign (and they had been included for thousands of years while the covenant sign was circumcision), it would naturally be assumed in the early church that infants were to be given the sign of the covenant.

History bears witness to this assumption. The first direct mention of infant baptism is around the middle of the second century A.D. What is noteworthy about this reference is that it assumes infant baptism to be the universal practice of the church. If infant baptism were not the practice of the first-century church, how and why did this departure from orthodoxy happen so fast and so pervasively? Not only was the spread rapid and universal, the extant literature from that time does not reflect any controversy concerning the issue.

In general, the New Covenant is more *inclusive* than the Old Covenant. Yet those who dispute the validity of infant baptism make it less inclusive with respect to children, despite the absence of any biblical prohibition against infant baptism.

Summary

1. The New Testament neither explicitly commands nor forbids infant baptism.
2. To make their case, opponents of infant baptism point to the differences between the Old and New Testaments and to the fact that baptism is a sign of faith.

Biblical passages for reflection:
Genesis 17:1-14
Acts 2:38-39
Acts 16:25-34

3. Advocates of infant baptism point out the continuity between circumcision and baptism as signs of faith.
4. Most baptisms in the New Testament were of first generation adult converts, who, of course, could not have been baptized as infants.
5. The record of baptisms in the New Testament includes "household" baptisms, which would seem to include children and infants.
6. Church history bears witness to the universal, noncontroversial practice of infant baptism in the second century A.D.

82 THE LORD'S SUPPER

Martin Luther rejected the Roman Catholic doctrine of transubstantiation, that is, that the Communion bread and wine are changed into the actual body and blood of Christ. Luther saw no need for this doctrine. Rather, he agreed that Christ's presence did not *replace* the presence of bread and wine but was *added* to the bread and wine. Luther maintained that the body and blood of Christ are somehow present in, under, and through the elements of bread and wine. It is customary to call the Lutheran view *consubstantiation* because the substance of the body and blood of Christ are present *with* (*con*) the substance of bread and wine. Lutheran theologians, however, do not like the term *consubstantiation* and protest that it is understood in terms that are too closely associated with the Roman Catholic doctrine of transubstantiation.

But it is clear that Luther insisted on the real physical and substantial presence of Christ in the Lord's Supper. He repeatedly cited Jesus' words of institution, "this is My body," to prove his point. Luther would not allow the verb *is* to be taken in a figurative or representative sense. Luther also adopted the doctrine of the communication of attributes by which the divine attribute of omnipresence was communicated to the human nature of Jesus, making it possible for His body and blood to be present at more than one place at the same time.

Zwingli and others argued that Jesus' words "this is My body" meant really "This *represents* My body." Jesus frequently used the verb *to be* in such a figurative sense. He said, "I am the door," "I am the true vine," etc. Zwingli and others argued that Christ's body is not present in actual substance at the Lord's Supper. The supper is a memorial only, with Christ's presence no different from His normal presence through the Holy Spirit.

John Calvin, on the other hand, when he debated with Rome and Luther, denied the "substantial" presence of Christ at the Lord's Supper. Yet when he debated with the Anabaptists, who reduced the Lord's Supper to a mere memorial, he insisted on the "substantial" presence of Christ.

On the surface it seems that Calvin was caught in a blatant contradiction. However, upon closer scrutiny we see that Calvin used the term *substantial* in two different ways. When he addressed Roman Catholics and Lutherans, he used the term *substantial* to mean "physical." He denied the physical presence of Christ in the Lord's Supper. When he addressed the Anabaptists, he insisted on the term *substantial* in the sense of "real." Calvin thus argued that Christ was *really* or *truly* present in the Lord's Supper, though not in a physical sense.

Because Calvin rejected the idea of the communication of attributes from the divine nature to the human nature, he was accused of *separating* and *dividing* the two natures of Christ and committing the Nestorian heresy, which was condemned at the Council of Chalcedon in A.D. 451. Calvin replied that he was not separating the two natures but *distinguishing* between them.

The human nature of Jesus is presently localized in heaven. It remains in perfect union with His divine nature. Though the human nature is contained in one place, the *person* of Christ is not so contained because His divine nature still has the power of omnipresence. Jesus said, "I am with you always, even to the end of the age" (Matthew 28:20). Despite its limitations, and at the risk of being misunderstood, we give the following picture to illustrate what we are saying.

JESUS

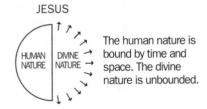

The human nature is bound by time and space. The divine nature is unbounded.

Human Nature in Heaven

Divine Nature
Omnipresent

The Church

**Biblical passages
for reflection:**
Matthew 26:26-29
1 Corinthians
    10:13-17
1 Corinthians
    11:23-34

Calvin taught that though Christ's body and blood remain in heaven, they are spiritually "made present" to us by Jesus' omnipresent divine nature.[1] Wherever the divine nature of Christ is present, He is truly present. This is consistent with Jesus' own teaching that He was "going away" yet would abide with us. When we meet Him at the Lord's Supper we commune with Him. By meeting us in His divine presence, we are brought into His human presence mystically, because His divine nature is never separated from His human nature. The divine nature leads us to the ascended Christ, and in the Lord's Supper we have a taste of heaven.

Summary

1. Luther taught that the body and blood of Christ were added in, under, and through the elements of bread and wine.
2. Zwingli taught the memorial view of the Lord's Supper.
3. Calvin denied the physical presence of Christ at the Lord's Supper, but affirmed the real presence of Christ.
4. Jesus' human nature is localized in heaven; His divine nature is omnipresent.

83

TRANSUBSTANTIATION

There is no more solemn or sacred moment in the life of the church than the celebration of the Lord's Supper. It is called Holy Communion because during this meal a special meeting takes place between Jesus and His people. At that moment Jesus is present with us in a unique way.

The question is, how is Christ present with us in the Lord's Supper? This question has been the topic of endless controversy among Christians. It has not only been a point of contention between Protestantism and Roman Catholicism, it was also an area of conflict that the leaders of the Reformation—Luther, Calvin, and Zwingli—failed to resolve among themselves.

The Roman Catholic church teaches the doctrine of transubstantiation. *Transubstantiation* means that during the Mass a miracle takes place by which the substance of the ordinary elements of bread and wine changes into the substance of the body and blood of Christ. To the human senses the bread and wine exhibit no perceivable change. But Roman Catholics believe that although the elements still look like bread and wine, taste like bread and wine, smell like bread and wine, etc., they become the actual flesh and blood of Christ.

To understand the miracle requires that we know something about the philosophy of Aristotle. Aristotle taught, in simple terms, that every object (entity) is made up of *substance* and *accidents*. The *substance* is the deepest essence, or "stuff," of a thing. *Accidents* refers to the outward, external, or surface *appearance* of an object. It refers to the qualities of an object we see, feel, smell, and taste.

For Aristotle there was always an inseparable relationship between an object and its accidents. An oak tree, for example, always has both the substance and the accidents of being an oak tree. For something to have the substance of one thing and the accidents of another thing would require a miracle.

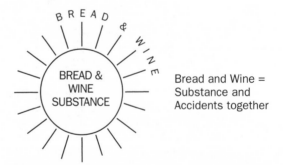

Substance = Essence
Accidents = Outwardly
perceivable
qualities

This is the miracle of transubstantiation. The elements of bread and wine change into the substance of the body and blood of Christ. Meanwhile, the accidents of bread and wine remain. Therefore, in the Mass we have the substance of the body and blood of Christ without the accidents of body and blood, and the accidents of bread and wine without the substance of bread and wine.

Before the miracle takes place, we have the substance and the accidents of bread and wine.

Bread and Wine =
Substance and
Accidents together

After the miracle takes place, we have the substance of Christ's body and blood with the accidents of bread and wine.

More important than the controversy surrounding transubstantiation was the issue concerning the human nature of Jesus. Body and blood belong to the humanity of Jesus, not to His deity. Since the Mass is celebrated in different parts of the world at the same time, the question is, how can the human nature of Jesus (body and blood) be at more than one place at the same time? The

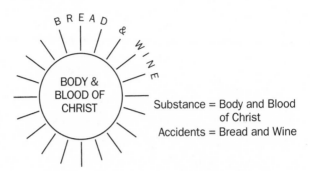

Substance = Body and Blood of Christ

Accidents = Bread and Wine

Biblical passages for reflection:
Mark 14:22-25
1 Corinthians 11:23-26

power to be omnipresent, of being equally present everywhere, is an attribute of deity, not humanity. For the human nature of Jesus to be spread over the world would require the deification of the human nature. Both Luther and Roman Catholics taught that the divine nature of Christ (which does have the attribute of omnipresence) communicates this power to the human nature so that the human nature, though normally localized, can be present at more than one place at the same time.

But to Calvin and others, this idea of the communication of divine attributes to the human nature was seen as a violation of the Council of Chalcedon (A.D. 451), which affirmed that the two natures of Christ, human and divine, are united in such a way as to be without mixture, confusion, separation, or division, *each nature retaining its own attributes.* So for Calvin and most of the Reformers, transubstantiation manifested a form of this heresy.

Summary

1. *Transubstantiation* means that during the Mass, the bread and wine are miraculously changed into the body and blood of Christ, while still appearing to the senses to be bread and wine.
2. *Substance* refers to the essence of a thing, while *accidents* refers to its outwardly perceivable qualities.
3. Transubstantiation requires the empowering of the human nature of Christ with divine attributes in order for His body and blood to be at more than one place at the same time.
4. Calvin rejected transubstantiation as a violation of the Council of Chalcedon.

84

THE SABBATH

The sanctity of the Sabbath was instituted at Creation. After His creative work of six days, God rested on the seventh day and hallowed it. By hallowing it, God set the seventh day apart. He consecrated it as holy. Proper observance of the Sabbath was one of the Ten Commandments given at Mount Sinai. It is important to remember that its institution was an integral part of the creation covenant. In the Old Testament, violation of the Sabbath was a capital offense.

Biblical passages for reflection:
Genesis 2:1-3
Exodus 20:8-11
Isaiah 58:13-14
Matthew 12:1-14
Acts 20:7
1 Corinthians
  16:1-2
Revelation 1:10

The word *Sabbath* means "seventh." That is why some insist that Saturday is the only proper day to celebrate the Sabbath, and that it is illegitimate to observe it on Sunday. However, historic Christianity has always observed Sunday as the Sabbath because in the New Testament it is "the Lord's day," the day of Christ's resurrection. The principle of Sabbath, one in seven, remains intact. The weekly Sabbath has been in perpetual effect since Creation and was observed by the apostles.

Questions of proper Sabbath observance continue to be debated among theologians. Most agree that the Sabbath includes a mandate to rest from all but necessary commerce or labor. The Sabbath is also a time for corporate worship and special attention to the study of God's Word. It is a special time of rejoicing in Christ's resurrection and in the hope of our Sabbath rest in heaven.

Disagreement centers on the role of recreation and works of mercy. Some regard recreation as a worldly violation of the Sabbath, while others insist it is an important part of rest and refreshment. The Bible nowhere explicitly promotes or prohibits recreation on the Sabbath, though the meaning of *pleasure* in Isaiah 58:13 may suggest that it is prohibited.

A less strident debate focuses on the issue of works of mercy. Many appeal to Jesus' example of special ministry on the Sabbath Day as an implicit command for Christians to be actively engaged in works of mercy on the Sabbath, such as visiting the sick. Others contend that Jesus' example proves that it is lawful and good to be so engaged, but that what is allowed is not necessarily required. (That such works of mercy are not limited to the Sabbath is clear.)

Summary

1. The Sabbath was instituted at Creation and is still in force.
2. *Sabbath* means "seventh." It refers to a cycle of one day in seven.
3. The early church celebrated the Sabbath on the Lord's Day, moving the Sabbath from Saturday to Sunday (the first day of the week).
4. The Sabbath requires cessation from regular labor (except necessary labor) and the assembly of saints in corporate worship.
5. There is disagreement over the propriety of recreation and the necessity of works of mercy on the Sabbath.

85 OATHS AND VOWS

As a boy I heard the fabled account of George Washington and the cherry tree. When young George was confronted by his distressed father concerning the wanton destruction of a cherry tree, the boy said, "I cannot tell a lie; I cut down the tree."

It took me years to figure out that Washington's confession was in fact a lie. To say "I cannot tell a lie" is to lie about one's ability to lie. There were many things George Washington could not do: he could not fly; he could not be in more than one place at the same time, etc. But George Washington could tell a lie. He was a man. All human beings are capable of telling lies. Scripture declares that "all men are liars" (Psalm 116:11). This does not mean that everyone lies all the time. We also have the ability to tell the truth. The problem arises when we are called upon to trust someone's word, and we do not know for sure if he is telling the truth.

To emphasize the importance of truth in the making of promises and the giving of important testimonies, we resort to the swearing of oaths and vows. Before offering testimony in a courtroom, the witness is sworn in. He or she promises to "tell the truth, the whole truth, and nothing but the truth, so help me God."

In the vow, appeal is made to God and to God alone as the supreme witness of the statement. God is the guardian of vows, oaths, and promises. He Himself is the fountainhead of all truth and is incapable of lying. What is false about George Washington is true of God; He cannot tell a lie (Titus 1:2; Hebrews 6:17-18). Neither can God abide with liars. He warns against taking rash or false vows: "Pay what you have vowed—better not to vow than to vow and not pay" (Ecclesiastes 5:4-5). The Ten Commandments include a law against bearing false witness (Exodus 20:16).

Since our entire relationship to God is based upon covenant promises, God sanctifies the matter of vows, oaths, and promises. Trust in human relationships (such as marriage and business agreements) is necessary for the welfare of society. A lawful oath is a part of worship wherein people, seeking to assure the veracity of what they speak, call upon God as a witness of what they assert and promise. The implication is that if those taking oaths are found to be lying, God will punish them with swiftness and severity.

The Christian church has always affirmed the value of oaths and vows. The Westminster divines listed the following scriptural boundaries and stipulations,

The name of God only is that by which men ought to swear, and therein it is to be used with all holy fear and reverence. Therefore, to swear vainly or rashly, by that glorious and dreadful Name, or, to swear at all by any other thing, is sinful, and to be abhorred. Yet, as in matters of weight and moment, an oath is warranted by the Word of God, under the New Testament as well as under the Old; so a lawful oath, being imposed by lawful authority, in such matters, ought to be taken.[1]

An additional stipulation is that an oath should not be made with equivocation or mental reservation. God does not accept crossed fingers, but expects honesty. An oath is not to be taken lightly. It should be saved for solemn occasions, for solemn promises. Even governments recognize this in insisting on oaths for weddings and before the giving of legal testimony. Even in less solemn instances, moreover, a believer is called to honesty— that one's yes be yes, and one's no be no. That is the responsibility of a faithful disciple of Christ.

Biblical passages for reflection:
Deuteronomy
    10:20
2 Chronicles
    6:22-23
Ezra 10:5
Matthew 5:33-37
James 5:12

Summary

1. Human beings have a capacity for telling lies.
2. God, the source of truth, cannot lie and is the guardian of truth.
3. Oaths and vows are a lawful part of worship.
4. Oaths should be sworn by God alone. No creature can be the ultimate witness of truth.
5. Vows should not be made rashly or with reservations.

Part
IX

SPIRITUALITY
AND LIVING
IN THIS AGE

86 THE FRUIT OF THE SPIRIT

The fruit of the Holy Spirit is one of the most neglected aspects of the biblical teaching on sanctification. There are various reasons for this:

1. *Preoccupation with externals.* Though students often murmur and grumble when facing tests in the classroom, there is a sense in which we really want to have them. Tests that measure skill, achievement, and knowledge are even standard fare in magazines. People like to know how they rate. Have I achieved excellence in a certain endeavor, or am I mired in mediocrity?

Christians are no different. We tend to measure our progress in sanctification by examining our performance against external standards. Do we curse? Do we drink? Do we go to movies? These standards are often used to measure spirituality. The real test—evidence of the fruit of the Spirit—is often ignored or minimized. This is the trap the Pharisees fell into.

We recoil from the real test because the fruit of the Spirit is too nebulous. It is far more demanding of personal character than superficial externals are. It is a lot easier to refrain from cursing than it is to acquire a habit of godly patience.

2. *Preoccupation with gifts.* The same Holy Spirit who leads us into holiness and bears fruit in us also gives spiritual gifts to believers. We seem to be far more interested in the gifts of the Spirit than the fruit, despite the clear biblical teaching that one may possess gifts while being immature in spiritual progress. Paul's letters to the Corinthians make that abundantly clear.

3. *The problem of righteous unbelievers.* It is frustrating to measure our progress in sanctification by the fruit of the Spirit when the virtues listed among the fruit are sometimes exhibited to a greater degree by non-Christians. We all know nonbelievers who exhibit more gentleness or patience than many Christians. If people can

have the "fruit of the Spirit" apart from the Spirit, how can we determine our spiritual growth in this manner?

There is a *qualitative* difference between the virtues of love, joy, peace, patience, etc., engendered in us by the Holy Spirit and those exhibited by nonbelievers. Nonbelievers operate from motives that are ultimately selfish. But when believers exhibit the fruit of the Spirit, they are exhibiting characteristics that are ultimately directed toward God and others. Being filled with the Spirit means that one's life is controlled by the Holy Spirit; nonbelievers can only exhibit these spiritual virtues to the extent of human ability.

Paul lists the fruit of the Spirit in his letter to the Galatians: "The fruit of the Spirit is love, joy, peace, longsuffering, kindness, goodness, faithfulness, gentleness, self-control" (Galatians 5:22-23). These virtues are to characterize the Christian life. If we are filled with the Spirit, we will exhibit the fruit of the Spirit. But, of course, this takes time. These are not superficial character adjustments that happen overnight. They involve a reshaping of the innermost dispositions of the heart, which is a lifelong process of sanctification by the Spirit.

Biblical passages for reflection:
Romans 12:1-21
1 Corinthians 12:1–14:40
Galatians 5:19-26
Ephesians 4:1–6:20

Summary

1. We tend to neglect the study of the fruit of the Spirit because: (1) we are preoccupied with externals; (2) we are preoccupied with spiritual gifts; and (3) we recognize that many nonbelievers exhibit the spiritual virtues better than Christians.
2. It is easier to measure spirituality by externals than by the fruit of the Spirit.
3. We can have spiritual gifts and still be immature.
4. There is a qualitative difference between the presence of the spiritual virtues in nonbelievers and believers. With nonbelievers, it is merely human effort. With Christians, it is God the Holy Spirit producing spiritual fruit in measure beyond mere human ability.

87 LOVE

In our society, love is usually spoken of in passive terms. That is, love is something that happens *to us* over which we have little or no control. We "fall" in love. We speak this way chiefly because we associate love with a particular feeling or emotion. Such emotion cannot be produced by pushing a button or by a conscious act of the will. We do not "decide" to fall in love with someone.

The Bible, however, speaks of love in far more active terms. The concept of love functions more as a verb than as a noun. Love is a duty—an action we are obliged to perform. God commands us to love our neighbor, to love our spouse, and even to love our enemies. It is one thing to conjure up feelings of love and affection for one's enemies; it is another thing to act in a loving manner toward them.

The Bible has a complex concept of love that is expressed in relatively few words. The Old Testament predominantly used one Hebrew word, *aheb,* to express love. The New Testament primarily used two Greek words for love—*phileo* and *agape. Phileo,* from which the city Philadelphia derives its name (meaning the "city of brotherly love"), is the Greek word that is used to denote the affection shared by friends. By contrast, the term *eros,* which is not used in the Bible, refers more to sexual or erotic love. It is the kind of love we often associate with romance. These two types of love are common to all human beings. These types of love have a tendency to be motivated by self-interest, self-gratification, and self-protection.

The New Testament, however, describes a third kind of love. *Agape* stands in contrast to the more basic affections. Its most distinguishing feature is a lack of self-interest. It proceeds out of a heart of care and concern for others. Its characteristics are enumerated by Paul in 1 Corinthians 13. Agape love is patient and kind. It neither boasts nor envies. It is not proud, rude, self-seeking, or easily angered. It is quick to forgive; it seeks the good and the true. It protects, trusts, hopes, and perseveres always. It never fails.

Biblical love is therefore more than a mere emotion. It is active. The calling of the Christian is not primarily to develop feelings of love for others. In many instances that is outside the Christian's control. However, we can control how we respond and act toward a given person. The Christian is to *be loving,* to mirror the selfless love of God.

Agape love, then, is the ultimate fruit of the Spirit. As Paul wrote, "now abide faith, hope, love, these three; but the greatest of these is love" (1 Corinthians 13:13).

Insofar as agape love mirrors and reflects the character of God's love for us, it may be called a steadfast love, a love that endures with loyalty. It is characterized by fidelity—the faithfulness that is built upon trust. Such love is incapable of being fickle; it is the love of permanent commitment.

Biblical passages for reflection:
Deuteronomy
6:4-5
Matthew 5:43-48
1 Corinthians
13:1-13
Ephesians 5:25-33
1 John 4:7-21

Summary

1. Biblical love is active love.
2. Biblical love is a duty commanded by God.
3. Of the various Greek words for love, three important ones need to be distinguished:
   (a) *phileo* = brotherly affection
   (b) *eros* = sexual or romantic love
   (c) *agape* = godly or spiritual love
4. Agape love reflects the steadfast love of God and is oriented toward *others.*

HOPE

There are many things in this world we "hope" for. We hope that we will receive a raise in our salary. We hope that our favorite team will win the World Series. This kind of hope expresses our personal desires for the future. We have hope concerning things that are uncertain. We don't know if our desires will come to pass, but we hold out hope that they will.

When the Bible speaks of hope, however, it has something different in view. Biblical hope is a firm conviction that the future promises of God will be fulfilled. Hope is not mere wish projection, but an *assurance* of what *will* come to pass. "This hope we have as an anchor of the soul, both sure and steadfast, and which enters the Presence behind the veil" (Hebrews 6:19).

Hope takes its place alongside faith and love as one of the Christian virtues that the apostle Paul sets forth in 1 Corinthians 13:13. Hope is faith directed toward the future.

Hope is used in two ways in the Bible. The less common usage points out the object of our hope. Christ is our hope of eternal life. The more common usage is as an attitude of assurance regarding the fulfillment of God's promises. The Christian is called to hope, that is, to have full assurance of the resurrection of God's people and the coming of God's kingdom. Hope is inextricably bound up with eschatology.

Paul reminds Christians that until the kingdom comes in its fullness, believers can only have an assured hope; they must "walk by faith, not by sight" (2 Corinthians 5:7). This hope is neither unfounded nor groundless. Though the life of the Christian is marked more by suffering than triumph (1 Corinthians 4:8-13; 2 Corinthians 4:7-18), the foundation for hope is in the Godhead.

First, the believer looks upon the death and resurrection of Christ. His death was the darkest hour for His disciples. The promised Messiah was dead, His kingdom

Biblical passages for reflection:

Job 13:15

Romans 5:1-5

Romans 8:18-25

Titus 2:11-14

1 John 3:1-3

apparently lost. With the Resurrection, that despair turned to hope. Alongside suffering, whether great or small, the Christian's hope must endure. God is always sufficient and faithful.

Second, the believer has the Holy Spirit as a down payment on the kingdom. His presence assures us that the kingdom will be fully consummated. The Spirit is not only a sign toward hope, but the sustainer of hope. He fulfills the role of Comforter, girding up the believer in strength and hope. It is the Spirit that encourages the believer to pray to the Father, "Your kingdom come."

Summary

1. Biblical hope is a matter of assurance rather than wishing.
2. Hope is a virtue, not a weakness.
3. Faith is trust in what God has already done. Hope is trust in what God promises for the future.
4. The resurrection of Christ gives us hope in the midst of suffering.
5. The Holy Spirit, the Comforter, gives us hope. His presence is a guarantee of the coming kingdom of God.

89

PRAYER

We are able to talk to God. He speaks verbally to us in His Word and nonverbally through His obvious providence. We commune with Him through prayer. Charles Hodge declared that "prayer is the converse of the soul with God." In and through prayer we express our reverence and adoration for God; we bare our souls in contrite confession before Him; we pour out the thanksgiving of grateful hearts; and we offer our petitions and supplications to Him.

In prayer we experience God as personal and powerful. He can hear us and act in response. The Scripture teaches both the sovereign foreordination of God and the efficacy of prayer. The two are not inconsistent with one another, for God ordains the means as well as the ends for His divine purposes. Prayer is a means God uses to bring His sovereign will to pass.

Prayer is to be addressed to God alone, either to God as Triune or to the distinct persons of the Godhead. To pray to creatures is idolatry.

Proper prayer has several requisites. The first is that we approach God with sincerity. Empty and insincere phrases are a mockery to Him. Such prayer, far from being an exercise of godly religion, is an offense against God.

The second is that we approach God with reverence. In prayer we must always remember to whom we are speaking. To address God in a cavalier, casual, or flippant manner, as we might speak with our earthly friends, is to treat Him with the contempt of familiarity. As people pay homage to a king by entering his presence with a posture of respect and obeisance, so we come before God in full recognition of His supreme majesty.

The third requisite, which follows from the previous ones, is that we approach God in humility. Not only must we remember who He is, but we must also remember who and what we are. We are His adopted children.

We are also sinful creatures. He invites us to come boldly before Him, but never arrogantly.

God instructs us to be earnest and fervent in our requests. At the same time, we come in willful submission. To say "Your will be done" is not an indication of a lack of faith. The faith we bring to prayer must include a trust that God is able to hear our prayers and that He is disposed to answer them. Yet when God says no to our requests, this faith also trusts in His wisdom. God's wisdom and benevolence must always and everywhere be assumed by those who entreat Him with petitions.

We pray in the name of Jesus because we do thereby acknowledge His office as Mediator. As our High Priest, Christ is our intercessor even as the Holy Spirit is our helper in prayer.

A helpful tool in learning to pray is the acrostic A-C-T-S. Each letter in the acrostic indicates a vital element of prayer.

A = Adoration
C = Confession
T = Thanksgiving
S = Supplication

By following this simple acrostic we are sure to include all of the proper elements of prayer.

Biblical passages for reflection:
Psalm 5:1-3
John 14:13-14
Romans 8:26-27
Philippians 4:6-7
1 John 5:14-15

Summary

1. Prayer is communion with God.
2. Prayer is to be addressed to God alone.
3. Prayer must be sincere, reverent, and humble.
4. We are commanded to be fervent and persistent in prayer.
5. The prayer of faith is a prayer trusting in God's wisdom and kindness.
6. The acrostic ACTS is an aid to prayer.

90 ANTINOMIANISM

There is an old rhyme that serves as something of an antinomian theme song. It says, "Freed from the law, O blessed condition; I can sin all I want and still have remission."

Antinomianism literally means "anti-lawism." It denies or downplays the significance of God's law in the life of the believer. It is the opposite of its twin heresy, legalism.

Antinomians acquire their distaste for the law in a number of ways. Some believe that they no longer are obligated to keep the moral law of God because Jesus has freed them from it. They insist that grace not only frees us from the curse of God's law but delivers us from any obligation to obey God's law. Grace then becomes a license for disobedience.

The astounding thing is that people hold this view despite Paul's vigorous teaching against it. Paul, more than any other New Testament writer, emphasized the differences between law and grace. He gloried in the New Covenant. Nevertheless, he was most explicit in his condemnation of antinomianism. In Romans 3:31 he writes, "Do we then make void the law through faith? Certainly not! On the contrary, we establish the law."

Martin Luther, in expressing the doctrine of justification by faith alone, was charged with antinomianism. Yet he affirmed with James that "faith without works is dead." Luther contested with his student Johann Agricola on this issue. Agricola denied that the law had any purpose in the life of the believer. He even denied that the law served to prepare the sinner for grace. Luther responded to Agricola with his work *Against the Antinomians* in 1539. Agricola later recanted his antinomian teachings, but the issue remained.

Subsequent Lutheran theologians affirmed Luther's view of the law. In the *Formula of Concord* (1577), the last of the classical Lutheran statements of faith, they outlined three uses for the law: (1) to reveal sin; (2) to establish general decency in the society at large; and (3) to provide a rule of life for those regenerated through faith in Christ.

Antinomianism's primary error is confusing justification with sanctification. We are justified by faith alone, apart from works. However, all believers grow in faith by keeping God's holy commands—not to gain God's favor, but out of loving gratitude for the grace already bestowed on them through the work of Christ.

It is a serious error to assume that the Old Testament was a covenant of law and the New Testament, a covenant of grace. The Old Testament is a monumental testimony to God's amazing grace toward His people. Likewise, the New Testament is literally filled with commandments. We are not saved by the law, but we demonstrate our love for Christ by obeying His commandments. "If you love Me," Jesus said, "keep My commandments" (John 14:15).

We frequently hear the statement, "Christianity isn't a lot of do's and don'ts; it is not a list of rules." There is some truth in this deduction, inasmuch as Christianity is far more than a mere list of rules. It is, at its center, a personal relationship with Christ Himself. Yet Christianity is also not less than rules. The New Testament clearly includes some do's and don'ts. Christianity is not a religion that sanctions the idea that everyone has the right to do what is right in his own eyes. On the contrary, Christianity never gives anyone the "right" to do what is wrong.

Biblical passages for reflection:
John 14:15
Romans 3:27-31
Romans 6:1-2
1 John 2:3-6
1 John 5:1-3

Summary

1. Antinomianism is the heresy that says Christians have no obligation to obey the laws of God.
2. The law reveals sin, is a foundation for decency in society, and is a guide for the Christian life.
3. Antinomianism confuses justification and sanctification.
4. Law and grace fill both the Old and New Testaments.
5. Though obeying God's law is not the meritorious cause of our justification, a justified person is expected to strive ardently to obey the commandments of God.

91

LEGALISM

Legalism is the opposite heresy of antinomianism. Whereas antinomianism denies the significance of law, legalism exalts law above grace. The legalists of Jesus' day were the Pharisees, and Jesus reserved His strongest criticism for them. The fundamental distortion of legalism is the belief that one can earn one's way into the kingdom of heaven. The Pharisees believed that due to their status as children of Abraham, and to their scrupulous adherence to the law, they were the children of God. At the core, this was a denial of the gospel.

A corollary article of legalism is the adherence to the letter of the law to the exclusion of the spirit of the law. In order for the Pharisees to believe that they could keep the law, they first had to reduce it to its most narrow and wooden interpretation. The story of the rich young ruler illustrates this point. The rich young ruler asked Jesus how he could inherit eternal life. Jesus told him to "keep the commandments." The young man believed that he had kept them all. But Jesus decisively revealed the one "god" that he served before the true God—riches. "Go, sell what you have and give to the poor, and you will have treasure in heaven" (Matthew 19:21). The rich young ruler went on his way saddened.

The Pharisees were guilty of another form of legalism. They added their own laws to the law of God. Their "traditions" were raised to a status equal to the law of God. They robbed people of their liberty and put chains on them where God had left them free. That kind of legalism did not end with the Pharisees. It has also plagued the church in every generation.

Legalism often arises as an overreaction against antinomianism. To make sure we do not allow ourselves or others to slip into the moral laxity of antinomianism, we tend to make rules more strict than God Himself does. When this occurs, legalism introduces a tyranny over the people of God.

Likewise, forms of antinomianism often arise as an overreaction to legalism. Its rallying cry is usually one of freedom from all oppression. It is the quest for moral liberty run amuck. Christians, in guarding their liberty, must be careful not to confuse liberty with libertinism.

Another form of legalism is majoring on the minors. Jesus rebuked the Pharisees for omitting the weightier matters of the law while they were scrupulous in obeying minor points (Matthew 23:23-24). This tendency remains a constant threat to the church. We have a tendency to exalt to the supreme level of godliness whatever virtues we possess and downplay our vices as insignificant points. For example, I may view refraining from dancing as a great spiritual strength while considering my covetousness a minor matter.

The only antidote to either legalism or antinomianism is a serious study of the Word of God. Only then will we be properly instructed in what is pleasing and displeasing to God.

Biblical passages for reflection:
Matthew 15:1-20
Matthew 23:22-29
Acts 15:1-29
Romans 3:19-26
Galations 3:10-14

Summary

1. Legalism distorts the law of God in the opposite direction of antinomianism.

Antinomianism ◄——————— GOD'S LAW ——————► Legalism

2. Legalism elevates human traditions to the level of divine law.
3. Legalism binds God's people where God has left them free.
4. Legalism majors on the minors and minors on the majors.

92 THE THREEFOLD USE OF THE LAW

Every Christian wrestles with the question, how does the Old Testament law relate to my life? Is the Old Testament law irrelevant to Christians or is there some sense in which we are still bound by portions of it? As the heresy of antinomianism becomes ever more pervasive in our culture, the need to answer these questions grows increasingly urgent.

The Reformation was founded on grace and not upon law. Yet the law of God was not repudiated by the Reformers. John Calvin, for example, wrote what has become known as the "Threefold Use of the Law" in order to show the importance of the law for the Christian life.[1]

The first purpose of the law is to be a mirror. On the one hand, the law of God reflects and mirrors the perfect righteousness of God. The law tells us much about who God is. Perhaps more important, the law illumines human sinfulness. Augustine wrote, "The law orders, that we, after attempting to do what is ordered, and so feeling our weakness under the law, may learn to implore the help of grace."[2] The law highlights our weakness so that we might seek the strength found in Christ. Here the law acts as a severe schoolmaster who drives us to Christ.

A second purpose for the law is the restraint of evil. The law, in and of itself, cannot change human hearts. It can, however, serve to protect the righteous from the unjust. Calvin says this purpose is "by means of its fearful denunciations and the consequent dread of punishment, to curb those who, unless forced, have no regard for rectitude and justice."[3] The law allows for a limited measure of justice on this earth, until the last judgment is realized.

The third purpose of the law is to reveal what is pleasing to God. As born-again children of God, the law enlightens us as to what is pleasing to our Father, whom we seek to serve. The Christian delights in the law as God Himself delights in it. Jesus said, "If you love Me, keep My commandments" (John 14:15). This is the highest function of the law, to serve as an instrument for the people of God to give Him honor and glory.

By studying or meditating on the law of God, we attend the school of righteousness. We learn what pleases God and what offends Him. The moral law that God reveals in Scripture is always binding upon us. Our redemption is from the curse of God's law, not from our duty to obey it. We are justified, not because of our obedience to the law, but in order that we may become obedient to God's law. To love Christ is to keep His commandments. To love God is to obey His law.

Biblical passages for reflection:
Psalm 19:7-11
Psalm 119:9-16
Romans 7:7-25
Romans 8:3-4
1 Corinthians 7:19
Galatians 3:24

Summary

1. The church today has been invaded by antinomianism, which weakens, rejects, or distorts the law of God.
2. The law of God is a mirror of God's holiness and our unrighteousness. It serves to reveal to us our need of a savior.
3. The law of God is a restraint against sin.
4. The law of God reveals what is pleasing and what is offensive to God.
5. The Christian is to love the law of God and to obey the moral law of God.

93

PERFECTIONISM

The doctrine of perfectionism holds that holiness or perfect love, brought about by the grace of God, is attainable by every Christian in this life and sets believers free from willful sin. The doctrine grew out of the teaching of John Wesley and continued through the early Pentecostal movement. This attainment of perfection is seen as a second work of grace that is wrought instantaneously in the heart of the believer.

Biblical passages for reflection:
Romans 5:8
1 Corinthians 15:42-57
2 Corinthians 7:1
Philippians 3:7-14
1 John 1:5-10

A more modified view is that after this second blessing the believer is more and more victorious over "willful sin." Whatever sin remains in such a person is either accidental sin or sin committed in ignorance. The difficulty with this view is that it stems from two primary errors. First, it diminishes the rigorous demands of God's law. Any real understanding of the breadth and depth of God's law would preclude the perfectionist position. Second, it has an inflated view of one's own spiritual achievement. To hold such a view one must necessarily overestimate one's righteousness.

The vast majority of evangelical churches throughout history, and the Reformed church in particular, find such a view abhorrent. Even the Neo-Pentecostal movement has nearly abandoned the doctrine. Martin Luther taught that regenerate human beings are at the same time justified and sinners. Believers are deemed just in the eyes of God by virtue of the Atonement and the imputed righteousness of Christ. God counts believers righteous "in Christ." In and of themselves, without regard to the work of Christ, believers remain sinners. Though the process of sanctification means that the believer is becoming less of a sinner, that process is not complete until death, when the believer is glorified.

Perfection is indeed a goal of the Christian life. That we fail to achieve it is not to be taken as an excuse for sin. As Christians we must continue to press forward to the mark of our high calling in Christ.

Summary

1. Perfectionism teaches that there is a second work of grace whereby believers experience perfect holiness or love in this life.
2. Modified perfectionism teaches that Christians can be victorious over willful sin.
3. Perfectionism rests upon a low view of the law of God and an exalted view of the performance of human beings.
4. God justifies us while we are yet sinners.
5. At the instant of justification, the lifelong process of sanctification begins.
6. Christians are only made perfect in glorification after death.

94 CIVIL GOVERNMENT

In America much is said and written about the separation of church and state. Originally this idea called attention to two distinct institutions both created by God, ordained by God, and accountable to or "under" God. Each institution had its distinctive tasks to perform and neither was to usurp the other's sphere of authority. It is the task of the church to preach the gospel, administer the sacraments, nurture the souls of its members, etc. These are not the tasks of the state. It is the state's responsibility to order society, raise taxes, govern business and society, maintain a standing army, protect life and property, etc. These are not the tasks of the church. The state is given the power of the sword, the church is not. The apostle Paul declares:

Let every soul be subject to the governing authorities. For there is no authority except from God, and the authorities that exist are appointed by God. Therefore whoever resists the authority resists the ordinance of God, and those who resist will bring judgment on themselves. For rulers are not a terror to good works, but to evil. Do you want to be unafraid of the authority? Do what is good, and you will have praise from the same. For he is God's minister to you for good. But if you do evil, be afraid; for he does not bear the sword in vain; for he is God's minister, an avenger to execute wrath on him who practices evil. (Romans 13:1-4)

In Paul's view, civil government is authorized by God. When a civil ruler is invested with power he is, in a sense, thereby "ordained" as a minister of God. His rule is not independent of God. The Westminster divines wrote:

God, the supreme Lord and King of all the world, hath ordained civil magistrates, to be, under him, over the people, for his own glory, and the public good: and to this end, hath armed them with the power of the sword, for the defense and encouragement of them that are good, and for the punishment of evil doers. . . . Civil magistrates may not assume to themselves the administration of the Word and sacraments; or the power of the keys of the kingdom of heaven; or, in the least, interfere on matters of faith.[1]

In our day, the concept of separation of church and state has been widely reinterpreted (and misinterpreted) to mean the separation of state and God. More and more, civil government seeks to be out from "under"God. It seeks autonomous power and authority. When the church cries "foul" the church is criticized for intruding into the domain of the state. The church, however, is not trying to be the state. The church, in offering prophetic criticism, is calling the state to be the state as God ordained it and rules over it.

There is one sense in which the gospel is unabashedly political. It declares that Jesus is the King of Kings and Lord of Lords. He sits in the seat of ultimate authority. All lesser magistrates are ultimately accountable to Him for how they exercise their rule.

The civil magistrate is given the power of the sword. The state is authorized to use force to insure justice and to defend its borders. Governments do not rule by request or suggestion. They rule by law, which is enforced by legal coercion. Although the government with the power of the sword is authorized to exert capital punishment and wage just war, its use of the sword is always accountable to God.

The Bible urges Christians to be models of civil obedience wherever possible. We honor Christ by praying for those in authority over us and for being submissive and obedient to their rule. We are to bend over backwards in our civil obedience. We must obey the magistrates unless they command us to do that which God forbids, or keep us from doing that which God commands. In both of these cases, we not only may, but we must disobey those in authority.

Summary

1. Church and state are two distinct institutions ordained by God and answerable to Him for their respective tasks.

Biblical passages for reflection:
2 Chronicles 26:16-20
Psalm 2:10-12
Romans 13:1-7
1 Timothy 2:1-4
1 Peter 2:13-17

2. Civil authority is ordained by God and is given the power of the sword.
3. No government is autonomous. No government can be separated from God.
4. When governments seek to be autonomous, it is the duty of the church to criticize them.
5. Obedience to governmental authority is a sacred duty for every Christian. Civil law must be scrupulously followed unless it is contrary to the Word of God.

MARRIAGE

The institution of marriage was ordained and instituted by God at Creation. Christ sanctified it by His presence at the wedding feast of Cana and by His instructions via His apostles in the New Testament. Most modern wedding ceremonies reflect this and acknowledge the divine origin of marriage. What is often ignored or overlooked in modern contracts is that marriage is regulated by God's commandments. God's law circumscribes the meaning and legitimacy of marriage.

Marriage is to be an exclusive relationship between one man and one woman wherein the two become "one flesh," being unified physically, emotionally, intellectually, and spiritually. It is intended to last for life. The union is secured by a sacred vow and covenant and consummated by physical union. Scripture lists only two situations under which the agreement may be dissolved—infidelity and abandonment.

Infidelity is forbidden in the marriage relationship. The institution of marriage was created by God so that men and women could mutually complete one another and take part in His creative work of procreation. The physical union necessary for procreation also has a spiritual significance. It points toward and illustrates the spiritual union of husband and wife. Paul uses this union to symbolize the relationship between Christ and His church even as the Old Testament described the covenant relationship between God and Israel by the figure of marriage. Fidelity, mutual cherishing, and support are to be at the core of the marriage relationship. Acts of infidelity break the covenant and, as such, allow the injured party to sue for divorce.

In addition, Paul in 1 Corinthians 7:12-16, says that if a believing spouse is abandoned, he or she is under no obligation to maintain the marriage covenant. Abandonment, like infidelity, is a fundamental violation of God's design for marriage.

Biblical passages for reflection:
Genesis 2:24
Matthew 19:1-9
1 Corinthians 7
Ephesians 5:21-33
1 Thessalonians 4:3-8
Hebrews 13:4

Marriage is a creation ordinance. One need not be a Christian in order to receive the common grace of the institution. While all men and women may marry, the Christian is called to marry only "in the Lord." Scripture is clear in its prohibition against Christians marrying non-Christians.

In the order of marriage, the husband is called to be the "head" of the wife. The wife is called to be in submission to her husband as to the Lord. The husband is called to love his wife and to give himself sacrificially to his wife as Christ loved His bride, the church, and gave Himself for it.

Summary

1. Marriage was instituted by God and is regulated by God.
2. Marriage is to be monogamous.
3. The physical union permitted and commanded in marriage mirrors the spiritual union of husband and wife.
4. The marriage estate is used figuratively in Scripture to illustrate the relationship between Christ and His church.
5. Marriage, being a creation ordinance, is given to all human beings. The church recognizes civil marriages. Christians, however, are commanded to marry "in the Lord."
6. God orders the structure of the marriage union. Each partner has specific commands of God to obey.

96

DIVORCE

The question of divorce has become urgent in a society where the incidence of divorce has reached epidemic proportions. Because of the radical proliferation of divorce and the legal and family problems it provokes, the law has moved to facilitate the process by providing for no-fault divorce. As divorce becomes easier and easier to obtain, the problem of its acceleration is exacerbated.

The Bible is not so superficial about divorce. Jesus' teaching on the subject is delivered in the context of a first-century debate between rabbinic schools. There was an ongoing disagreement between liberals and conservatives about the legitimate grounds of divorce. Jesus was confronted by the issue:

The Pharisees also came to Him, testing Him, and saying to Him, "Is it lawful for a man to divorce his wife for just any reason?" And He answered and said to them, "Have you not read that He who made them at the beginning 'made them male and female,' and said, 'For this reason a man shall leave his father and mother and be joined to his wife, and the two shall become one flesh'? So then, they are no longer two but one flesh. Therefore what God has joined together, let not man separate." (Matthew 19:3-6)

We notice that when the Pharisees asked Jesus about a liberal divorce law, He immediately took them back to Scripture and God's original institution of marriage. He stressed that marriage is intended to be for life. He underscored the union of husband and wife into one flesh that cannot be dissolved by human decrees. Only God is authorized to determine the grounds of dissolving marriage.

The debate continued:

They said to Him, "Why then did Moses command to give a certificate of divorce, and to put her away?" He said to them, "Moses, because of the hardness of your hearts, permitted you to divorce your wives, but from the beginning it was not so. And I say to you, whoever divorces his wife except for sexual immorality, and marries another, commits adultery; and whoever marries her who is divorced commits adultery." (Matthew 19:7-9)

If we look closely at Jesus' answer we see that He disputed the Pharisees' understanding of Old Testament law. Moses did not "command" but *allowed* divorce on specified grounds. (Moses, of course, was God's spokesman. It was God who permitted this deviation from His original intent because of the presence of sin that violates marriage.) Jesus reminded them that even this permission was given only because of sin (hardness of heart) and did not as such nullify the original intent of marriage.

Jesus then gave His own pronouncement on the matter—forbidding divorce except on the grounds of sexual immorality. His enigmatic words about remarriage and adultery must be understood in relation to invalid and illegitimate divorces. If people grant divorces where God does not, then the couple is still married in the sight of God. Therefore, remarriage of illegitimately divorced people constitutes entering into an adulterous relationship.

Later, as we said in the previous chapter, Paul extended permission to divorce in the case of the believer being abandoned by the unbeliever (1 Corinthians 7:10-15). The Westminster Confession summarizes the matter. It reads:

In the case of adultery after marriage, it is lawful for the innocent party to sue out a divorce; and after the divorce, to marry another as if the offending party were dead. . . . Although the corruption of man be such as is apt to study arguments unduly to put asunder those whom God hath joined together in marriage; yet, nothing but adultery, or such willful desertion as can no way be remedied by the church, or the civil magistrate, is cause sufficient of dissolving the bond of marriage; wherein, a public and orderly course of proceeding is to be observed; and the persons concerned in it not left to their own wills, and discretion, in their own case.[1]

Biblical passages for reflection:
Matthew 5:31-32
Matthew 19:3-9
Romans 7:1-3
1 Corinthians
   7:10-16

Summary

1. The Bible does not condone "no-fault" divorce.
2. Jesus repudiated the Pharisees' liberal view of divorce.
3. Moses allowed, but did not command, divorce.
4. Jesus allows divorce in the case of sexual immorality.
5. Jesus taught that the remarriage of illegitimately divorced persons constitutes adultery.
6. Paul adds desertion by the unbeliever as grounds for divorce.

Part
X

END TIMES

97 THE ANTICHRIST

The biblical portrait of the Antichrist has evoked much interest not only in Christian circles but in secular culture, being grist for the mill of Hollywood movies and bizarre novels. The Antichrist is the ultimate villain, the supreme "black hat" who embodies to the nth degree all that is evil.

The New Testament portrait of the Antichrist is somewhat enigmatic. There is much confusion and debate that focuses upon his role and nature. The term *anti-* that is used to describe him (or it) can mean either "against" or "in place of." The Antichrist is one who not only opposes Christ, but seeks to usurp the rightful place of Christ. He seeks to substitute himself for Christ. The Antichrist, therefore, is a false Christ, who seeks to deceive people into thinking that he is the true Christ.

Debate has ensued about the identity of the Antichrist. Is the Antichrist a person, a power, or an institution? Is the Antichrist a religious or a political figure, or both? Is there only one Antichrist, or are there many? The Antichrist has been identified at times by Christians as a particular person in history such as Nero, Hitler, and Mussolini, just to name a few. Many Protestants have identified the papacy of Rome as the institution of antichrist, while others look to a yet unrevealed figure or power to be the Antichrist.

John speaks of "many antichrists" (1 John 2:18) and of the "spirit of Antichrist" that was "already in the world" (1 John 4:3). We can conclude from this that during the period between the apostolic age and the return of Christ there are to be many manifestations of antichrist, at least in spirit and power.

The apostle Paul indicates that a special manifestation of antichrist will appear before the final coming of Christ. This "man of sin" will come in accordance with the working of Satan and will have his seal of power in the "temple of God"

(2 Thessalonians 2:1-12). Some believe this can only occur if temple worship is restored to the nation of Israel, others interpret it as a reference to an appearance in the New Testament "temple," the Christian church.

The coming of the Antichrist is linked with a great apostasy in the church. Perhaps an alliance between secular government and religious institutions is in view. The goal of the Antichrist is to make war on the people of God and to seek the destruction of Christ and His Kingdom. The Bible assures us, however, that despite the tremendous power and influence of the Antichrist, his defeat, judgment, and doom are sure. He is no match, in the final analysis, for the true and living Christ.

Biblical passages for reflection:
2 Thessalonians 2:1-12
1 John 2:18-23
1 John 4:1-6
2 John 1:7

Summary

1. The Antichrist works both "against" and "in place of" Christ.
2. Antichrist has been manifested throughout church history in persons and institutions.
3. The Bible foretells a special manifestation of antichrist with extraordinary power and influence at the end of the age.
4. The Antichrist will be defeated by Christ.

98 THE RETURN OF CHRIST

The church of all ages has looked with joyous anticipation to the promised future return of Christ. As His first advent secured our redemption, so His second advent is the blessed hope of the church for the full consummation of His kingdom.

Biblical passages for reflection:
Matthew
    24:1–25:46
Matthew 26:64
Luke 21:5-36
Acts 1:4-11
1 Thessalonians
    4:13–5:11
Titus 2:11-14

The New Testament term most often used to point to Christ's return is the *Parousia.* The Parousia refers to the "appearing," "manifestation," or "coming" of Jesus in glory at the end of the age. It refers to the church's expectation of the promised Second Coming or Second Advent of Christ.

The Bible teaches that Jesus' coming will be both personal and visible. Though His coming will be with power, it will include more than a visitation of His power. It will include His very person. His coming will be neither secret nor invisible. His appearance will be accompanied by clouds of glory in like manner to His departure at the Ascension. There will be a heavenly fanfare of audible shouting, accompanied by the voice of an archangel.

At the coming of Christ, the church will experience a rapture—being taken up in the air to meet Christ as He comes. The rapture will not be secret but open and manifest. Its purpose will not be to whisk the elect away from the earth for a while until Christ returns for a "second" Second Coming. The purpose of the rapture is to allow the saints to meet Jesus in the air as He returns and be included in His entourage during His triumphal descent from heaven. His coming in this manner will be attended by the general resurrection, the final judgment, and the end of the world.

Christians of every generation are called to be vigilant in their watch for the Parousia in order that His coming will not be a surprise to us, like an unexpected thief in the night. We are also urged to remind ourselves of this marvelous future manifestation as an encouragement in our present labors.

No one knows the day or hour of Christ's return. Many have tried to calculate the time, only to be embarrassed by the failure of their specific predictions to come true. The call of Scripture is to vigilance. We need to keep watch for the signs of His nearness. Though Christ has tarried for centuries, causing the hopes of some to wane, each day that passes brings us closer to His awaited return.

Summary

1. The church has the assurance of the promised return of Christ.
2. Christ's parousia will be personal and visible.
3. Christ will return as He departed in His ascension—with clouds of glory.
4. The church will meet Christ to accompany Him in His triumphal reentry to earth.
5. The church must be vigilant in its watch for Christ's return, yet careful to avoid the folly of dogmatic predictions of the day and hour of His coming.

99 THE KINGDOM OF GOD

World history has witnessed a multitude of divergent forms of government. The most common types have been dictatorships ruled by military strength, republics ruled by law, democracies ruled by majority vote, and two types of monarchies—constitutional monarchies (in which the monarch's powers are limited) and absolute monarchies (in which the monarch's word is law).

The kingdom of God is an absolute monarchy. God has no external constitution to bind Him. He needs no consent from the governed to rule over them. He is not limited by referenda or by majority vote. His word is law; His rule is absolutely sovereign.

In any monarchy, the virtues of honor and loyalty to the throne are exceedingly important. There is no monarchy where these elements are more vital than in God's kingdom. Yet the fundamental sin of the human race is grounded in our refusal to honor God as God (Romans 1:21) and in our disloyalty to the King of Kings.

The theme of the kingdom of God is a central motif that runs as a thread through both Old and New Testaments. The theme accents God's reign over His people. The coming Messiah is announced as God's anointed King who will be enthroned in heaven as the King of Kings and Lord of Lords.

The Old Testament points to the kingdom as coming in the future. The New Testament opens with the announcement of John the Baptist that "the kingdom of heaven is at hand" (Matthew 3:2). The historical situation is described in images such as "the ax is laid to the root of the trees" (Matthew 3:10) and "His winnowing fan is in His hand" (Matthew 3:12), both indicating radical nearness. It was the breakthrough into history of God's kingdom that heralded the New Testament gospel. John's message that "the King is coming" signaled the urgency of the times.

The accent of Jesus' own preaching also falls on the

announcement of the gospel of the kingdom. He declares that the kingdom has come with power and is in the midst of His people. At His ascension, Jesus commanded His disciples to be His witnesses in the world. They are to witness to the reign of Jesus as King of Kings. Jesus' current status as cosmic King is invisible. The world is either ignorant of His sovereignty or denies it. It is the task of the church to give visible witness to the invisible kingdom.

Jesus inaugurated the kingdom of God. He has already been enthroned in heaven. But it is as though He is a King in exile with few loyal subjects. At His return He will fully consummate His reign.

The New Testament indicates that the kingdom of God is both present and future. There is an "already" and a "not yet" to the kingdom. Both aspects must be understood and embraced by Christians. To view the kingdom either as already totally realized or as totally futuristic is to do violence to the message of the New Testament. We serve a King who has already been enthroned. Yet we await His triumphal return in glory when every knee will bow before Him.

Biblical passages for reflection:
Psalm 10:16-18
Psalm 22:27-31
Daniel 2:44
John 18:36
Hebrews 1:8-14

Summary

1. God's kingdom is by absolute rule.
2. The theme of God's kingdom links the Old and New Testaments.
3. The New Testament announces the inauguration of the kingdom of God with Jesus' appearance and subsequent enthronement.
4. The kingdom of God exists already but will be fully consummated at His glorious return.

100

HEAVEN

A contemporary ballad declares, "This is heaven . . . when I'm with you." Being in close communion with a loved one is indeed a blessing. Yet as there are no earthly situations worthy of comparison to the misery of hell, so there are no earthly joys suitable to serve as accurate analogies of the marvels of heaven.

As we find grim and ghastly biblical images for hell, so we find rich and promising biblical images for heaven. It is likened to paradise, to the bosom of Abraham, and to a glorious city that comes down from heaven. The New Jerusalem is described in terms of translucent streets of gold, a place with walls of precious gemstones, and a setting of perpetual and everlasting joy.

What is most notable about heaven is what is absent from it as well as what is present in it. Things that will be absent include: (1) tears, (2) sorrow, (3) death, (4) pain, (5) darkness, (6) ungodly people, (7) sin, (8) temples, (9) the sun or moon, and (10) the curse from Adam's sin (see Genesis 3:14-19).

What will be present in heaven includes: (1) the saints, (2) the river of the water of life, (3) healing fruit, (4) the Lamb of God, (5) worship, (6) the wedding feast of the Lamb and His bride, (7) the unveiled face of God, and (8) the Sun of Righteousness.

Heaven is where Christ is. It is the eternal bliss of communion with the God-man. Jonathan Edwards, in trying to give voice to the joy believers will find in heaven writes that the saints will

swim in the ocean of love, and be eternally swallowed up in the infinitely bright, and infinitely mild and sweet beams of divine love; eternally receiving the light, eternally full of it, and eternally compassed round with it, and everlastingly reflecting it back again to its fountain.[1]

While the saints will delight in fellowship with their God and Savior, there is no reason to believe that they will not recognize and fellowship with saints they knew on earth. Heaven is the abode of all good things.

There will be degrees of blessedness in heaven. Paul uses a metaphor of the stars of differing brilliance shining in the same heaven to describe this. There are, however, several clarifying points that need to be made. First, all the stars will shine. That is to say, there is no unhappiness in heaven. All are blessed beyond our most insightful imaginations. Second, the atoning work of Christ has the same saving efficacy for all saints. Finally, the "works" of the believer, which "merit" greater or lesser blessedness, are not good in themselves. Rather, it is the sovereign pleasure of God to regard these works as meritorious. He does so for Christ's sake only. While the greatest horror of hell is its eternality, one of the greatest joys of heaven is the assurance that it will never end. The last enemy, death, will be no more. Luke 20:34-38 assures the believer that this reward of heaven is everlasting.

The greatest joy of heaven is the beatific vision, seeing the face of God. This unspeakable joy, however, comes through the eyes of the soul. God is spirit, and in spirit the elect shall see Him. This is the reward, earned by Christ, enjoyed by His children.

Biblical passages for reflection:
1 Corinthians 15:50-57
2 Corinthians 5:1-8
1 Peter 1:3-9
Revelation 21–22

Summary

1. Heaven will include the absence of all that brings pain and death.
2. Heaven will be a place without sin and the effects of sin.
3. Heaven will be a place where believers will enjoy the immediate presence of Christ.
4. Heaven will include the beatific vision, the glorious experience of gazing at the face of God, which is not possible in this life.
5. Heaven will be a place to enjoy God's rewards forever.
6. No earthly knowledge or experience will be able to dim the fullness of joy we will have in heaven.

101 THE BEATIFIC VISION

There is a story told of a little boy who struggled with the idea of God that he was learning from his parents. What bothered him most was that he was told God is invisible. How could he worship and serve a God he could not see? Already he was aware of the maxim "Out of sight, out of mind." In frustration to the theology of an invisible God, he cried out, "I want a God with skin on!"

Perhaps the desire for a God with skin is one factor that prompts humankind to the worship of idols. Idols of stone or wood, though altogether deaf and dumb and utterly powerless to help us, are at least visible. They are a substitute designed to satisfy the craving of our eyes for the majesty of God.

Paul wrote that mankind is guilty of changing the "glory of the incorruptible God into an image made like corruptible man" (Romans 1:23), and of "exchang[ing] the truth of God for the lie, and worship[ing] and serv[ing] the creature rather than the Creator, who is blessed forever. Amen" (Romans 1:25).

Even the disciples expressed a desire to see the face of God directly. They too were plagued by the elusive invisibility of God. When Jesus met with His disciples for the Last Supper in the upper room, Philip said, "Lord, show us the Father, and it is sufficient for us" (John 14:8). Philip spoke for every believer. Our sufficiency would be altogether met by one glimpse of the unveiled face of God. To see Him in His holy splendor would be enough. It would satisfy the soul and calm the troubled spirit.

If Jesus ever expressed annoyance or impatience with the questions of His disciples, it was with this request. He replied, "Have I been with you so long, and yet you have not known Me, Philip? He who has seen Me has seen the Father; so how can you say, 'Show us the Father'?" (John 14:9).

**Biblical passages
for reflection:**
Exodus
    32:1–33:23
Numbers 6:24-26
Matthew 5:8
John 14:1-11
Revelation 22:1-5

Earlier in his earthly ministry, Jesus preached the Sermon on the Mount, beginning with the Beatitudes. Here He pronounced His blessing on the pure of heart, with the attending promise that they would see God. That God cannot presently be seen in His glory and that He remains invisible to our eyes is a burden to humans who long to view the One who is the supreme object of our devotion and love. From the time that He barred access to Eden with an angel wielding a flaming sword, it has been God's command that no human can see Him unveiled. Even to Moses, who requested to see God's unveiled glory, God replied, "My face shall not be seen" (Exodus 33:23).

Yet the redeemed long for the moment when they can look beyond the veil and gaze directly upon the purity of God's splendor. The reason we cannot perceive it now is not due to a deficiency in our eyes, but to a lack of purity in our hearts. When we are glorified in heaven and our hearts are purified we shall enjoy the unspeakable bliss of beholding Him as He is in glory.

The beatific vision is so called because it is the promise of the vision of God that carries with it the ultimate blessedness of the human soul. The highest benediction of Israel was, "The LORD bless you and keep you; the LORD make His face shine upon you, and be gracious to you; the LORD lift up His countenance upon you, and give you peace" (Numbers 6:24-26).

John promises us that though mystery attends much of what lies before us in heaven, of this much we can be sure: that "we shall be like Him, for we shall see Him as He is" (1 John 3:2).

This promise assures us that in heaven God will display Himself to us in a way that will go beyond a theophany (an external manifestation of God's glory such as the burning bush). The vision will transcend that of a burning bush or a pillar of cloud. We will see more than an outward representation or a reflected image. We will see Him "as He is." We will peer, somehow, into His very essence. Then there will be no need for skin.

Summary

1. God's invisibility is often the occasion for human acts of idolatry.
2. Christ displayed the perfect image of God; to see Him is to see the Father.
3. The vision of God is promised to the pure in heart.
4. No mortal can see the face of God until we are purified in heaven.
5. The future vision of God is called "beatific" because it will flood our souls with blessedness.

102

HELL

We have often heard statements such as "War is hell" or "I went through hell." These expressions are, of course, not taken literally. Rather, they reflect our tendency to use the word *hell* as a descriptive term for the most ghastly human experience possible. Yet no human experience in this world is actually comparable to hell. If we try to imagine the worst of all possible suffering in the here and now we have not yet stretched our imaginations to reach the dreadful reality of hell.

Hell is trivialized when it is used as a common curse word. To use the word lightly may be a halfhearted human attempt to take the concept lightly or to treat it in an amusing way. We tend to joke about things most frightening to us in a futile effort to declaw and defang them, reducing their threatening power.

There is no biblical concept more grim or terror-invoking than the idea of hell. It is so unpopular with us that few would give credence to it at all except that it comes to us from the teaching of Christ Himself.

Almost all the biblical teaching about hell comes from the lips of Jesus. It is this doctrine, perhaps more than any other, that strains even the Christian's loyalty to the teaching of Christ. Modern Christians have pushed the limits of minimizing hell in an effort to sidestep or soften Jesus' own teaching. The Bible describes hell as a place of outer darkness, a lake of fire, a place of weeping and gnashing of teeth, a place of eternal separation from the blessings of God, a prison, a place of torment where the worm doesn't turn or die. These graphic images of eternal punishment provoke the question, should we take these descriptions literally or are they merely symbols?

I suspect they are symbols, but I find no relief in that. We must not think of them as being *merely* symbols. It is probable that the sinner in hell would prefer a literal lake of fire as his eternal abode to the reality of hell represented in the lake of fire image. If these images are indeed symbols, then we must conclude that the reality is worse than the symbol suggests. The function of symbols is to point beyond themselves to a higher or more intense state of actuality than the symbol itself can contain. That Jesus used the most awful symbols imaginable to describe hell is no comfort to those who see them simply as symbols.

A breath of relief is usually heard when someone declares, "Hell is a symbol for separation from God." To be separated from God for eternity is no great threat to the impenitent person. The ungodly want nothing more than to be separated from God. Their problem in hell will not be separation from God, it will be the presence of God that will torment them. In hell, God will be present in the fullness of His divine wrath. He will be there to exercise His just punishment of the damned. They will know Him as an all-consuming fire.

No matter how we analyze the concept of hell it often sounds to us as a place of cruel and unusual punishment. If, however, we can take any comfort in the concept of hell, we can take it in the full assurance that there will be no cruelty there. It is impossible for God to be cruel. Cruelty involves inflicting a punishment that is more severe or harsh than the crime. Cruelty in this sense is unjust. God is incapable of inflicting an unjust punishment. The Judge of all the earth will surely do what is right. No innocent person will ever suffer at His hand.

Perhaps the most frightening aspect of hell is its eternality. People can endure the greatest agony if they know it will ultimately stop. In hell there is no such hope. The Bible clearly teaches that the punishment is eternal. The same word is used for both eternal life and eternal death. Punishment implies pain. Mere annihilation, which some have lobbied for, involves no pain. Jonathan Edwards, in preaching on Revelation 6:15-16 said, "Wicked men will hereafter earnestly wish to be turned to nothing and forever cease to be that they may escape the wrath of God."[1]

Hell, then, is an eternity before the righteous, ever-burning wrath of God, a suffering torment from which there is no escape and no relief. Understanding this is crucial to our drive to appreciate the work of Christ and to preach His gospel.

Summary

1. The suffering of hell is beyond any experience of misery found in this world.
2. Hell is clearly included in the teaching of Jesus.
3. If the biblical descriptions of hell are symbols, then the reality will be worse than the symbols.

Biblical passages for reflection:
Matthew 8:11-12
Mark 9:42-48
Luke 16:19-31
Jude 1:3-13
Revelation
    20:11-15

4. Hell is the *presence* of God in His wrath and judgment.
5. There is no cruelty in hell. Hell will be a place of perfect justice.
6. Hell is eternal. There is no escape through either repentance or annihilation.

NOTES

Introduction

1. J. V. Langmead Casserley, *Apologetics & Evangelism* (Louisville: Westminster, 1970).
2. John Stott, *Christ the Controversialist* (Downers Grove, Ill.: InterVarsity Press, 1970).
3. John Bunyan, *Pilgrim's Progress* (Carol Stream, Ill.: Tyndale House Publishers, Inc. 1991), 11-15.
4. Allan Bloom, *The Closing of the American Mind* (New York: Simon & Schuster, 1987).
5. C. S. Lewis, "On the Reading of Old Books," in *God in the Dock: Essays on Theology and Ethics* (Grand Rapids: Eerdmans, 1970), 204-205.

Chapter 3

1. John Calvin, *Institutes of the Christian Religion,* trans. Henry Beveridge, 2 vols., bk.I (Grand Rapids: Wm. B. Eerdmans, 1975), 43.

Chapter 9

1. Roland H. Bainton, *Here I Stand: A Life of Martin Luther* (Nashville: Abingdon Press, 1978).

Chapter 20

1. *Westminster Confession of Faith* (Committee for Christian Education & Publication, Presbyterian Church in America, 1990), chap. 5, sec. 1.

Chapter 26

1. *Westminster Confession,* chap. 8, sec. 1.

Chapter 33

1. Calvin, *Institutes,* bk. II, 1:448.

Chapter 35

1. Calvin, *Institutes,* bk. II, 1:425-429.

Chapter 39

1. Martin Luther, *Bondage of the Will* (Old Tappan, NJ: Revell, 1957), 70.
2. Calvin, *Institutes,* bk. I, 1:71-72.

Chapter 44

1. William Shakespeare, *The Complete Works of Shakespeare,* ed. David Bevington, 3d ed. (Glenview, Ill.: Scott, Foresman and Co., 1980), act 5, sc. 5, lines 24-28, p. 1247.

Chapter 50

1. *Westminster Larger Catechism* (Committee for Christian Education and Publication, Presbyterian Church in America, 1990), question #24.
2. Calvin, *Institutes,* bk. II, 1:362.

Chapter 51

1. *Westminster Confession,* art. 6:1.
2. *Westminster Confession,* art. 6:1-4.

Chapter 53

1. Roland H. Bainton, *Here I Stand: A Life of Martin Luther* (Nashville: Abingdon Press, 1978).

Chapter 60

1. Charles Colson, *Born Again* (Old Tappan, N.J.: Revell, 1977).

Chapter 63

1. Jonathan Edwards, *The Freedom of the Will,* ed. Paul Ramsey (New Haven: Yale University Press, 1973), 137.
2. Edwards, *The Freedom of the Will,* 156.

Chapter 78

1. Calvin, *Institutes,* bk. IV, 2:XII.
2. *Westminster Confession,* art. 30:3.

Chapter 82	1. Calvin, *Institutes,* bk. IV, 2:XVII.
Chapter 85	1. *Westminster Confession,* art. 22:3.
Chapter 92	1. Calvin, *Institutes,* bk. II, 1:304-310.
	2. Calvin, *Institutes,* bk. II, 1:306.
	3. Calvin, *Institutes,* bk. II, 1:307.
Chapter 94	1. *Westminster Confession,* art. 23:1, 3.
Chapter 96	1. *Westminster Confession,* art. 24:5, 6.
Chapter 100	1. Jonathan Edwards, *The Works of Jonathan Edwards,* vol. 2 (Carlisle, Pa.: Banner of Truth, 1979), 29.
Chapter 102	1. John H. Gerstner, *Heaven & Hell* (Orlando: Ligonier Ministries, 1991), 75.

SUGGESTED READING

BEGINNING

I. REVELATION

North, Gary. *The Hoax of Higher Criticism.* Tyler: Institute for Christian Economics, 1989.

Radmacher, Earl D. *Can We Trust the Bible?* Carol Stream, Ill.: Tyndale House Publishers, Inc., 1979.

II. THE NATURE AND ATTRIBUTES OF GOD

Brown, Stephen. *If God Is in Charge.* Nashville: Thomas Nelson, Inc., 1983.

Colson, Charles W. *Loving God.* Grand Rapids: Zondervan, 1987.

III. THE WORKS AND DECREES OF GOD

Ramsbottom, B. A. *Bible Doctrines Simply Explained.* London: Gospel Standard Trust Publications, 1986.

Robertson, O. Palmer. *Covenants: God's Way.* Phillipsburg: Presbyterian & Reformed Publishing Company, 1987.

IV. JESUS CHRIST

Lloyd-Jones, D. M. *The Cross of Christ.* Downers Grove, Ill.: InterVarsity Press, 1986.

McDowell, Josh. *More Than a Carpenter.* Carol Stream, Ill.: Tyndale House Publishers, Inc., 1980.

Sproul, R. C. *Following Christ.* Carol Stream, Ill.: Tyndale House Publishers, Inc., 1991.

V. THE HOLY SPIRIT

Green, Michael. *I Believe in the Holy Spirit.* Grand Rapids: William B. Eerdmans Publishing Company, 1989.

Stott, John R. *The Baptism and Fullness of the Spirit.* Downers Grove, Ill.: InterVarsity Press, 1976.

VI. HUMAN BEINGS AND THE FALL

Allen, Ronald B. *The Majesty of Man: The Dignity of Being Human.* Sisters, Oreg.: Multnomah, 1984.

Brand, Paul, and Philip Yancey. *Fearfully & Wonderfully Made.* Grand Rapids: Zondervan, 1987.

Lewis, C. S. *The Abolition of Man.* New York: Macmillan Publishing Company, Inc., 1978.

VII. SALVATION

Horton, Michael Scott. *Putting Amazing Back into Grace: An Introduction to Reformed Theology.* Nashville: Thomas Nelson, Inc., 1991.

Palmer, Edwin H. *The Five Points of Calvinism: A Study Guide.* Grand Rapids: Baker Book House, 1972.

Stott, John R. *Basic Christianity.* Grand Rapids: William B. Eerdmans Publishing Company, 1957.

VIII. THE CHURCH AND SACRAMENTS

Barrs, Jerran. *Shepherds and Sheep: A Biblical View of Leading and Following.* Downers Grove, Ill.: InterVarsity Press, 1983.

Sartelle, John P. *Infant Baptism: What Christian Parents Should Know.* Phillipsburg: Presbyterian & Reformed Publishing Company, 1985.

IX. SPIRITUALITY AND LIVING IN THIS AGE

Kelly, Douglas. *If God Already Knows, Why Pray?* Brentwood: Wolgemuth & Hyatt Publishers, Inc., 1989.

Sproul, R. C. *Following Christ.* Carol Stream, Ill.: Tyndale House Publishers, Inc., 1991.

———. *The Intimate Marriage.* Carol Stream, Ill.: Tyndale House Publishers, Inc., 1986.

X. END TIMES

Clouse, Robert G., ed. *The Meaning of the Millenium: Four Views.* Brethren Missionary Herald Inc., 1978.

Erickson, Millard J. *Contemporary Options in Eschatology: A Study of the Millenium.* Grand Rapids: Baker Book House, 1977.

INTERMEDIATE

I. REVELATION

Sproul, R. C. *Knowing Scripture.* Downers Grove, Ill.: InterVarsity Press, 1977.

Stott, John R. *The Authority of the Bible.* Downers Grove, Ill.: InterVarsity Press, 1974.

II. THE NATURE AND ATTRIBUTES OF GOD

Packer, J. I. *Knowing God.* Downers Grove, Ill.: InterVarsity Press, 1973.

Pink, Arthur W. *Attributes of God.* Grand Rapids: Baker Book House, 1975.

Sproul, R. C. *One Holy Passion: The Consuming Thirst to Know God.* Nashville: Thomas Nelson, Inc., 1987.

———. *The Holiness of God.* Carol Stream, Ill.: Tyndale House Publications, Inc., 1985.

Storms, C. Samuel. *The Grandeur of God.* Grand Rapids: Baker Book House, 1984.

III. THE WORKS AND DECREES OF GOD

Boice, James M. *Our Sovereign God.* Grand Rapids: Baker Book House, 1977.

Bridges, Jerry. *Trusting God.* Colorado Springs: NavPress, 1991.

Robertson, O. Palmer. *The Christ of the Covenants.* Phillipsburg: Presbyterian & Reformed Publishing Company, 1981.

IV. JESUS CHRIST

Bruce, F. F. *Jesus: Lord and Savior.* Downers Grove, Ill.: InterVarsity Press, 1986.

Sproul, R. C. *The Glory of Christ.* Carol Stream, Ill.: Tyndale House Publications, Inc., 1990.

Stott, John. *The Cross of Christ.* Downers Grove, Ill.: InterVarsity Press, 1986.

Warfield, Benjamin B. *The Savior of the World.* Carlisle, Pa.: Banner of Truth, 1960.

V. THE HOLY SPIRIT

Packer, J. I. *Keep in Step with the Spirit.* Tarrytown: Fleming H. Revell Co., 1984.

Palmer, Edwin H. *The Holy Spirit: His Person and Ministry.* Phillipsburg: Presbyterian & Reformed Publishing Co., 1985.

Sproul, R. C. *The Mystery of the Holy Spirit.* Carol Stream, Ill.: Tyndale House Publishers, Inc., 1990.

VI. HUMAN BEINGS AND THE FALL

Machen, J. Gresham. *The Christian View of Man.* Carlisle, Pa.: Banner of Truth, 1984.

Packer, J. I. *Knowing Man.* Wheaton, Ill.: Good News Publishers, 1979.

Sproul, R. C. *The Hunger for Significance.* Ventura, Calif.: Gospel Light Publications, Inc., 1991.

VII. SALVATION

Murray, John. *Redemption: Accomplished and Applied.* Grand Rapids: William B. Eerdmans Publishing Company, 1961.

———. *The Sovereignty of God.* Edited by Jacob T. Hoogstra. Grand Rapids: Zondervan, 1940.

Pink, Arthur W. *The Sovereignty of God.* Carlisle, Pa.: Banner of Truth, 1988.

Sproul, R. C. *Chosen by God.* Carol Stream, Ill.: Tyndale House Publications, Inc., 1986.

VIII. THE CHURCH AND SACRAMENTS

Adams, Jay E. *The Meaning and Mode of Baptism.* Phillipsburg: Presbyterian & Reformed Publishing Company, 1975.

Kuiper, R. B. *The Glorious Body of Christ.* Carlisle, Pa.: Banner of Truth, 1987.

Stott, John. *One People: Helping Your Church Become a Caring Community.* Harrisburg: Christian Publications, 1982.

IX. SPIRITUALITY AND LIVING IN THIS AGE

Bridges, Jerry. *The Pursuit of Holiness.* Colorado Springs: NavPress, 1978.

Ferguson, Sinclair. *A Heart for God.* Carlisle, Pa.: Banner of Truth, 1987.

Pratt, Richard L. Jr. *Pray with Your Eyes Open: Looking at God, Ourselves, and Our Prayers.* Grand Rapids: Baker Book House, 1988.

Sproul, R. C. *Pleasing God.* Carol Stream, Ill.: Tyndale House Publishers, Inc., 1988.

X. END TIMES

Campbell, Roderick. *Israel and the New Covenant.* Tyler: Geneva Ministries, 1982.

Gerstner, John H. *Jonathan Edwards on Heaven and Hell.* Grand Rapids: Baker Book House, 1980.

Gilmore, John. *Probing Heaven.* Grand Rapids: Baker Book House, 1989.

Hendriksen, William. *The Bible on the Life Hereafter.* Grand Rapids: Baker Book House, 1959.

ADVANCED

I. REVELATION

Bruce, F. F. *The Foundation of Biblical Authority.* Edited by James M. Boice. Grand Rapids: Zondervan, 1978.

———. *Canon of Scripture.* Downers Grove, Ill.: InterVarsity Press, 1988.

Montgomery, John Warwick. *God's Inerrant Word.* Minneapolis: Bethany Fellowship, 1974.

Warfield, B. B. *The Inspiration and Authority of the Bible.* Grand Rapids: Baker Book House, 1964.

II. THE NATURE AND ATTRIBUTES OF GOD

Bavinck, Herman. *The Doctrine of God.* Translated by W. Hendricksen. Carlisle, Pa.: Banner of Truth, 1977.

Boice, James. *Foundations of the Christian Faith.* Downers Grove, Ill.: InterVarsity Press, 1986.

Charnock, Stephen. *The Existence and Attributes of God.* Grand Rapids: Baker Book House, 1979.

Clark, Gordon. *The Trinity.* (Trinity Papers: No. 8.) Jefferson: The Trinity Foundation, 1985.

III. THE WORKS AND DECREES OF GOD

Ames, William. *The Marrow of Theology.* Durham: The Labyrinth Press, Inc., 1983.

Bates, William. *Harmony of the Divine Attributes.* Harrisonburg: Sprinkle Publications, 1985.

Warfield, B. B. *Counterfeit Miracles.* Carlisle, Pa.: Banner of Truth, 1986.

Witsius, Herman. *The Economy of the Covenants between God and Man.* Distributed by Phillipsburg: Presbyterian & Reformed Publishing Company, 1990.

IV. JESUS CHRIST

Morris, Leon. *The Apostolic Preaching of the Cross.* Grand Rapids: Willliam B. Eerdmans Publishing Company, 1976.

———. *The Cross of Jesus.* Grand Rapids: William B. Eerdmans Publishing Company, 1988.

Owen, John. *The Death of Death in the Death of Christ.* Carlisle, Pa.: Banner of Truth, 1989.

Smeaton, George. *The Doctrine of the Atonement according to the Apostles.* Peabody: Hendrikson Publications, Inc., 1988.

Warfield, B. B. *The Person and Work of Christ.* Distributed by Grand Rapids: Baker Book House; published by Phillipsburg: Presbyterian & Reformed Publishing Company, 1950.

V. THE HOLY SPIRIT

Kuyper, Abraham. *The Work of the Holy Spirit.* Grand Rapids: William B. Eerdmans Publishing Company, 1956.

Owen, John. *The Holy Spirit, His Gifts & Power.* Melbourne: Kregel Publications, 1977.

Smeaton, George. *The Doctrine of the Holy Spirit.* Carlisle, Pa.:
Banner of Truth, 1988.

VI. HUMAN BEINGS AND THE FALL

Clark, Gordon H. *The Biblical Doctrine of Man.* Jefferson: The
Trinity Foundation, 1984.

Cosgrove, Mark P. *The Essence of Human Nature.* Grand Rapids:
Zondervan, 1977.

Hoekema, Anthony. *Created in God's Image.* Grand Rapids: William
B. Eerdmans Publishing Company, 1986.

Machen, J. Gresham. *The Christian View of Man.* Carlisle, Pa.:
Banner of Truth, 1984.

VII. SALVATION

Crampton, Kenneth, and Gary Talbot. *Calvinism, Hyper-
calvinism and Arminianism.* Lakeland: Whitefield Publishing,
1990.

Morris, Leon. *The Atonement.* Downers Grove, Ill.: InterVarsity
Press, 1983.

Wallace, Ronald S. *The Atoning Death of Christ.* Wheaton, Ill.: Good
News Publishers, 1981.

VIII. THE CHURCH AND SACRAMENTS

Bannerman, D. Douglas. *The Scripture Doctrine of the Church.*
Grand Rapids: William B. Eerdmans Publishing Company,
1955.

Marcel, Pierre. *The Biblical Doctrine of Infant Baptism.*
Translated by James Clarke. London: James Clarke &
Company, 1953.

McNair, Donald J. *The Challenge of Eldership: A Handbook for the
Elders of the Church.* Philadelphia: Great Commission
Publications, 1984.

Murray, John. *Christian Baptism.* Phillipsburg: Presbyterian &
Reformed Publishing Company, 1980.

IX. SPIRITUALITY AND LIVING IN THIS AGE

Burroughs, Jeremiah. *The Rare Jewel of Christian Contentment.*
Carlisle, Pa.: Banner of Truth, 1979.

Edwards, Jonathan. *Charity and Its Fruits.* Carlisle, Pa.: Banner of
Truth, 1978.

Owen, John. *The Grace and Duty of Being Spiritually Minded:
Stated and Practically Improved.* Grand Rapids: Baker Book
House, 1977.

Warfield, Benjamin B. *Perfectionism.* Grand Rapids: Baker Book
House, 1981.

X. END TIMES

Hoekema, Anthony A. *The Bible and the Future.* Grand Rapids:
William B. Eerdmans Publishing Company, 1979.

Ridderbos, Herman. *The Coming of the Kingdom.* Phillipsburg:
Presbyterian & Reformed Publishing Company, 1962.

Vos, Geerhardus. *The Kingdom of God and the Church.* Phillipsburg:
Presbyterian & Reformed Publishing Company, 1972.

CLASSIC THEOLOGY

Anselm of Canterbury. *Why God Became Man.* Edited by Jasper Hopkins and Herbert Richardson. Lewiston: Edwin Mellen Press, 1980.

———. *The Virgin Conception and Original Sin.* (Anselm of Canterbury series, Vol. 3) Translated by Jasper Hopkins and Herbert Richardson. Lewiston: Edwin Mellen Press, 1976.

Aquinas, St. Thomas. *The Summa Contra Gentiles.* Notre Dame: University of Notre Dame Press, 1975.

———. *Summa Theologica.* Translated by the Dominican Fathers of the English Province. Westminster: Christian Classics Inc., 1981.

Augustine, St. *Confessions of St. Augustine.* Grand Rapids: Baker Book House, 1977.

———. *City of God.* Edited by R. V. Tasker and translated by John Healey. Totowa: Biblio Distribution Center, 1973.

———. *The Trinity.* (Fathers of the Church series, Vol. 45). Translated by Stephen McKenna. Baltimore: Catholic University of America Press, 1963.

Calvin, John. *Institutes of the Christian Religion.* Translated by Ford L. Battles. Grand Rapids: William B. Eerdmans Publishing Company, 1986.

Edwards, Jonathan. *Freedom of the Will.* Edited by Arnold S. Kaufman and William K. Frankena. New York: Irvington Publications, 1982.

———. *Religious Affections: How Man Will Affect His Character before God.* Edited by James M. Houston. Sisters, Oreg.: Multnomah Press, 1990.

———. *Original Sin.* (Works of Jonathan Edwards series, Vol. 3) Edited by Clyde A. Holbrook. New Haven, Conn.: Yale University Press, 1970.

Hodge, A. A. *Outlines of Theology.* Carlisle, Pa.: Banner of Truth, 1983.

Hodge, Charles. *Systematic Theology.* Grand Rapids: William B. Eerdmans Publishing Company, 1960.

Luther, Martin. *The Bondage of the Will.* Translated by J. I. Packer. Tarrytown: Fleming H. Revell Company, 1990.

SCRIPTURE INDEX

Genesis 1 60
Genesis 1:1-2 110
Genesis 1:1–2:3 106
Genesis 1:1–2:25 135
Genesis 1:3ff 106
Genesis 1:26-27 131
Genesis 1:27 . . . . 129, 132
Genesis 2:1-3 240
Genesis 2:17 74
Genesis 2:24 266
Genesis 3:1-24 146
Genesis 3:14-19 279
Genesis 9:6 132
Genesis 15 72
Genesis 15:7-21 72
Genesis 17:1 41
Genesis 17:1-14 229
Genesis 18:25 54
Genesis 27:30-46 193
Genesis 50:20 62
Exodus 3:1-6 48
Exodus 4:1-9 66
Exodus 7:1-5 167
Exodus 20 72
Exodus 20:2 71
Exodus 20:1-17 18
Exodus 20:8-11 240
Exodus 20:16 241
Exodus 32:1–33:23 283
Exodus 33:23 282
Exodus 34:6-7 . . . . . 51, 54
Numbers 6:24-26 . . . 282, 283
Numbers 11 118
Deuteronomy 6:4 . . . . 35, 36
Deuteronomy 6:4-5 248
Deuteronomy 6:4-9 xxi
Deuteronomy 10:20 242
Deuteronomy 18:15-22 . . . 20
Deuteronomy 29:29 32
Deuteronomy 30:6 172
Deuteronomy 30:19-20 . . . 181
1 Samuel 2:2 48
1 Kings 8:27 44
1 Kings 16:29-34 156
1 Kings 17:21-24 66
2 Chronicles 6:22-23 . . . 242
2 Chronicles 26:16-20 . . . 263
Ezra 10:5 242

Nehemiah 8:8 28
Nehemiah 9:32-33 54
Job 1:6-12 140
Job 11:7-9 44
Job 13:15 250
Job 38:1–41:34 . . . . 32, 63
Job 42:2 40
Psalm 2:10-12 263
Psalm 5:1-3 252
Psalm 8:3-5 128
Psalm 10:16-18 278
Psalm 14:1 5
Psalm 19:1-14 . . . . . . 6, 13
Psalm 19:7-11 258
Psalm 22:27-31 278
Psalm 25:8-10 51
Psalm 33:1-9 60
Psalm 51 129
Psalm 51:5 146
Psalm 51:10, 17 194
Psalm 90:2 38
Psalm 99:1-9 48
Psalm 100:1-5 51
Psalm 104:24-26 60
Psalm 110 102
Psalm 115:3 . . . . . . 18, 41
Psalm 116:11 241
Psalm 119 16
Psalm 119:9-16 258
Psalm 119:105 115
Psalm 139:1-18 32
Psalm 139:7-8 110
Psalm 139:7-10 44
Psalm 145:17 54
Psalm 147:5 46
Proverbs 16:4 . . . . 163, 167
Ecclesiastes 5:4-5 241
Ecclesiastes 9:10 16
Ecclesiastes 12:7 135
Isaiah 6 20
Isaiah 6:1-13 48
Isaiah 7:10-16 86
Isaiah 40:3 92
Isaiah 42:1-4 102
Isaiah 55:8-9 32
Isaiah 58:13 239
Isaiah 58:13-14 240
Isaiah 61:1 92

Jeremiah 10:1-16	60	Matthew 19:3-9	268
Jeremiah 17:9	146, 149	Matthew 19:7-9	267
Jeremiah 23:23-24	44	Matthew 19:21	255
Jeremiah 31:31-34	72	Matthew 23:22-29	256
Jeremiah 34:18	72	Matthew 23:23-24	256
Ezekiel 11:5	46	Matthew 24:1–25:46	276
Ezekiel 18:30-32	194	Matthew 26:26-29	233
Ezekiel 36:26-27	160, 170, 172	Matthew 26:36-41	138
Daniel 2:44	278	Matthew 26:34	276
Daniel 4:34-35	63	Matthew 28:19	36
Daniel 7	105	Matthew 28:19-20	224
Joel 2:28-29	119	Matthew 28:20	232
Joel 2:28-32	20	Mark 1:1-5	92
Zephaniah 1	160	Mark 1:21-28	142
Matthew 1:21	177	Mark 2:1-12	78
Matthew 1:23	86	Mark 2:10	105
Matthew 3:2	277	Mark 2:28	77, 78, 105
Matthew 3:10	277	Mark 9:42-48	287
Matthew 3:12	277	Mark 13:11	122
Matthew 3:13-17	92	Mark 13:24-27	94
Matthew 3:15	80, 84	Mark 14:22-25	237
Matthew 3:16-17	36	Luke 1:26-38	102
Matthew 4:1-11	26, 140	Luke 1:34	85
Matthew 4:4	15	Luke 1:35	85
Matthew 5:8	283	Luke 1:37	40, 85
Matthew 5:17-20	18	Luke 8:5-8	198
Matthew 5:31-32	268	Luke 8:15	198
Matthew 5:33-37	242	Luke 8:49-56	207
Matthew 5:43-48	248	Luke 8:52	205
Matthew 7:1-5	222	Luke 10:17-20	142
Matthew 7:15-20	20	Luke 11:14-26	142
Matthew 7:21-23	203	Luke 11:39-44	152
Matthew 8:11-12	287	Luke 16:19-31	287
Matthew 9:1-8	106	Luke 20:34-38	280
Matthew 10:28	133, 135	Luke 21:5-36	276
Matthew 10:39	8	Luke 22:20	72
Matthew 11:20-24	144	Luke 22:31	140
Matthew 12:1-14	240	Luke 23:34	154
Matthew 12:22-32	154	Luke 23:43	205, 207
Matthew 12:31-32	153	Luke 24:44-45	24
Matthew 13:11	9	Luke 24:46-47	194
Matthew 13:24-43	218	Luke 24:50-53	97
Matthew 15:1-20	256	John 1:1	105
Matthew 16:13-21	106	John 1:1-3	77
Matthew 16:19	221	John 1:1-5	38
Matthew 16:25	9	John 1:1-14	78, 82
Matthew 17:1-9	94	John 1:1-18	89, 106
Matthew 18:3	188	John 1:14	87, 88
Matthew 18:15-17	220	John 1:18	88
Matthew 18:15-20	221	John 2:11	66
Matthew 19:1-9	266	John 2:17	79, 83
Matthew 19:3-6	267	John 3:1-21	203

John 3:3 171
John 3:6 138
John 3:16 177
John 3:16-17 160
John 4:34 . . . . 80, 83
John 5:30 80
John 6:35-40 199
John 6:44, 65 181
John 7:37-39 119
John 8:34-36 181
John 8:58 78
John 10:27-30 . . . . . 177, 199
John 10:35 15
John 13:18 163
John 14:1-11 283
John 14:8 281
John 14:9 281
John 14:13-14 252
John 14:15 . . . . . 254, 258
John 14:16 121
John 14:16-18 122
John 15:1-8 196
John 15:5 181
John 15:13 114
John 15:26 124
John 16 111
John 16:13 . . . . . 111, 112
John 16:13-15 116
John 17:9-12 177
John 17:12 199
John 17:13-23 212
John 17:17 . . . . . . 15, 16
John 18:36 278
John 19:11 69
John 20:23 221
John 20:28 78
Acts 1:4-11 276
Acts 1:9-11 95
Acts 2:1-11 119
Acts 2:16-21 118
Acts 2:22-24 63
Acts 2:38-39 229
Acts 2:40-47 224
Acts 3:17-26 102
Acts 5:3-4 . . . . . . 109, 110
Acts 5:32 114
Acts 7:55-56 97
Acts 8 118
Acts 10 118
Acts 10:47 118
Acts 14:8-18 129
Acts 15:1-29 256

Acts 15:15-16 26
Acts 15:18 46
Acts 15:28 114
Acts 16:25-34 229
Acts 17:16-34 13
Acts 17:22-31 . . . 38, 44, 129
Acts 17:28 . . . . 38, 134
Acts 19 118
Acts 19:1-7 122
Acts 20:7 240
Acts 20:17-21 194
Acts 20:28 177
Romans 1:1-6 216
Romans 1:3-4 86
Romans 1:16-17 160
Romans 1:16-32 185
Romans 1:18-23 . . . 4, 13, 129
Romans 1:20 184
Romans 1:21 277
Romans 1:23 281
Romans 1:25 281
Romans 2:1-11 144
Romans 2:4 194
Romans 2:12-16 . . . . 12, 152
Romans 2:14-15 13
Romans 2:15 151
Romans 3:9–4:8 192
Romans 3:10-12 148
Romans 3:10-26 . . . . 144, 146
Romans 3:19-26 256
Romans 3:20 189
Romans 3:20-26 74
Romans 3:21-28 . . . . 174, 190
Romans 3:23 . . . . . 143, 147
Romans 3:27-31 254
Romans 3:31 253
Romans 4:1-8 196
Romans 4:11-12 226
Romans 5:1 100
Romans 5:1-5 . . . . . 196, 250
Romans 5:1-11 185
Romans 5:8 260
Romans 5:12-19 . 144, 146, 190
Romans 5:17-19 174
Romans 5:18-21 84
Romans 6:1-2 254
Romans 6:1-4 224
Romans 6:3-4 226
Romans 7:1-3 268
Romans 7:7-25 . . . . 18, 258
Romans 7:13–8:17 138
Romans 7:14 148

Romans 7:23 148
Romans 8 198
Romans 8:1-11 149
Romans 8:3-4 258
Romans 8:5-8 181
Romans 8:9-17 110
Romans 8:11 210
Romans 8:15-17 203
Romans 8:16 . . . . 114, 201
Romans 8:18-23 135
Romans 8:18-25 250
Romans 8:26-27
. . . . 121, 122, 252
Romans 8:28 50
Romans 8:28-39 51
Romans 8:29 132
Romans 8:29-30 . . . 211, 212
Romans 8:30
. . . . . 163, 170, 172, 177, 198
Romans 8:31-39 199
Romans 8:33-34 100
Romans 8:34 97
Romans 8:37 122
Romans 8:39 198
Romans 9 167
Romans 9:10-12, 16 162
Romans 9:14 54
Romans 9:14-15 162
Romans 9:14-18 69
Romans 9:14-33 54
Romans 9:15 54
Romans 10:5-13 . . . 74, 188
Romans 10:14-17 185
Romans 11:13 216
Romans 11:13-24 220
Romans 11:33-36 . . 32, 46, 63
Romans 11:36 41
Romans 12:1-21 246
Romans 13:1-4 261
Romans 13:1-7 263
Romans 14:9-10 97
Romans 14:23 . . . . 151, 152
Romans 16:25-27 9
1 Corinthians 1:10-31 220
1 Corinthians 1:26-31 160
1 Corinthians 2:6-16 32
1 Corinthians 2:7 9
1 Corinthians 2:9 . . . 209, 210
1 Corinthians 2:9-11 115
1 Corinthians 2:9-16 116
1 Corinthians 2:10-11 109
1 Corinthians 4:8-13 249

1 Corinthians 5 222
1 Corinthians 6:19-20 . . . 110
1 Corinthians 7 266
1 Corinthians 7:10-15 . . . 168
1 Corinthians 7:10-16 . . . 269
1 Corinthians 7:19 258
1 Corinthians 7:12-16 . . . 265
1 Corinthians 9:2 216
1 Corinthians 9:27 197
1 Corinthians 10:13-17 . . 233
1 Corinthians 10:14-23 . . 156
1 Corinthians 10:14-24 . . 142
1 Corinthians 11:23-26 . . 237
1 Corinthians 11:23-34
. . . . 224, 233
1 Corinthians 11:27-32 . . 222
1 Corinthians 12 119
1 Corinthians 12:1–14:40 . 246
1 Corinthians 12:12-14
. . . . 218, 226
1 Corinthians 13 . . . . 247, 248
1 Corinthians 13:11 . . . xii, xx
1 Corinthians 13:12 209
1 Corinthians 13:13 . . 248, 249
1 Corinthians 14:20 . . xii, xxi
1 Corinthians 14:26-33 . . 119
1 Corinthians 14:33 9
1 Corinthians 15:1-58 . . . 210
1 Corinthians 15:3-8 24
1 Corinthians 15:9 216
1 Corinthians 15:35-55 . . 135
1 Corinthians 15:42-57
. . . . 132, 260
1 Corinthians 15:45-49 . . . 86
1 Corinthians 15:50-54 . . 212
1 Corinthians 15:50-57 . . 280
1 Corinthians 15:53 211
1 Corinthians 16:1-2 . . . 240
2 Corinthians 1:12 203
2 Corinthians 3:17-18 . . . 124
2 Corinthians 3:18 212
2 Corinthians 4:7-18 . . . 249
2 Corinthians 5:1-8 280
2 Corinthians 5:1-10 . 206, 207
2 Corinthians 5:7 249
2 Corinthians 5:16-21 . . . 190
2 Corinthians 5:17-19 . . . 196
2 Corinthians 5:19 174
2 Corinthians 5:21 . . . . 84, 92
2 Corinthians 6:14-18 . . . 156
2 Corinthians 7:1 260
2 Corinthians 7:8-12 . . . 194

2 Corinthians 13:14
. . . . 36, 110, 111, 112
Galatians 2:11-21 190
Galatians 3:1-14 . . . . 156, 185
Galatians 3:10-14 . . . . 74, 256
Galatians 3:13 173
Galatians 3:23-29 18
Galatians 3:24 258
Galatians 3:26-29 224
Galatians 4:4 . . . . . . 82, 86
Galatians 4:6 . . . . 122, 124
Galatians 5:16-18 114
Galatians 5:19-26 246
Galatians 5:22-23 246
Ephesians 1:3-6 167
Ephesians 1:3-14 163
Ephesians 1:7 174
Ephesians 1:7-12 170
Ephesians 1:11 . . . . . 41, 69
Ephesians 1:22-23 220
Ephesians 2:1 148
Ephesians 2:1-3 . 138, 149, 170
Ephesians 2:1-10 148, 171, 190
Ephesians 2:3 148
Ephesians 2:4-10 188
Ephesians 2:8-9 . . . . 185, 196
Ephesians 2:19-22 . . 110, 218
Ephesians 3:1-13 6
Ephesians 4:1-6 218
Ephesians 4:1–6:20 246
Ephesians 4:7-8 97
Ephesians 4:11-16 . . . 20, 26
Ephesians 4:17-19 149
Ephesians 5:21-33 266
Ephesians 5:25-33 248
Philippians 1:6 . . . . 198, 199
Philippians 1:19-26 . . 206, 207
Philippians 2:5-8 80
Philippians 2:5-11 82
Philippians 2:9 104
Philippians 2:9-11 . . . . 77, 78
Philippians 2:12-13
. . . . xix, 124, 192
Philippians 3:7-11 190
Philippians 3:7-14 260
Philippians 3:8-9 174
Philippians 3:20-21 210
Philippians 4:6-7 252
Colossians 1:9-14 69
Colossians 1:15 . . . . . 87, 132
Colossians 1:15-19 89
Colossians 1:15-20 38

Colossians 1:18 218
Colossians 1:19 78
Colossians 2:8 . . . . . xiv, 156
Colossians 2:11-15 226
1 Thessalonians 1:6-10 . . 160
1 Thessalonians 1:10 . 159, 174
1 Thessalonians 2:13 . 16, 188
1 Thessalonians 4:3-8 . . . 266
1 Thessalonians 4:13-18
. . . . 207, 210
1 Thessalonians 4:13-5:11 276
2 Thessalonians 2:1-12 . . 274
2 Thessalonians 2:5-10 . . 140
2 Thessalonians 2:13-14 . 170
2 Thessalonians 2:13-15 . 163
1 Timothy 1:18-20 222
1 Timothy 2:1-4 263
1 Timothy 2:5 100
1 Timothy 4:1 112
1 Timothy 4:8 133
1 Timothy 5:19-20 222
2 Timothy 1:8-12 170
2 Timothy 2:14-19 199
2 Timothy 2:15 28
2 Timothy 3:14-17 . . . . 6, 28
2 Timothy 3:15-17 16
2 Timothy 3:16 15
2 Timothy 3:16-17 24
Titus 1:2 241
Titus 1:15 . . . . . . 146, 152
Titus 2:11-14 . . . . . 250, 276
Titus 3:1-7 174
Titus 3:3-7 226
Titus 3:4-7 . . . . . . 172, 196
Hebrews 1:1-2 4
Hebrews 1:1-3 94
Hebrews 1:1-4 . . . . . . 6, 28
Hebrews 1:1-14 89
Hebrews 1:3 . . . . . . 41, 132
Hebrews 1:5 88
Hebrews 1:8-14 278
Hebrews 2:1-4 66
Hebrews 2:3-4 66
Hebrews 2:14-18 82
Hebrews 3:1 216
Hebrews 3:3-6 100
Hebrews 4:13 46
Hebrews 4:15 . . . . . . 82, 83
Hebrews 5:5-6 102
Hebrews 5:8-10 80
Hebrews 5:12-14 xi
Hebrews 6 197

Hebrews 6:13-18 69
Hebrews 6:17-18 241
Hebrews 6:18 39
Hebrews 6:19 249
Hebrews 7:20-25 100
Hebrews 7:26 84
Hebrews 8 72
Hebrews 9:11-15 199
Hebrews 9:11-22 100
Hebrews 9:23-28 97
Hebrews 10:5-10 80
Hebrews 11:1 184
Hebrews 11:3 60
Hebrews 13:4 266
Hebrews 13:20-21 72
James 1:12-15 144
James 1:13-15 181
James 1:14-15 83
James 1:17 . . . . 49, 51
James 2:1 78
James 2:10 144
James 2:14 187
James 2:14-26 . . . . 185, 188
James 2:17 187
James 2:18-24 192
James 2:19 184
James 4:5 112
James 5:12 242
1 Peter 1:2 36
1 Peter 1:3-9 280
1 Peter 1:15-16 . . . . 123, 124
1 Peter 1:23 171
1 Peter 2:9-10 220
1 Peter 2:11 138
1 Peter 2:13-17 263
1 Peter 3:18 84
1 Peter 4:8 222
1 Peter 5:8 140
1 Peter 5:8-11 140
2 Peter 1:5-11 192
2 Peter 1:10 201
2 Peter 1:16 183
2 Peter 1:16-21 26

2 Peter 1:19-21 24
2 Peter 1:20-21 . . . . . 16, 28
2 Peter 1:21 116
2 Peter 3:9 69
2 Peter 3:14-16 24
2 Peter 3:14-18 26
1 John 1:5-10 260
1 John 1:8-10 . . . . 144, 149
1 John 1:9 194
1 John 2:1 121
1 John 2:2 176
1 John 2:3-6 . . . 192, 203, 254
1 John 2:18 273
1 John 2:18-23 274
1 John 2:19 197
1 John 3:1-3 250
1 John 3:2 282
1 John 4:1-6 . . . . 142, 274
1 John 4:3 273
1 John 4:4 140
1 John 4:7-11 192
1 John 4:7-21 248
1 John 5:1-3 254
1 John 5:6 112
1 John 5:13 203
1 John 5:14-15 252
1 John 5:16 154
1 John 5:19-21 156
2 John 1:7 274
Jude 1:3-13 287
Jude 1:4 167
Revelation 1:8 38
Revelation 1:10 240
Revelation 4:1-11 48
Revelation 6:15-16 286
Revelation 7:9-10 218
Revelation 19:11-16 106
Revelation 20:11-15 287
Revelation 21–22 280
Revelation 21:23 93
Revelation 22:1-5 283
Revelation 22:4-5 94

DR. R. C. SPROUL, theologian, pastor, and teacher, is chairman of the board of Ligonier Ministries. Dr. Sproul also presides on the board of SERVE International and has taught at several seminaries. He has a daily radio ministry, *Renewing Your Mind,* and preaches at Saint Andrew's Chapel in the Orlando area. His many books include *The Holiness of God; Now, That's a Good Question!; Chosen by God; The Mystery of the Holy Spirit; Pleasing God; Faith Alone;* and *The Consequences of Ideas.*